STUART McHARDY is a writer, musician, folklorist, storyteller and poet, and has lectured on many aspects of Scottish history and culture both in Scotland and abroad. Combining the roles of scholar and performer gives McHardy an unusually clear insight into tradition. As happy singing old ballads as analysing ancient legends, he has held such posts as Director of the Scots Language Resource Centre and President of the Pictish Arts Society. McHardy is a prolific author, and has had many books published, including *A New History of the Picts, Tales of Edinburgh Castle, The Quest for the Nine Maidens, On the Trail of Scotland's Myths and Legends* and *Edinburgh and Leith Pub Guide*. McHardy lives in Musselburgh with his wife Sandra.

By the same author:

Tales of Whisky and Smuggling (House of Lochar, 2002)
Scots Poems to be Read Aloud (ed.) (Luath Press, 2003)
MacPherson's Rant and other tales of the Scottish Fiddle (Birlinn, 2004)
The Silver Chanter and other tales of Scottish Piping (Birlinn, 2004)
School of the Moon (Birlinn, 2004)
Tales of the Picts (Luath Press, 2005)
On the Trail of Scotland's Myth's and Legends (Luath Press, 2005)
The Well of the Heads and other Clan Tales (Birlinn, 2005)
The White Cockade and other Jacobite Tales (Birlinn, 2006)
On the Trail of The Holy Grail (Luath Press, 2006)
Tales of Edinburgh Castle (Luath Press, 2007)
Edinburgh and Leith Pub Guide (Luath Press, 2008)
Tales of Loch Ness (Luath Press, 2009)
Tales of Whisky (Luath Press, 2010)
Speakin o Dundee (Luath Press, 2010)
A New History of the Picts (Luath Press, 2011)
Tales of Bonnie Prince Charlie & the Jacobites (Luath Press, 2012)
Arthur's Seat (Luath Press, 2012) with Donald Smith
Scotland the Brave Land (Luath Press, 2012)
Pagan Symbols of the Picts (Luath Press, 2012)
Calton Hill (Luath Press, 2013) with Donald Smith
Edinburgh Old Town (Luath Press, 2014) with John Fee & Donald Smith
Scotland's Democracy Trail (Luath Press, 2014) with Donald Smith
Scotland's Future History (Luath Press, 2015)
Scotland's Future Culture (Luath Press, 2017)
The Stones of the Ancestors (Luath Press, 2020) with Douglas Scott

THE NINE MAIDENS

Priestesses of the Ancient World

STUART McHARDY

Luath Press Limited
EDINBURGH
www.luath.co.uk

First published as *The Quest for the Nine Maidens* 2003
This revised and updated edition 2023

ISBN: 978-1-80425-091-4

The author's right to be identified as author of this book under the Copyright, Designs and Patents Act 1988 has been asserted.

The paper used in this book is recyclable. It is made from low chlorine pulps produced in a low energy, low emission manner from renewable forests.

 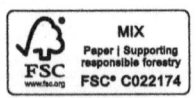

Printed and bound by Severnprint, Gloucester

Typeset in 10.5 point Sabon by Lapiz

© Stuart McHardy 2003, 2023

This book is dedicated to my wife Sandra Davidson in whom, for me, the Goddess walks.

Contents

Nine Maidens – Approximate Timeline		9
Nine Maidens Perspective – Significant Sites		10
Preface		13
Introduction		15
CHAPTER 1	Dragonslayer	22
CHAPTER 2	The Goddess Bride	37
CHAPTER 3	The Nine Maidens in Welsh Tradition	58
CHAPTER 4	The Nine Maidens in Irish Tradition	83
CHAPTER 5	Sisters of Avalon	93
CHAPTER 6	Islands of Women	106
CHAPTER 7	Sagas and Sea Spirits	127
CHAPTER 8	Muses, Maenads and beyond	145
CHAPTER 9	The Number Nine in Folklore, Literature and Ritual	170
CHAPTER 10	The Nine Maidens	195
CHAPTER 11	Mythical and Legendary Figures Associated with Nine Maidens	209
Bibliography		231

NINE MAIDENS – APPROXIMATE TIMELINE

Time	CELTIC	NORSE	GREEK	SHAMANIC	OTHER
20th CENTURY	Abernethy St Brides Well Rites Sanquhar			9 Daughters of Solboni	Raratonga
	Closure of Pittempton Well			9 Daughters of Ulgan	'Nus Tarian'
16th CENTURY REFORMATION					Kogi 9 Mamas Venezuela
1000 AD	Corryvreckan Tales				
	Cerridwen	Thidrandi Volva			Kikuyu 9 Sisters
	Pictish 9s	Heimdall			
BIRTH OF CHRIST	Maidens of Avalon	Menglod Valkyries			
500 BC GREEK CIVILISATION		Mill Maidens	Apollo and Muses		
3200 BC EGYPTIAN EMPIRE					Ennead of Heliopolis
3500 BC MEGALITHIC PERIOD	9 Maidens Stone Circles				
15000 BC					Cogul Dancing Maidens

Preface

IN THE TWENTY years since the *Quest for the Nine Maidens* was published I have continued researching the topic. This in turn has led to a greater understanding of the extent to which mythological constructs have survived in the oral traditions of Scotland and elsewhere. Part of this understanding relates directly to new ways of seeing the landscape, which in turn has given rise to a new approach to analysing past societies, which I have called Geomythography. Over the past three years I have taught courses on Scottish Geomythography at the University of Edinburgh's Centre for Open Learning.

In this new edition, in order to avoid confusion and to properly reflect on how my thinking has developed I have added new information and analyses within the original framework of the text, rather than just bolting on appendices and in particular chapter three now gives extended relevant material from Ireland.

I must give heartfelt thanks to Gavin MacDougall and the staff at Luath Press, to many students over the years who have helped clarify my thinking and particularly to Donald Smith, Director of the Traditional Arts Centre, Scotland, for his ongoing support and encouragement, as well as being the first person to describe me as a geomythographer, for which no blame should be attached, to him at least.

Introduction

THE THEME OF this book is the existence of groups of nine women who were involved in healing, prophecy, weather-working and what appears to have been ritual activity over a remarkably wide geographical and chronological range. Their activities suggest they are probably best understood as priestesses. Such groups of nine women exist in the mythologies and oral traditions of many different cultures throughout the world. Although I first came across them in my native Scotland, the search for the Nine Maidens has involved material from many locales, some of them well beyond Europe and originating from many periods. What is clear is that the Nine Maidens functioned as discrete groups within many different societies, some of which have the Nine Maidens at the centre of their mythologies. Mythology can be understood as the process which gives rise to the earliest stories humans told each other and which were attempts to explain life in ways that are meaningful and understandable.

A Goddess?

Many of the different traditions of the Nine Maidens associate them with what are apparently goddess-type figures, and this reflects a very widespread early belief in the world having been created by an essentially female force. Many commentators have thought this to have been the basis for the earliest forms of human religion and the fact that we all have mothers is probably why humans first developed the idea of a supreme Mother Goddess, giver of life and death. I am reluctant to suggest there was an ancient Mother Goddess religion, precisely because in the modern world the very term religion has connotations developing from the reality that most of the contemporary dominant religions are undeniably patriarchal, often aggressively so, and hierarchical, with highly structured dogmas and the connotations of this are potentially a hindrance to trying to understand the beliefs of the far past. Likewise, as a result of ongoing research I now use the term pre-Christian rather than pagan, as the latter term has contemporary connotations that are not necessarily helpful. However the Compact Edition of the *Oxford English Dictionary* tells us on p.2052 that the term pagan originally meant 'villager, rustic' and as most people throughout the past lived in small localised communities it has become obvious to me that human culture is derived from the social, intellectual and spiritual activities of such small communities. Ideas which were shared over vast distances and long periods of time were experienced, both communally and individually, at a local level. I would further suggest that culture both precedes and supersedes the relatively modern ideas of what constitutes civilisation. That the material concerning the Nine Maidens is concerned with both belief and ritual is undeniable but to try to fit this in with modern ideas of how religions operate may well be to miss the point.

The material from Scotland, where our story starts, can be interpreted as supporting the idea of the existence of an ancient dual goddess figure who can be portrayed in terms of light and dark, summer and winter, life and death. This duality is much more like the eastern concept of yin and yang than the later simplified Christian idea of the battle between good and evil. In some Scottish traditions the goddess of Winter, the Hag, actually becomes the golden goddess of Summer, Bride, the pre-Christian precursor of St Bride or Bridget, who in both Britain and Ireland is associated with a range of material concerning the Nine Maidens. I will be dealing with this subject in depth, in a forthcoming work.

In traditions furth of Scotland we see the Nine Maidens associated with, amongst others, the Norse goddesses Menglod and Ran, the Welsh Cerridwen, her Breton counterpart Korrigan, in Siberian shamanic traditions, in a foundation legend from Kenya and of course in the case of the Greek Muses, the most obvious of all the Nine Maidens groups, we see them associated with a god, Apollo. While it is impossible to prove that the association with such male god figures came later than their link to goddess figures, we can be sure that their association with a single male figure is very ancient indeed. The earliest dateable reference to the Nine Maidens is in a Magdelanian cave painting from Catalonia which is perhaps as much as 17,000 years old. This painting which has nine female figures dancing round a decidedly priapic male figure has been interpreted as representing some kind of fertility ritual. The reality that some indigenous Australian Dreamtime stories refer to creatures that have been extinct for over 30,000 years, shows the potential for oral traditions to hold on to very old realities and in terms of the Nine Maidens, given their widespread provenance and the existence of one tradition from close to Africa's Great Rift Valley where the oldest humans have been located, may even suggest the Nine Maidens stories originally came out of Africa with the first humans.

The association with the Mother Goddess might account for the existence of many Nine Maidens Wells in Scotland, water itself being the fount of all life. In one particular case, at Sanquhar in southern Scotland, nine white stones were still being placed in St Bride's Well in the 20th century, in memory of the Nine Maidens.

Languages

The stories of the Nine Maidens survive in many lands in many tongues. I begin with a short place poem in Scots, still the first spoken language of at least a third of Scotland's population. Many of the versions of the tale in Scotland must have also been told in earlier forms of Celtic languages, Scottish Gaelic and Brythonnic, variants of which it is believed were spoken by all the tribal groupings of Scotland outside of the Gaelic heartland in the west. Without going into too much detail, Scotland at the time the Romans left was populated by a variety of tribes who spoke two basic different kinds of Celtic language, Q-Celtic, surviving in modern Irish, Scottish Gaelic and the reborn Manx tongue, and P-Celtic which lives on as Welsh, Breton and the also reborn Cornish. Early Roman sources suggest that at least some of these peoples were in regular, if sporadic, contact with Germanic-speaking tribes in mainland Europe and/or Scandinavia, and it is at least possible some of these latter groups were also based in the British Isles, or were frequent visitors. Overly Romantic interpretations of the histories of Ireland, Scotland and Wales have led to some unfortunate assumptions about language and ethnicity. The notion of ethnic purity is a racist concept and the fact that we know people were travelling the whole of the eastern Atlantic littoral on a regular basis as far back as 5,000 years ago shows that contact between widely-spread societies has been going on for a long time. One example should illustrate this. Many scholars have noted the great flowering of Gaelic culture within the Lordship of the Isles in the mediaeval period. The culture of this society, which clearly saw itself as separate from the growing Scottish nation-state, was a combination of what is known as Gall-Gael traditions and learning. The Gall here is Norse, the Gael, Celtic. Attempting to separate how these two strands intertwined and grew is an exercise in futility – like many human societies, the mixture of ideas, languages, social mores and skills emanating from different sources made the combination more vibrant and dynamic. An analogy might be found in the selective breeding of livestock.

Geographical spread

We can be sure that Scotland and Ireland were still primarily inhabited by people living in tribal societies before and after the Romans took control of England. However, in other areas society was much more centralized and from the city-states of Greece we have early written sources that tell us of the best known of the Nine Maidens groups, the Muses. As will become clear, there are grounds for seeing their god Apollo as originating in the north, but this is not of primary importance. What is important is that the extensive Greek sources show many Muse-like groups associated with mountaintops, springs and islands, just like many other Nine Maidens groups across the world. Within the Celtic-speaking areas of Europe in Roman times we have references from Scotland, Ireland and Wales and a striking early literary reference to a group of Druidesses in Brittany. These are not the only such groups in Breton tradition but the source gives them a definite historical provenance. It is striking that the Nine Maidens also show up in British Arthurian tales, which were part of the cultural inheritance of the P-Celtic-speaking tribes of south and central Scotland.

Within the Germanic-speaking world, and we should remember that contact between Britain and Scandinavia and the Netherlands goes back to long before Megalithic times, we have various groups like the Valkyries and the Nine Maidens of the Mill, who clearly belong to the realm of mythology, while Icelandic traditions carry memories of what appear to have been practising pre-Christian priestesses. We will also consider material from Romania, Africa and the Far East which focuses on groups of nine women. This remarkable spread is paralleled by the magic use of nine which seems in fact to have been almost universal. While the link between the use of the number in ritual and the actual and mythological groups of nine women is unclear, it seems more than likely that there is some underlying concept common to both. Suggestions have been made that there is an underlying lunar aspect to this widespread usage of the number nine in ritual.

Literature and oral transmission

Western education has for a long time been based almost exclusively on literacy. However even in the modern world literacy is not yet universal and just a few hundred years ago only a tiny minority of human beings were able to read. For the majority of our time on this planet all knowledge was passed on by word of mouth, and example. Scholars have tended to be dismissive of oral transmission and historians in particular consider the lack of written sources an insuperable problem in understanding the past. This attitude is now being severely challenged. There are examples from Australian aboriginal tradition that show the capacity of oral transmission to carry accurate data for tens of thousands of years (Isaacs 1980). If the indigenous peoples of Australia were capable of this, why should we think our own ancestors were any different? I believe that there is much we can learn from traditional tales, particularly when used critically in conjunction with other disciplines such as archaeology and place-name studies. Oral material is of course different from literary material – the old cliché about history being written by winners is of particular relevance when dealing with remnants of pre-Christian religion that have survived in written sources from the pens of Christian scribes. However, though history may be written by winners this has never meant that the defeated have abandoned the telling of their own stories. Within tribal societies, the transmission of knowledge by word of mouth to the young was an integral part of everyday existence and what worked would always be of more relevance than what was strictly accurate in terms of the precise date, personnel etc. This is not to diminish the relevance of such material only to show that it has its limitations, as of course, all literary history has. An example of this can be seen by reading American and Soviet histories of the Second World War. One side says the victory was achieved by the armed proletariat the other that it was effectively achieved by the entrepreneurial and creative capacities of capitalism. Which one is the more accurate? When one also considers how the British and their Commonwealth Allies saw their role in the same conflict it is clear that history is not a definitive science. In this sense all history has to be treated critically. Oral tradition arises within communities sharing a common culture, and springs directly from that shared experience as opposed to literature which, in the West arose from specific individuals working to a pre-set, Christian, agenda. The material of oral tradition survives within communities because of its ongoing relevance to society and in pre-literate societies ideas have to be transmitted from tongue to ear, or by practical example. The vast amounts of mythological and genealogical data that are common to most tribal societies were – like the lore of healing, birthing, cooking, food-gathering, planting, hunting and all other activities – passed down from generation to generation by word of mouth. This meant that people passing on and receiving such information used their memories differently than we do (Kelly 2017). We write things down to remember them; oral societies with highly developed mnemonic skills did not need that. What is clear is that myth, legend and folklore retain a great deal of human knowledge from a very long stretch of the human story on this planet.

Most of what I have gathered about the Nine Maidens groups has of course been gathered from literary sources, but these literary sources vary in how close the original writers were to actual oral tradition. In Norway and Iceland the pre-Christian religion lasted till circa 1000AD and there we have clear representations of Nine Maidens as pre-Christian priestesses. In Scotland we have early medieval sources presenting the Nine Maidens as a particular group of Pictish saints. In Greece the various nine female groups on islands and hilltops, though occurring in literary sources, were also based on earlier oral traditions. What is also often ignored is that European literature, from about the 4th century CE onwards, and thus history, was created by monks who had a vested interest in obscuring, hiding or ignoring non-Christian traditions. In this light it is perhaps a testament to the tenacity of both pre-Christian belief and the institution of the Nine Maidens themselves that we have so many literary sources for them. It is a fact that oral tradition continues after literacy is introduced, a point that will be dealt with in the text, and this can account for some of the survivals. What I hope I prove here beyond dispute is that the institution of groups of nine women, involved in some kind of sacral behaviour, and regularly associated with sometimes a single supernatural female or a single male figure, was something known over a very wide geographical area for a remarkable length of time.

Stuart McHardy
Fisherrow

CHAPTER 1

Dragonslayer

THE ORIGINAL STIMULUS for this book was a simple four-line poem, in Scots (a Germanic language distinct from English), which survived in oral tradition as the explanation of the creation of Martin's Stane, a Pictish Symbol Stone just to the north of Dundee. The Picts were the tribal people who occupied most of Scotland from Roman times till merging with their cousins, the Scots of Argyll, to form Alba, later Scotland, towards the end of the First Millennium CE. This is the poem as recorded in Andrew Jervise's *Epitaphs and Inscriptions*:

> It was tempit at Pittempton
> Draggelt at Badragon
> Stricken at Strikemartin
> An killt at Martin's Stane (p.206)

The story is of a group of nine sisters who lived with their father at Pittempton, now within the northern edge of Dundee, and who were all killed by a dragon-like creature, or a pair of dragons in some versions, that appeared at the nearby well. The stone with which the tale is associated, known as Martin's Stane, stands in the shadow of the Sidlaw hills a few miles north of Dundee. Here is the story as told by Jervise in *The Land of the Lindsay*s:

> Long, long ago, the farmer of Pittempton had nine pretty daughters. One day their father thirsted for a drink from his favourite well, which was in a marsh

at a short distance from the house. The fairest of the
nine eagerly obeyed her father's wish by running to
the spring. Not returning within a reasonable time, a
second went in quest of her sister. She too tarried so
long that another volunteered, when the same result
happened to her and to five other sisters in succession. At last the ninth sister went to the spring, and
there, to her horror, beheld, among the bulrushes,
the dead bodies of her sisters guarded by a dragon!
Before she was able to escape, she too fell into the
grasp of the monster, but not until her cries had
brought people to the spot. Amongst these was her
lover, named Martin who, after a long struggle with
the dragon which was carried on from Pittempton
to Balkello, succeeded in conquering the monster. It
is told that Martin's sweetheart died from injuries
or fright; and the legend adds that in consequence
of this tragedy, the spring at Pittempton was named
the Nine Maidens' Well, and the sculptured stone
at Strathmartine also St Martin's Stane at Balkello,
were erected by the inhabitants to commemorate
the event. (p.162)

Balkello is the name of a farm near where the stone stands. Local tradition has it that the original name of Kirkton of Strathmartine was Strikemartin as in the poem, and the name has been reported as surviving in a medieval charter. There are also records attesting to the existence of a piece of another Pictish Symbol Stone with the figure of a man with a great club over his shoulder which used to be built into the wall of a nearby barn. It has been suggested that there were at one time around a dozen Pictish symbol stones in the immediate area but only three have survived. Such a collection of stones, like the collections elsewhere at Meigle and St Vigean's both less than 20 miles from Dundee, may suggest an important, early Christian religious foundation in the area. It is a striking fact that many of the Pictish symbol stones have been found in conjunction with Christian church or burial sites. Given that it was common practice for the early church to take over the temples or sites of earlier ritual activity, it is likely that somewhere around Strathmartine there was a significant pre-Christian ritual site.

Suggestions have been made that the story is merely an attempt to explain the meaning of the symbols on Martin's Stane. Until very recently the symbols on the Pictish stones were thought to be indecipherable, but modern research is now coming up with plausible, if not definitive, interpretations linking them with dynastic symbols or totems and with pre-Christian supernatural concepts. Some of the symbols – adder, deer cauldron, lunate crescents – have strong associations with ancient goddess figures, both within the myths and legends of the Celtic-speaking peoples and other European peoples (McHardy 2012 passim). The representative and decorative styles of the Pictish symbol stones are now recognised to have had a seminal influence on what has become known as Late Insular Celtic Art, perhaps best known in *The Book of Kells*. This great masterpiece of illuminated manuscript art was begun on the Scottish holy island of Iona, if not by Pictish artists, then by artists who had been exposed to the art of the Picts.

The place-names in the Martin's Stane rhyme suggest there is more to this story than the pursuit and killing of a maiden-eating dragon, fascinating as that might be. Pittempton on the northern outskirts of the city of Dundee, appears to be a name combining the Pictish place name *Pit* with the Gaelic *tiompan* – a drum – giving the place of the drum. Drums have been used in sacred rituals in societies all over the world for as far back as memory can tell and so the name supports the idea of some sort of cult or ritual practice taking place in the immediate area. Baldragon is Gaelic for the township of the dragon, or hero, either of which meanings could be seen as deriving from the story.

Although the verse is in Scots, still spoken by hundreds of thousands of people in Scotland today, the place-names are in Celtic tongues – Pictish and Gaelic. Pictish was probably, like the ancestor of modern Welsh, a P-Celtic language, while Gaelic, like Irish, is a Q-Celtic language. The P-Celtic and

Q-Celtic forms are thought to have developed separately from the same root. One of the most obvious differences is that where the Q-Celtic has a hard 'C' sound, the P-Celtic languages have a 'P' sound. Compare the Welsh Owen Map Owen with the Gaelic Ewen Mac Ewen – with *map* and *mac* both meaning 'son of'. Linguists believe that in the east of Scotland, Pictish was the predominant native language before being superseded by Gaelic between the 9th and 12th centuries after which Gaelic was in turn replaced by Scots. Some scholars think that there were several languages spoken by the Picts and have even theorised that this might have included some form of Germanic language. It is possible that the story of Martin's Stane existed in both Pictish and Gaelic before being told in Scots, but as we have no written record of it before the 18th century it is impossible to confirm. Recent analysis of Pictish carving has led to the suggestion that their creation started as early as the 4th century but in *Stones of the Ancestors* (Scott & McHardy 2020) the case is made for a much longer cultural development of the use of symbols carved in stone in Scotland.

The meaning of the Martin's Stane story has been interpreted in various ways, one suggestion I was given is that it was told to mark the end of whatever 'power' was associated with the stone. In 1985 I saw the stone being dowsed to see if there was a ley line running under it. Ley lines are thought by some to be a kind of weak electromagnetic current that links together ancient sites in straight lines, many of the sites being of greatly differing ages. What ley lines signify, if anything at all, is unclear. The dowser, the late American-Scottish artist Marianna Lines, used a cut crystal ball on a revolving mount fixed to a silver chain which she held between the fingers of her right hand, palm upwards. As soon as she got close to the stone, the ball began to whirl furiously and the silver chain flew up to the horizontal. It was remarkable seeing the ball rotate at high speed on the end of this rigid chain. The conclusion of the people there that day was that there was certainly some kind of power in evidence. It is worth noting that the Chinese name for what we call ley lines is dragon lines. In his *Hill of the Dragon*, Newman makes the point that stories of dragons eating maidens are often references to the passing away of the older religions in the face of Christianity.

The fame of the Nine Maidens Well at Pittempton lasted a long time. As late as the 1870s, according to Jervise, the farmer at Pittempton, fed up with people tramping across his fields to visit the well every first of May, the ancient feast day of Beltane, covered it over with a sheet of iron which he then buried. This survival of ritual activity at the well is remarkable testimony to the tenacity of the Nine Maidens story and the continuity of the ancient pilgrimage tradition to Scotland's holy wells. People had been visiting this site for over a thousand years. Jervise in *Epitaphs and Inscriptions* further writes,

> people still alive in the parish recall of nine graves, near the east end of the old kirk of Strathmartine which were pointed out as those of the nine sisters; and it is uniformly added that the stone with two serpents carved upon it [now in Dundee Museum] stood at the head of one of these mounds. I am also told that no interments have been made in these graves during the recollection of the oldest inhabitants. (p.206)

This last remark suggests a considerable degree of veneration by the locals for these nine graves. As interest grows in the beliefs and habits of our distant ancestors it is possible that the Nine Maidens Well might one day be re-opened. After all, the statue of a dragon, inspired by the story, now stands in the centre of Dundee.

When I first began to look into the Nine Maidens story I soon came across other material referring to them close to Martin's Stane. Just over Balluderon hill to the north lies the head of Glen Ogilvy nestling in the Sidlaw Hills. It is said that in the 6th century St Donald lived here with his nine daughters, following a simple life of contemplation and prayer, eating one plain meal of barley bread and water a day. St Donald was widely respected for his holiness and when he died, his daughters carried on as before. Their reputation for holiness grew, and, in time came to the attention of the King at Abernethy. The story tells us that the king was called Garnard (a Garnard appears in the Pictish king list, one of few early Scottish documents to have survived down the centuries). We are told Garnard invited the Nine Maidens to come and live in his capital at Abernethy which is about 20 miles to the south-south-west of Martin's Stane and on the south bank of the river Tay. There he built them an oratory and there they lived out their days in sanctity and prayer. It is said that they were buried at the foot of a large oak. This is how Bellenden translates Henry Boece's Latin *History and Chronicle of Scotland*:

> thir holy virginis, efter deceis of thair fader, come to Garnard, King of Pichtis, desiring sum place quhare thay micht leif ain solitar life, in the honour of God. Garnard condescendit to thair desiris and gaif thaim ane hous in Abernethy with certane rentis to be takin up of the nixt landis, to thair sustentation quhare thay leiffit ane devote life and war buryit at the rute of ane aik, quhilk is haldin yit in great veneration amang the pepil. (ix ch xxxv)

Burial at the foot of a large oak has potential pre-Christian connotations. The story of this group of Nine Maidens was told in a series of carved wood panels in an oratory on the north side of the churchyard in Abernethy, which are said to have survived till they were destroyed in the mindless vandalism that accompanied the Protestant Reformation in Scotland in the 16th century. In a version of the story quoted in the *Aberdeen Breviary* (1854) the Nine Maidens are said to have come, at the request of the Pictish king, to Abernethy from Ireland with St Brigid, a major figure in the Early Irish Church derived from the older goddess Bride common to Scotland, Ireland and certain parts of England, of whom more later. These Nine Maidens crop up in a variety of early Scottish sources as a group of Pictish saints. They are unusual within Christian tradition in that they are known collectively. Forbes, in his *Kalendars of Scottish Saints* has this in the entry for 18 July:

> the nine virgine dochters to S. Donewalde under King Eugenius VII in Scotland . . . He spent a most holy life in the Glen of Ogilvy, and on his death his daughters entered the monastery at Abernethy . . . (p.420)

The names of three of them survive, Mayota or Mazota, Fincana and Fyndoca. All three are referred to as individual saints. In Stewart's *Metrical Version of Boece*, written in the early 16th century a few years after Boece's work appeared in Latin, he says 'The eldest hecht Mazota to her name /The secund sister callit Fyncana;' (p.329). St Mazota, sometimes also known as St Mayoca, the eldest of the Nine Maidens, was commemorated on 22 December and had the parish of Drumoak originally Dalmaik, in Aberdeenshire, called after her. There was an old well here called St Maik's Well and it is likely it too was a pilgrimage well, visited at certain significant times of the pre-Christian year.

Boece's history tells that one day in Glen Ogilvy, Mazota came to a field where geese were feeding on recently sown barley and charmed them into flying off and leaving the crop. This power over birds is reminiscent of the powers associated with goddesses and priestesses in many locations around the world and is told in Bellenden's translation of the *History and Chronicle of Scotland*:

> His [St Donald's] eldest daughter, Mayo, maid inhibition to the wild geese, to eat hir fader's corne, and thy obey hir holy monitions, and therefore, wild geese was never seen efftir on that ground . . . (p.116)

This appears to be a reference to Mazota and 22 December is the winter solstice, the shortest day of the year, a time of great importance in lands where the winter days are short and the weather is often severe. It has long been the time of great fire festivals which are believed to be the origin of the modern festivities of Christmas. The association with this date suggests not only antiquity but also that Mazota was a figure of some importance to the ancient peoples of Scotland. The Midwinter or Yule festivals of northern Europe celebrate the fact that from this time on the days grow longer, bringing the promise of the spring and summer to come. In countries where daylight lasts only a few hours at this time, midwinter has always been a time when people were in need of celebration. Within such festivities there was a strong undercurrent of supplication to the gods, or the Goddess, to carry on the turning of the seasons. The use of fire as a symbol of fertility and renewal continues to this day in Scotland, with the Burning of the Clavie at Burghhead, the whirling of fire-balls at Stonehaven and the Shetland festival of Up Hellya, when the festivities culminate in the burning of a replica of a Viking longship. Other fertility rituals have survived with the decking of houses with boughs of evergreen trees and the hanging up of the once sacred mistletoe. Today's kisses under the mistletoe are probably a remnant of something much more earthy in the distant past. Seasonal Affective Disorder Syndrome (SADS) is the modern term for depression due to the long periods of darkness in winter. Our ancestors seem to have realised that in the darkest months it is psychologically beneficial to have a major feast or festival celebrating the forthcoming return of the sun, and a pretty good excuse for a party.

St Fyncana had a church dedicated to her at Echt in Aberdeenshire and the parish of St Fink near Blairgowrie in Perthshire was supposedly named after her. Her name survives there in the place-name Chapelton of St Fink, where there are the remains of an ancient burial ground and a chapel. St Fyndoca is believed to have had a dedication at Dunblane and her name is also thought to have survived in the Perthshire parish of Findo Gask, where, according to the *Aberdeen Breviary*, she founded a church. There are also references to a church dedicated to Fyndoca on the island of Innishail in Loch Awe in Argyll. F

Marian McNeill in her marvellous exposition of Scottish folklore and folk belief, *The Silver Bough*, tells us:

> One of the Nine Maidens, St Fyndoca, erected a sanctuary on the lovely peaceful island of Innishail on Loch Awe, in the shadow of Ben Cruachan, and hither for centuries the clans of the adjoining territories – Campbells, MacArthurs, MacCalmans, MacCorkindales and others – brought their dead for burial. (1 p.175)

JF Mackinlay stated, in his article 'Traces of the Cultus of the Nine Maidens' in the *Proceedings of the Society of Scottish Antiquaries* of 1905-6, that he believed all references and dedications to the Nine Maidens were in the east of Scotland in the old counties of Perthshire, Forfarshire and Aberdeenshire, all within the ancient bounds of Pictland. In fact, Nine Maidens references are not limited to the Pictish area, or to Scotland, or even to the British Isles. Loch Awe itself is outside what is traditionally considered the Pictish area of Scotland. The MacArthur clan from this area claim descent from an ancestor who some think might have been the original of King Arthur, and as we shall see Arthurian legends contain a wealth of Nine Maidens connections. The generally accepted history of Scotland has Gaelic-speaking Scots coming into mainland Scotland not many miles from Loch Awe, from Ireland, around 500AD. Though this has recently been comprehensively debunked (Campbell 2001), it was the case that trading and cultural contacts over the Irish Sea have been continuous from the Stone Age onwards – both ways. Another interpretation of the available evidence would be that the Scots homeland of Dalriada was the heartland of a thalassocracy, or sea-based polity that encompassed both Argyll on Scotland's west coast, Ulster, the northern province of Ireland and many of the islands in between. That the Nine Maidens were known in both Ireland and Scotland is inarguable.

We have already travelled a fair distance from Martin's Stane and the association of the Nine Maidens with the oak tree at Abernethy suggests links with widespread ancient belief. The oak was widely venerated throughout the pre-Christian societies of Europe and is often associated with that shadowy priesthood of the Celtic-speaking peoples, the Druids. Oak groves were sites of ritual activity among both the Celtic- and Germanic-speaking tribal peoples of northern and western Europe. Place-name evidence has been utilised to locate a whole series of such sacred enclosures in ancient Scotland (Barrow 1997). The association of the Nine Maidens in various tales with the oak, and the dragon, which, like the serpent, is associated with pre-Christian belief, is highly significant, reinforcing the idea that the Nine Maidens are derived from truly ancient times.

Several wells in Scotland were dedicated to the Nine Maidens, and some of these were the subject of particular rituals at specific times of the year. Even into the 20th century young women were visiting Bride's Well at Sanquhar in south-west Scotland and placing nine white stones in it at Beltane (see p.49), one of the great feast days of the tribal peoples of ancient Britain and beyond. The veneration of water is much older than the ritual of Christian baptism; within the old pre-Christian religion it is conceivable that water could have been understood as the very life blood of the Mother Goddess – all life requires water, and she was apparently seen as the fount of all life.

In Scotland during the Reformation in the second half of the 16th century many of the new Presbyteries are recorded as passing acts condemning a variety of rituals we now perceive as pre-Christian, though then they were seen as 'Popish'. The village of Glamis, just a couple of miles from the foot of Glen Ogilvy and with its own Nine Maidens Well provides an example. Mackinlay in *Ancient Church Dedications in Scotland* says:

> Even in the seventeenth century the fame of the oak at Abernethy was such that an enactment was passed by the Kirk Session of Glamis forbidding maidens to go to it on pilgrimage. (p.16)

In parish after parish, acts or bye-laws were passed banning people from a whole range of activities including well and tree worship and the Beltane rites – and these acts had to be re-enforced for many years. The people hung on to the old ways, which have never been totally forgotten and in the 1990s in Edinburgh, the annual Beltane fires were revived on Calton Hill. Calton is from Gaelic *Calltunn*, Hazel, which was a significant tree in traditional Scottish lore and the ceremonies on the hill now attract thousands of people every year. Perhaps this revival is symptomatic of people turning to the past to try and make sense of their lives in an increasingly impersonal and greed-dominated world where the pursuit of wealth has replaced spirituality for so many. Today's quest for spirituality and a sense of rootedness are perhaps all the stronger because we have for so long turned our backs on the past – telling ourselves that material progress is an endlessly beneficial process – while global warming and widespread environmental devastation suggest the opposite – and thereby failing to realise that some human concepts and activities are themselves rooted in practices from the very dawn of time. Whatever the reason, Calton Hill named for an ancient sacred tree and with strong links to the fairies, seems the perfect location for people to celebrate fertility just as their ancestors used to.

The dedications to the Nine Maidens at wells in such places as Cortachy, Finavon and Dundee in Angus, at Newburgh and Abernethy in Fife, at Loch Tay and Murrayshall in Perthshire, at Tough and Pitsligo in Aberdeenshire suggest that these collective saints, or their predecessors, were popular in early Scotland. Around three and a half kilometres south-east of the Nine Maidens' Well at Pitsligo is Nine Maidens' Hill, a small knoll surrounded by a ditch, which is probably worth further investigation, particularly as there are interesting crop-marks nearby. Local tradition was that it got its name from a nearby well. The name Ninewells crops up over a much wider area than ancient Pictland. Some interpret the name as meaning 'many wells'; others think the name derives from Ninian, the 5th century Christian cleric, who is said to have converted at least some of the Picts to the new religion. There is perhaps a case for at least some of the Ninewells having originally been Nine Maidens wells. A further complication is that in Gaelic one word for maiden is *nighean*, pronounced nee-an. If the motif of the Nine Maidens is as ancient as I suggest, it would be quite possible for the original meaning to become overlaid with similar-sounding names, particularly if such names possessed their own associations with sanctity.

A well in Aberdeenshire has a story very similar to the story of Martin's Stane. A great Pictish warrior called Ochonochar, the ancestor of the modern family of Forbes, was called to the parish of Auchendoir in Aberdeenshire because a giant bear was terrorising the district. It had slaughtered Nine Maidens by the time he arrived and after a short, but bloody battle, Ochonochar killed the fearsome beast. The Nine Maidens Well here is at Logie on the river Don (Canmore 146106) and at nearby Kildrummy, at the confluence of the Mossat Burn with the river Don, there is the Nine Maidens' Green where tradition says the Nine Maidens are buried. Near to this there is a church dedicated to St Bride, which like many other early Christian sites has been built on a mound, potentially an even earlier site of ritual activity (McHardy 2012, p.140). There are reports that there was also a Pictish Symbol Stone there, but this has not survived. The name Forbes, in a piece of spurious local folklore etymology, is said to have come from Ochonochar shouting 'For Bess', as he slew the bear, Bess having been his beloved among the slain Nine Maidens. This motif of the hero loving one of the Nine Maidens parallels the story of Martin's Stane.

Near Forfar, at Finavon (a Gaelic-derived name meaning the white water), there was a chapel dedicated to the Nine Maidens. Jervise, in his *Lands of the Lindsays*, says that although some local people thought the Ninewell was a corruption of St Ninian's well

> as the 'Nine virgin dochters of St Donewalde who lived as in a hermitage in the Glen of Ogilvy at Glamis' were canonised as the Nine Maidens, perhaps

> the fountain and the kirk had been inscribed to
> them. Like most of the primitive saints they were
> remarkable for industry and humility, and are said
> to have laboured the ground with their own hands
> and to have eaten only once a day, and then but
> barley bread and butter. (p.162)

The common name for the church at Finavon among the locals was 'the kirk of Aikenhatt', a clear reference to the oak tree, and again possibly harking back to earlier pre-Christian traditions at the site. Nearby is Aberlemno a site where there are several remarkable Pictish symbol stones, including one now thought to be a representation of the Battle of Dunnichen in 685AD, when the Picts destroyed an invading army of Angles from the northern English kingdom of Northumbria. A few miles west, at Cortachy, the Nine Maidens Well was renamed the Duchess Well by some local aristocrat indifferent to tradition. Mackinlay in his *Ancient Church Dedications* suggested that there was once a Nine Maidens altar in the kirk here.

Another Nine Maidens location exists at the far end of the Sidlaw Range from Martin's Stane. Overlooking Strathmore just above Perth is Maidenwell on Parkside farm. This was previously the site of a 'wishing well', which can be seen as a reference to the sanctity of a particular well in the past; and it was named Nynmaidenwell in a document from 1536. Even in the 20th century it was called Nynwell.

One particular story from Perthshire demonstrates a Nine Maidens theme we will return to, the location of Nine Maidens groups on an island. At the village of Kenmore at the east end of Loch Tay there was for many years a fair known as the *Feill nam Bann Naomh* – the fair of the Holy Women, nuns who were said to have lived on the crannog or artificial island now known as Priory Island, but formerly *Eilean nam Bann Naohma* – the Island of the Holy Women. The story has been interpreted as being a Nine Maidens story, perhaps originally due to an early reference to the fair being held on the Nine Virgins' Day (see

Chapter 6). However many aspects of this tradition fit precisely with recurring motifs in the Nine Maidens stories:

> The 'Holy Women's Fair' used to be opened with great state and ceremony. We have it from one who, in his youth, less than fifty years ago, was a delighted spectator of the scene, that the ground officer, carrying a drawn sword, walked in state, preceded by a piper, and followed by a dozen or so young men walking in regular order, each carrying a halbert. On the procession arriving at the cross or centre of the market the official proclaimed the 'Peace of the Fair'. Once this was cried there was perfect liberty. The debtor could not be taken up for his debt, or the reiver for his theft; even the fugitive bondman was free from arrest on that day, and though his owner met him in the fair he dared neither 'chase nor tak him', nor apprehend him on his way home. And besides there was unrestricted free trade, while at other times only those privileged to sell could do so. (Maclean p.45)

This echoes what we know of ancient pre-Christian festivals and some medieval fairs, during which the normal rules of society would be suspended. This was also a regular occurrence at the ancient feast days of Beltane and Samhain, midwinter and midsummer. Before moving to the island, the Holy Women of the island in Loch Tay are said to have been based at Inchadney, a mile or so downriver. This church was dedicated to the Nine Maidens. Not far off, on the other side of the river Tay, is the noted prehistoric stone circle of Croft Moraig. The nuns were said to have been driven off the island after a scandal involving a young man. In several cases folklore traditions of nunneries in Scotland cannot be substantiated through charters or other written documents; this suggests to me that such traditions might well derive from memories of pre-Christian female religious groups preserved in local story.

Other dedications to the Nine Maidens in Scotland support the contention that at the very least there was some sort of Nine Maidens cult as suggested by Mackinlay in his 1910 article 'Traces of the Cultus of the Nine Maidens'. A grouping of nine women, often associated with a single male, is a motif that occurs over a wide geographic and chronological spread which suggests the saintly Nine Maidens of the Pictish Church were in fact a Christianised version of a grouping that stems from the very far past. Their connections with wells and other aspects of the Nine Maidens stories underline links with ancient ritual and belief.

That the saintly Nine Maidens appear to be a Christianised idea of a much older concept is hardly surprising. At the dawn of the 7th century Bishop Mellitus was told by Pope Gregory to take over the temples of pre-Christian worship and preach the word of God therein (Bede, pp. 86-7). Many early Celtic saints seem to have developed from earlier pre-Christian figures; it has been suggested that even the much-vaunted St Columba was as much a druid as a Christian priest. The Nine Maidens of Glen Ogilvy and Abernethy fit this pattern. It is conceivable that the concept of the Nine Maidens, and associated cultic practices, came into Britain with the earliest settlers after the end of the last Ice Age. While some of the Scottish traditions concerning the Nine Maidens refer to groups of priestesses in specific locales, elsewhere they are often closely linked to important mythological figures. Some of these other groups are closely associated with a single male figure. However there are also extremely significant female figures to whom we find them linked in traditions from the British Isles.

As we shall see there are magic practices associated with the number nine that occur in societies all over the world just like the groups of Nine Maidens themselves. And at least one example of a group of nine women, involved in some sort of ritual, dates from the time when Scotland and the rest of the British Isles were under the ice.

CHAPTER 2

Bride and Monenna

IN BOWER'S *SCOTOCHRONICON*, a 13th century historical work, the story is told of St Bridget coming over from Ireland at the request of King Gartnait or Garnard:

> King Brude was succeeded by Garnard, son of Domnach . . . who founded and built the collegiate church of Abernethy after blessed Patrick brought blessed Bridget together with her nine virgins; just as we find in a certain chronicle of the church of Abernethy . . . Those nine virgins died within five years and were buried in the north part of the said church. (2 p.303)

St Bridget has been commonly seen as the Irish precursor of the Scottish Bride, handmaiden of Mary in Gaelic lore. There are many Bride place-names in once Pictish areas of Scotland which are accepted as having been Christianised by the Gaelic-speaking Columban church from the 6th century onwards. One would therefore expect such place-names to contain the term 'St Bride' or 'St Bridget'. However in many cases they are simply 'Bride' names, suggesting that these names predate the arrival of the Columban church. It appears that Bride was one of the mother goddesses of pre-Christian Scotland, as much at home in Scotland, where Gaelic and Pictish, and other north Brythonnic dialects were spoken in the 6th century, as in Gaelic-speaking Ireland. In Ireland St Bridget is quite clearly a modernised version of a pre-Christian goddess figure. Her central shrine was said to be at Kildare meaning the 'cell of the oak tree', and there a perpetual flame was kept alive within a fenced area into which no male might pass. Within the enclosure Bride's sacred flame was tended by Nine Maidens. Some versions say the fire was tended by nineteen maidens – a number with strong lunar, and therefore female, associations; the moon repeats its cycle of crossing the skies every 18.6 years. As we will see later, the lunar association with the number nine is also significant.

Bride is a figure common to both Scotland and Ireland; and remembering that there was a tribe called the Brigantes in what is now northern England, it would seem that any attempt to trace her to a single, locatable place of origin is an exercise in futility. The many commentators who have insisted on her originating in Ireland are implicitly expressing a prejudice in favour of the idea that if you have no records you have no history, thus ignoring what we can learn from oral tradition. In Britain the dominant model for interpreting the past arises from a militaristic, hierarchic and masculine perspective. Much of what we currently conceive of as history was written at the behest of kings and other powerful military or religious figures and it is thus their version of history. Oral history gives us some alternative to this history of winners. Another distorting bias in standard British history is that it is really little more than English history with a few sops to Scottish, Welsh and Irish sensibilities. Among these 'nations' this has led to a romanticised view of a glorious Celtic, rather than British past, but such ideas of 'Celticism' are no older than the 18th century.

Commentators tell us that the early literary material from Ireland is much more influenced by the written traditions of Christian literacy than by the mores of pre-Christian society and thus all we can find in such old tales are museum pieces of dead pre-Christianism. This argument is extensively presented in Kim McCone's *Pagan Past and Christian Present in early Irish Literature*. There is some sense in this position – when the Christian monks began writing down the stories of Ireland (as they probably did in Scotland too, but due to the efforts of

Edward I, the Protestant Reformers and the followers of Oliver Cromwell, very few old Scottish texts have survived) – they were the only ones who could read and write. Until the 19th century, most people throughout the world weren't literate and continued to pass on knowledge through the telling of the old tales, generation to generation. To this day previously unrecorded tales are still being gathered in Scotland and elsewhere. If the oral tradition can keep stories intact for millennia as is clear from Australian experience, we should pay more attention to our indigenous oral traditions. In Australia the fossil remains of Diprotodons, giant extinct marsupials, were discovered in the 19th century in several locations. Until these fossilised remains were found, the educated approach to aboriginal stories which told of ancestor peoples hunting such animals was to consider them fantasy. These animals became extinct over 30,000 years ago, but the stories of them continued to be told by the aboriginal peoples into the 20th century. Other material too survived in such traditions. As Jennifer Isaacs tells us in *Australian dreaming; 40,000 years of Aboriginal history*;

> From the Pleistocene era to as late as 5000 B.P. [before the present] the awe-inspiring sight of erupting volcanoes was witnessed by aboriginal people in the southern part of the content. A myth collected many years ago may well describe the eruption of mount Wilson in the Blue Mountains near Sydney. (p.29)

In Europe, in areas like the Balkans, stories are still being told that are accepted as being over 2,000 years old and in tribal societies in various parts of our planet the oral tradition continues. Given the evidence from Australia we have to at least consider the possibility that oral transmission in other parts of the world could contain material of the same level of antiquity.

A story that Loch Moan in south-west Scotland was where King Arthur returned his magic sword to the waters was told me by a student who first heard it over 30 years ago from an old uncle who told her the story had been handed down through their family for generations. In this way such remnants of ancient lore survive where people still inhabit the lands of their ancestors. Additionally stories would travel virtually intact with emigrants to new lands where they would be told as happening within the new physical environment. There is a view that many such stories are a result of literacy – i.e. people originally reading them and then setting them in their own landscape in their retelling. What is now understood about storytelling traditions throughout the world suggests that this analysis is putting the cart before the horse, presenting as authoritative what is essentially supposition. Imparting knowledge from one generation to another is fundamental to human society, and in pre-literate societies all basic knowledge and ideas are passed on through stories, myth and legend. In order to have the maximum relevance and impact such material is given within the local landscape of the audience which makes it easier to learn or absorb. So wherever we find Bride or Nine Maidens stories being told, we can be pretty sure that they were part of the lore of the people who inhabited that environment. Such lore can encompass memories of actual events, individuals and groups, as well as the more fundamental and essentially sacred concepts that underpin mythology, the basis of religion. The Nine Maidens seem to belong to both these strata of orally transmitted tradition.

Whatever their origin, Bride and her Nine Maidens are placed securely in the Pictish capital of Abernethy by early Scottish historians such as Boece, Wyntoun etc. Abernethy seems for a time to have been the most important Christian centre in Dark Age Scotland till perhaps as late as the 11th century. However, as noted by Mackinlay, there were numerous dedications to these Nine Maidens elsewhere in eastern Scotland. Small, in *Interesting Roman Antiquities* (p.171), mentions Bride and her Maidens as coming not from Ireland but from Glenesk which lies in the mountainous parts of Angus on the north side of the river Tay, and which has the intriguing place-name Bride's Bed at the head of Loch Lee. A mountain location is certainly something that occurs again and again with both the Nine Maidens and the Mother Goddess.

The association of Bride names with prehistoric sites in areas once inhabited by the Picts further suggests that this goddess was common to both Picts and Scots. In Angus alone there are Bride's Bed, Bride's Coggie and Bride's Ring and several wells dedicated to her, though wells dedicated to Bride are found all over Scotland. It has been noted already that in general Scottish historians accepted, till recently, that Gaelic did not come into Scotland till around 500CE, and spread over the rest of the land as the power and influence of the Scots of Dalriada increased. As Campbell shows this is not sustainable but it is apparently the case that the Gaelic language spread throughout Scotland as part of the process of Christianisation that is said to have followed the arrival of St Columba in the 6th century. As the Picts and Scots were apparently not totally united before the middle of the 9th century, it is fair to assume that the farthest parts of Pictland from Columba's base in Argyll would be the last to be Gaelicised. In that case, we would expect the Pictish province of Circinn, corresponding to the area of Angus and the Mearns, to be influenced late and it would therefore seem unlikely that Gaelic-speaking Christian monks would give the name of a pre-Christian goddess to sites in Pictland, and as it has been noted, many of these place-names are not St Bridget, or St Bride names, but Bride names. This would suggest that Bride is not an imported figure but is indigenous to Scotland, a view shared by the historian Henry Chadwick according to his wife in her Introduction to his *Early Scotland*:

> [He] certainly suspected that St Brigit had her origin in Scotland or northern Britain, and was originally connected with a heathen Goddess Brigantia. For this of course he was not, originally responsible. (xii)

This is not to deny that Bride, or Bridget, existed in Ireland, but the idea that she must have come to Scotland from Ireland is due to the aforementioned tendency of Scottish historians to be blinded by the notion that all truly indigenous Scottish culture stems from Irish Gaelic tradition. The references we have that Bride brought the Nine Maidens over from Ireland are from sources written long after the Christianising of the Picts by the Columban church based on Iona. The languages of the Columban church were Latin and Gaelic. St Columba and his original followers were Irish and the combination of the story of Irish Dalriadic origins and the power of the new church has led to the notion that Ireland is the original homeland of Scottish culture. This is an assumption that flies directly in the face of the evidence as Campbell has pointed out (Campbell 2001). The Picts did not disappear from the face of Scotland because dynastic rule passed into the hands of a Dalriadic family who, following monkish precedent did trace their roots back to Ireland. The evidence suggests it is possible that the name 'Scots' originated in Argyll and Ulster in the prehistoric period. Given that Northern Ireland and several parts of western Scotland are within sight of each other, that we know the earliest peoples of Britain had boats, and that the archaeological record shows no great variation between these areas, the idea that this people came from Ireland to Scotland for the first time in the 6th century is unsustainable. We would be better thinking of the people on both sides of the water here as being in regular contact from the Stone Age onwards. It seems more than possible that Argyll in Scotland, much of the Inner Hebrides and Ulster formed a common a cultural and political unit, a thallassocracy or sea-based polity, that for much of its existence was independent of the tribal power bases of both Ireland and Scotland. The Norse polities, or kingdoms known as the Sudereys and Nordereys which later encompassed the islands from Man to Lewis, and sections of the mainland, after the arrival of the Vikings, can be seen as a continuance of this reality. Whatever the case we can be sure that the traditions and beliefs of the various tribes who made up the population of the new kingdom of Scotland in the 9th century did not disappear.

Given the importance of Bride/St Bridget to the search for the Nine Maidens we must now look at certain aspects of

Scottish tradition concerning her. The preponderance of Nine Maidens locations in east Scotland, well away from the Gaelic west, reinforces the idea that they did not come into Scotland from Ireland, either as a mythological or actual group.

Two important motifs concerning Bride are her portrayal as the goddess of summer and the tale of the Cailleach changing into Bride after drinking from a sacred well on Imbolc (Feb 1st), the day dedicated to Bride and St Bridget. This is how Marian McNeill gives these stories in *The Silver Bough*:

> Bride is kept prisoner all winter in Ben Nevis where she awaits her rescuer, Aengus of the White Steed, Aengus the Ever-Young, who has his home in that green island of perpetual summer that drifts about on the silver tide of the Atlantic. Aengus beholds Bride in a dream, and sets out to succour her, riding on his milk-white steed with flowing mane over the Isles and over the Minch. The Cailleach strives in vain to keep them apart, and the Day of Bride celebrates their union.
>
> Another legend shows the Cailleach and Bride not as two contending personalities, but as one and the same. On the Eve of Bride, the Cailleach repairs to the Isle of Youth in whose mysterious woods lies the Well of Youth. There, at the first glimmer of dawn, before any bird has sung or any dog barked, she drinks of the water that bubbles in a crevice of a rock, and having renewed her youth, emerges as Bride, the fair young goddess at the touch of whose wand the dun grass turns to vivid green, starred with the white and yellow flowers of spring. (2 p.21)

A similar duality is expressed in the traditional Gaelic concept of the sun as having two seasons – the time of the Big Sun and the time of the Little Sun. These seasons were separated by the great feast days of Beltane and Samhain, which today we know as Mayday and Halloween. Given the widespread human experience of having early foundation mythology explaining the creation of the seasons, the weather, and the formation of the land in terms of a goddess, here we appear to be dealing with a very ancient motif.

Over millennia ideas do develop as societies change and we should therefore not be surprised to see some variation in even the most ancient and fundamental of concepts. This does not diminish the capacity for the oral tradition to preserve remnants of a wide range of ancient belief and practice over remarkable time scales, but does show the necessity for maintaining a critical approach. Mackenzie gives us another version of the same story:

> Another conception was that the Cailleach changed from a fierce old hag to a beautiful maiden. In a folk-story which was connected with the Fians, she appears one night as a creature of uncouth appearance who claims hospitality. Fionn and Oisean [Ossian] refuse to let her under their coverings. Diarmaid pleads that she should be allowed to come to the warmth of the fire. Soon afterwards she sought to be under the warmth of the blanket together with himself. Diarmaid turned a fold of the blanket between them. Before long he gave a start, for the hag had transformed herself into the most beauteous woman that men ever saw. (p.138)

Here a clear duality is expressed, with the Cailleach changing into a desirable young woman, akin to story of the Cailleach going to the well at Imbolc and becoming Bride. This duality is clearly differentiated from the more usually noticed triple aspect of so many motifs in early European societies which has been treated extensively by many commentators. I suggest this dual motif is the older. In a lecture to the Pictish Arts Society in 1999 Dr Emily Lyle of the School of Scottish Studies at Edinburgh University, presented a model for potential matrilineal succession among the Picts in which one female line provided direct succession for the queen while another gave a line of mothers of kings who attained sovereignty by marrying the queen. Such a structure could ultimately have derived from precisely such a duality. The story of the Cailleach turning into Bride would appear to be a remnant of this that has passed into Gaelic from a source of great antiquity.

Mackenzie mentions a Romanian tale, in which a hag called Malvinia, based on a mountaintop, had eight witch companions (p.173). This is a clear example of the Nine Maidens motif, in that we have the nine women as witches, situated on a mountain called Silash, and actively involved in spreading winter. In a further echo of Scottish traditions, these nine witches were turned to stone on the mountaintop, echoing the widespread British tales of standing stones and stone circles being witches, or sometimes Sabbath revellers, who were turned to stone.

The Cailleach is closely associated with mountains. Before the growth of major cities, people were more aware of their natural environment. They would have observed mountains as the points around which changes in the weather originated. An early meaning of *Cailleach* is 'the veiled one'. This meaning of veiled is presumably what led to the term becoming the word for a nun in modern Gaelic. If you watch the clouds gather around Scottish mountains at almost any time of the year you will see this idea made remarkably explicit in the landscape. And not just Scottish mountains. Just as the Cailleach is veiled, so, often, are the mountains she inhabits. She is strongly associated with Ben Nevis, the highest mountain in the British Isles, notable for its dramatic and ever-changing weather patterns, and many other Scottish mountains and hills. The Corryvreckan, the remarkable whirlpool on the west coast of Scotland between the islands of Scarba and Jura is said to be where the Cailleach washed her plaid (the one-piece traditional garment of the Highlands, generally tartan) in late autumn and then spread it out over the mountains to dry. As she was the oldest creature her plaid was pure white: so the story explains both the period of heaviest activity of the whirlpool and the first serious snow fall of the year.

F Marian McNeill tells us in *The Silver Bough*:

> The Cailleach is the genius of winter and the enemy of growth. Her chief seat is Ben Nevis She ushers in winter by washing her great plaid in the whirlpool of Corryvreckan (Coire Bhreacain – the Cauldron of the Plaid) Before the washing, it is said, the roar of a coming tempest is heard by people on the coast for a distance of twenty miles, for a period of three days until the cauldron boils. When the washing is over, the plaid of old Scotland is virgin white. (2 p.20)

Here the Cailleach's cauldron is the whirlpool of the Corryvreckan and the cauldron is associated with Nine Maidens groups in other traditions as we shall see. Surviving folklore also refers to this whirlpool as being the breath of the Goddess beneath the waves. Only since humans have achieved space flight has it become known that the oceans contain eddies, up to 20 kilometres across, which circulate warm surface water into the depths thus releasing life-sustaining nutrients. This gives the motif of the whirlpool as the cauldron of the Mother Goddess, a whole new level of meaning. Mythology explains the physical universe and its attributes in human terms. Such material can often contain sophisticated observations and insights. In order to give lore and tradition the strongest possibility of being remembered, and to ensure that the moral lessons as well as its practical applications would be appreciated, tradition bearers would present their material within the environment familiar to their listeners. This accounts for the widespread instances of names in the Scottish landscape like *Allt na Cailleach* (Stream of the Old Woman), a name that can be interpreted as originally meaning the stream of the Goddess. The Cailleach is also said to have created a range of places across Scotland by dropping a creel, or apron full of peat and rocks. Her relation to the physical world, to seasonal change and to weather, shows we are dealing with a fundamental mythological construct.

The figure of the Cailleach in Gaelic tradition is paralleled in Scots tradition by the Gyre Carlin, also often portrayed as a winter hag and linked to the traditions of the witches which survive in many areas. Donald Mackenzie in *Egyptian Myth and Legend* writes:

> One of the many versions of the Scottish Hag story makes her the chief of eight big old women or witches. This group of nine suggests Ptah and his eight earth gnomes, the nine mothers of Heimdal the Norse god and the Ennead of Heliopolis (p. xxxviii)

In this association of the Cailleach with a group of nine she is one of the nine whereas most of our Bride references are to Bride and nine others. Mackenzie goes further and compares this group to the nine mothers of Heimdall in Norse myth and the Ennead of Heliopolis in Egypt. He makes the point, 'A people seldom remember their early history, but they rarely forget their tribal beliefs . . .' This is a particularly relevant statement for Scotland where Celtic-speaking, warrior tribes were in existence till 250 years ago and had retained many of the characteristics of Iron Age society.

More support for the Scottish provenance of Bride in Scotland comes from Jhone Leslie who writes in his 16th century *Historie of Scotland*:

> The Scottis, Peychtes, Britanis, Inglismen & Irishmen with sik veneratione in ilk place have honoured S Brigida, that innumerable kirkes erected to God, amang them ale, to her, ye sal se; yie and mae to her than to ony of the rest: the Irland men contendes that her haly body thay have with thame in that toune quhilke thay cal Dun, in quhilke place the body of thair Apostle S. Patrik is keipet. our cuntrey men ascrynes the same Glore unto thame, quha thinkes, that hitherto thay have honouret it in the Chanrie of Abernethie, & richtlie have done thay think. (1 p.229)

> The Scots, Picts, Britons, Englishmen and Irishmen with such veneration in every place have honoured St Brigid, that innumerable churches erected to God, among them all, to her, you shall see; yes and more to her than to any of the rest. The Irish people contend that her holy body they have with them in that town which they call Dun, in which place the body of their Apostle St Patrick is kept. Our countrymen ascribe the same Glory unto themselves, who think, that hitherto they have honoured it in the Chancery of Abernethy and have done so rightly to their own thinking. (translation)

In referring to the different tribal confederations/statelets of Dark Age northern Britain, Leslie is clearly differentiating between Britons and Englishmen. By Britons he appears to mean the P-Celtic people of Strathclyde, and probably the people of Manau Gododdin, known to the Romans as the Votadini, inhabiting the lands from East Lothian to possibly as far as the headwaters of the Forth, and perhaps as far south as the Tyne at some point. He is making it clear that St Brigid was known to both the P- and Q-Celtic tribes and to the Germanic-speaking peoples in what we now call Scotland. This supports of the idea of Bride being indigenous to Scotland and clearly points to a cult of St Bride/Bridget among Christians in Scotland in the pre-Reformation period. The belief that Brigid is buried at Abernethy in no way precludes her Irish provenance, but, taken together with the other evidence, this appears to be part of a continuum of belief which was indigenous to Scotland.

F Marian McNeill describes the following ritual in *The Silver Bough*:

> The parish church at Sanquhar in Dumfries-shire, stands on the site of a chapel dedicated to the saint, and not far off is St Bride's Well, where the young girls of the district used to repair on Beltane morning,

> each bringing an offering of nine white stones, symbolic of the traditional nine virgin attendants of the saint. (2 p.29)

The use of white stones here is perhaps a variation on the ancient practice of including white pebbles in burials – a practice that started in pre-Christian times and carried on into the early Christian period in Scotland; the use of the nine stones here was in honour of the Nine Maidens.

McNeill gives several examples of rituals performed in honour of Bride and St Bridget, whose importance in the Gaelic tradition is emphasised in her title as Handmaiden to Mary, or Birthmaiden to Christ. This would seem to be a transference of an established Goddess figure into the pantheon of a new religion – it was always the practice for the early Christian church to absorb some elements of previous belief when they moved into a new area. Even today, many of the fiestas of Mediterranean Europe appear to contain ideas that are closer to ancient belief than conventional Christianity. The Scottish Hebrides have been interpreted as the Eilean-Bride – the islands of Bride, and were said to have been created by the Cailleach, though the etymological derivation from Bride has been considered unlikely. Within Gaelic tradition one association with Bride that stands out as a strong echo of pre-Christian thought is her association with the serpent. The serpent in Christian terms is of course a symbol of evil but it is cast in a different light in several rhymes. In these traditions Bride's association is specifically with the adder, Scotland's only indigenous snake. The adder is also supposed to be linked with various Druidic traditions. McNeill gives this version of a hymn to the adder emerging from its hibernation on Imbolc, St Bride's Day, 1 February:

> Today is the day of Bride
> the serpent shall come from the hole
> I will not molest the serpent
> Nor will the serpent molest me. (2 p.27)

This hymn to the adder has been regarded as a relic of serpent worship by several commentators, but it is probably more accurate to say that the serpent/adder is a symbol associated with the Mother Goddess. In many cultures the serpent has been seen as symbol of knowledge. It is particularly fitting as a symbol of fertility, more specifically regeneration, as it seems to disappear into the earth through the winter, like seeds that are planted in autumn, lie dormant and come up in the spring. The annual replacement of its skin is also symbolic of rebirth and regeneration. The so-called worship of the dead, in rituals associated with ancient chambered cairns and other prehistoric sites, can be interpreted as prayers to the departed spirits of the ancestors – who have returned to the earth – to work their magic on the planted seeds to ensure next year's harvest grows. This idea is discussed in Hutton's *The Pre-Christian Religions of Prehistoric British Isles*. A variety of serpent/adder representations on many Pictish symbol stones suggests that the Picts too saw the serpent as a powerful symbol and it is at least possible that they associated it with Bride herself.

McNeill, quoting from *Carmina Gadelica* (Carmichael) tells us of other rites associated with Bride. It seems that in Rutherglen, nowadays a district of Glasgow, on the Eve of Bride's Day, groups of women (we are not told how many) would gather together and make an oblong basket they called *leaba Bride*, the bed of Bride, which they would decorate. Then, taking a selected sheaf of corn, they would fashion it into the shape of a woman and then they would 'deck this ikon with gay ribbons from the loom, sparkling shells from the sea, and bright stones from the hill.' The figure was called Bride:

> When it is dressed and decorated, one woman goes to the door of the house and, standing on the step with her hands on the jambs, calls softly into the darkness, 'Bride's bed is ready.' To this a ready woman behind replies, 'Let Bride come in. Bride is welcome.' The woman at the door again addresses Bride, 'Bride come thou in, thy bed is made. Preserve

the house for the Trinity.' The women then place the ikon of Bride with great ceremony in the bed. They place a small straight white wand (the bark being peeled off) beside the figure. The wand is generally of birch, broom, bramble, white willow or other sacred wood, 'crossed' or banned wood being carefully avoided. The women then level the ashes on the hearth, smoothing them carefully. In the early morning, the family closely scan the ashes. If they find the mark of the wand of Bride they rejoice, but if they find lorg Bride, the footprint of Bride, their joy is very great, for this is a sign that Bride was present with them during the night, and is favourable to them, and that there is increase in family, in flock, and in field in the coming year. Should there be no marks on the ashes, the family are dejected. It is a sign that she is offended and will not hear their call. To propitiate her and gain her ear the family offer oblations, and burn incense on the hearth.
(2 p.26)

It should be remembered that these practices are recorded as happening in communities that had been ostensibly Christian for over a thousand years. They underline the hold that the idea of Bride, an aspect of the Mother Goddess, continued to have on both community and individual until relatively recently.

Just as Bride is associated with the serpent, the Cailleach is associated with the cauldron, another symbol often found on the Pictish symbol stones. There are literally dozens of Bride and St Bride place-names not only in the Western Isles but all over Scotland and a good exposition of these can be found in Mackinlay's *Ancient Church Dedications in Scotland*. Further, as works on Scottish folklore such as Dalyell's *The Darker Superstitions of Scotland* and Gregor's *Folklore of North-East Scotland* show, pre-Christian beliefs have never been totally eradicated in Scotland. Bride and the Nine Maidens maintained a strong hold on the imagination of people in those communities where the oral tradition continued to play a strong role.

The attendance at the Nine Maidens Well at Pittempton until the 1870s, mentioned in Chapter 1, and the survival of the rite at Bride's Well in Sanquhar are cases in point. During the Second World War a group of young women enacted a pageant based on Bride and the Nine Maidens in Abernethy and one of my students told me of a fragment of surviving local folklore linking a story of nine witches with the Pictish tower there that she had been told by her grandmother.

As has been noted, the early history of the British Isles is full of individuals portrayed as saints who, like Bridget, are based on earlier pre-Christian figures. The Nine Maidens themselves after all are entered in the *Aberdeen Breviary* as being Pictish saints and there are other figures who seem to be part of similar traditions. One of these is St Monenna who appears under a variety of names including Darerca, Modwenna and Moninne, and the same figure seems to be behind the saints Edana and Medana. Like the Nine Maidens, she does not appear in the official Roman Catholic lists and therefore must be seen as indigenous to the British Isles. Monenna is said to have been a friend of St Bridget's, who came to Scotland from Ireland with eight virgins, a widow and the widow's son. Forbes' *Kalendars of Scottish Saints* has the following:

> When St Patrick came to her neighbourhood she presented herself before him, and received from him the virgin habit near the pool of Brigius, the translation of which means abundance. She proceeded to associate herself with eight virgins and one widow, with her baby named Luger, whom Darerca adopted, and who afterwards became a bishop. (p.404)

Here Monenna, like Bridget, is associated with a group of Nine Maidens and as is often the case, there is mention of a single male, as in the stories of Martin's Stane and of Ochonochar. This association of Nine Maidens with one male figure crop ups again and again. Stories which have it that this single male is born to one, or all, of the Nine Maidens occur mainly in Norse tradition (Chapter 6). Modwenna was baptised in a pool of abundance, echoing the pre-Christian traditions of fertility, specifically of cauldrons of abundance. In his *The Early Christianizing of Scotland*, Knight gives the following story from Galloway where there are several place-names associated with Modwenna:

> The legend states that the maiden and her companions took to a rock in the sea, which by her prayers, became a boat and carried them over the thirty miles to Farnes, now a part of Glasserton parish on the east side of Luce Bay. Still her admirer followed her and tracked her down. Climbing into a tree, she asked, 'What is it that you see in me that excites your passion?', ' Your face and eyes,' he said. Instantly she tore out her eyes and flung them at his feet! Horror-struck and filled with remorse, the soldier departed, and Modwenna descending from the tree, washed her face in a spring that had miraculously gushed up. (p.250)

The same story is told of the supposed saint Triduana, whose well at Restalrig in Edinburgh was known far and wide for its efficacy in curing disease of the eyes! There is an ancient motif concerned with eyes and healing behind these tales, but the Christianised versions have left us with little more than a bloody horror story. OGS Crawford in *The Eye Goddess* has written extensively on the link between the Goddess and the eye symbol. The great Australian scholar and poet Alexander Hope in his delightful *A Midsummer Eve's Dream* makes the point that Triduana was in fact the name of a three-day fast in the Celtic Church and was associated with three female figures, the others being Potencia and Emeria. He saw them as deriving from a tripartite protective goddess of a sacred well.

The list of churches Monenna is said to have founded in what we now call Scotland is given in Skene's *Celtic Scotland*:

> [S]he is said to have founded seven churches in Scotland: one at Chilnecase in Galloway, a second on the hill of Dundonald in Ayrshire, a third on Dumbarton rock, a fourth in the castle of Strivelyn or Stirling, a fifth at Dunedene which in Anglic is called Edinburgh, a sixth on the hill of Dunpelder in East Lothian, and the seventh at Lanfortin or Longforgund in Gowrie, where she is said to have died. (1 p.37)

Edinburgh, the capital of Scotland, was a major site in the Dark Ages as were; Dumbarton, the fort of the Britons, associated with the legendary Arthur; Stirling Rock, a major site of the Gododdin or Votadini, who are the subject of Britain's oldest extant heroic poem *The Gododdin;* Traprain Law a hilltop settlement/ritual site of the Votadini in Roman times and home of the legendary King Loth, brother-in-law to Arthur and grandfather of St Kentigern. Dundonald was also a supposed hill-fort and may well have been a site of local significance, while Chilnecase is interpreted as being Candida Casa, the site of the foundation of Scotland's earliest Christian saint St Ninian, who lived in the 5th century and with whom Monenna was said to have been in contact. These are all important, possibly communal/ritual centres except Longforgan (Longforgund) on the north bank of the Tay, which as far as I can tell has had no great place in history. However this is not to say that it was not important, merely that we have no record of the fact, nor any particular traditions to fall back on.

Such locations suggest the intriguing possibility that there were groups of Nine Maidens at sites of major ritual or communal. perhaps even sacral, importance to the various tribal peoples of Dark Age Scotland, just as the Pictish centre of Abernethy had its Nine Maidens, who were possibly pre-Christian priestesses involved in augury and healing. In support of this contention a name for Edinburgh Castle from 12th century written sources is *Castella Puellarum* – the Castle of the Maidens – and a local tradition said it was where the Picts kept their daughters. The term 'Picts' was for a long time a generic or catch-all word for 'the ancestors' in popular culture throughout Scotland. The term 'Castle of Maidens' is used for Edinburgh, or Holyrood Abbey, in several 12th and 13th century chronicles (Anderson 1990, II pp. 224, 297,303, 304, 498, 581,690). It is particularly noticeable that the term 'Castle of Maidens' is the most common one used for Edinburgh in this period. 'Castle of Maidens' was also used extensively by the writers of European Arthurian romances in the Middle Ages. As we shall see the Nine Maidens motif occurs extensively within Arthurian tradition. JS Glennie in his *Arthurian Localities in Scotland* was the first relatively modern writer to draw attention to the rootedness of Arthurian traditions in Scotland and gives well-argued locations for all of King Arthur's supposed battles here. Skene gives an 8th century P-Celtic name for Edinburgh Castle as *Mynyd Agned* (p.76), translated as the Mount or Castle of Maidens. With the figure of Arthur being common to the mythology and legendary traditions of all the P-Celtic speakers, the tales would also have been known amongst the Picts, accounting for the survival of the story of Arthur and Vanora (Guinevere) at Meigle in Perthshire. The first datable reference to Arthur is in the 6/7th century epic poem *The Gododdin* detailing a disastrous battle expedition purportedly to northern England by a group of warriors from near the Forth. This has been widely suggested as having been originally composed on Edinburgh's Castle Rock which plays a prominent part in the poem.

The location of these Nine Maidens groups on significant hilltops is reminiscent of the Vestal Virgins on Capitol Hill in Rome, and there are many references to groups of priestesses similarly located on hilltops in classical sources. This corresponds to the association of the Cailleach with mountaintops in Scotland. We can also see some correlation in such groups being close to seats of temporal power like the Vestals, and the above sites were all certainly sites of some local importance in Dark Age Scotland. It might even be that ritual, even sacral, functions predated any military use of these sites. Most European hilltop excavations to date have concentrated on the sites' military usage. James Grant, in his *Old and New Edinburgh* tells us of St Monenna:

> The site of her edifice is supposed to be that now occupied by the Chapel of St Margaret, the most ancient piece of masonry in the Scottish capital; and it is a curious circumstance, with special reference to the fable of the Pictish princesses that close by it, as recorded in the *Caledonian Mercury* of 20 September 1853, when some excavations were made, a number of human bones, apparently all females, together with some coffins, were found. (1 p.15)

He also tells us that according to the 16th century English historian Camden:

> The Britons called it Mynydh Agnedh – the maidens' or virgins' castle – because certain young maidens of royal blood were kept there in olden times. (Ibid.)

Wilson, in his *Memorials of Edinburgh in the Olden Time* has the following:

> According to Father Hay's apocryphal account, certain nuns attached to the royal chapel, and from whom the castle derived the name Castrum Puellarum, were thrust out by St David, and in their place canons introduced by the Pope's dispense, as fitter to live among soldiers. (2 p.4)

The discovery of female bodies and the name *Mynydh Agnedh* both support the possibility that Edinburgh Castle could have been a Nine Maidens site and in the story of the expulsion of the nuns from Edinburgh Castle we can perhaps discern echoes of other stories about other Nine Maidens being expelled or punished for sexual misbehaviour. There are traditions in several parts of Scotland where nunneries were said to have been established but for which there is no historical evidence. These may be Christianised versions of tales about earlier priestess groups. One example is Inchncailloch in Loch Lomond which tradition says housed a nunnery. A tale was told here of a priest killing a nun who planned to escape the island with her lover. The idea of the nunnery perhaps arises from the use of the term Cailleach itself, meaning the hooded one, for nuns. Sites of priestess groups worshipping a Mother Goddess figure might easily retain the name of the Goddess. It is also possible that such groups of pre-Christian priestesses could be interpreted as nuns by later, Christianised society.

The motif of Nine Maiden groups living in communities on hilltop sites or on islands occurs repeatedly and not only in Scotland. That there were specific groups of Nine Maidens associated with culturally, and politically, important Dark Age sites in Scotland is clear, and it is tempting to see such groups as being part of a common social structure that existed across tribal boundaries in contemporary Scotland and beyond.

The term 'Maiden Castle' is relatively common and it is strikingly obvious that these 'castles' are not all defensive structures. Hope makes an interesting connection:

> The shapes of certain hills may by themselves suggest such names as the Maiden-pap in Perthshire or the Hill with the Paps (Bennachie) in Aberdeenshire. But the Paps of Anu in Kerry remind us that not only were such hills sometimes named for their likeness to breasts but because they were thought to be the breasts of a Goddess. (p.37)

While Edinburgh Castle Rock is not one of this particular type of site, the association with St Monenna, the discovery of female bodies, and the name Castle of the Maidens all strengthen the possibility of it as a Nine Maidens site. Given the suggested link from earlier Goddess worship, it is interesting that the castle has become so closely associated with St Margaret, the foremost of Scottish female saints. The links between the Cailleach figure and so many different mountain locations in Scotland suggest that the choice of hilltop locations for priestess groups is not just fortuitous, just as the concept of mountaintops being sacred places is commonplace throughout human societies.

CHAPTER 3

The Nine Maidens in Welsh Tradition

THE GREATEST SURVIVING collection of early mythological material from Wales is *The Mabinogion*, which, along with the works of the semi-mythical bard Taliesin, contain much of what we know regarding the beliefs and ideas of the P-Celtic speaking tribes of Britain. These included not only the Welsh and Cornish peoples and the Picts but the tribal confederations in most of the west of Britain south of the Clyde and south-east Scotland. Many historians think that the whole population of what is now England, Scotland and Wales spoke variants of P-Celtic languages when the Romans first arrived in Britain in 55BC. It is quite likely however that the picture was considerably more complicated than that. With the relative ease of travel by sea at certain times of the year, there was trade in such commodities as amber and gold between Ireland and Scandinavia in prehistoric times and there was ongoing contact between the peoples adjoining the Irish and North Seas and along the Atlantic coasts from Megalithic times on. There seems no reason to doubt that the people of these islands were the direct descendants of the people who had raised the Megalithic monuments from Stonehenge to Calanais and from New Grange to Maes Howe in Orkney which show a cultural continuity over most of the north-eastern Atlantic littoral. Trading links between the east coast of Scotland and the Baltic have survived till the present day. Strong similarities between certain aspects of legendary and mythological material in Britain, Scandinavia, Gaul and Greece suggest either a common origin or strong ongoing cultural contacts, or indeed both.

The oldest surviving poem in Welsh is *The Gododdin* originating around the year 600CE in Scotland amongst the P-Celtic speaking people of Lothian. It describes a tragic raid by a group of warriors from Edinburgh, generally interpreted as going south into what is now England – a raid which saw virtually the entire force wiped out. The poem would appear to have been known amongst the P-Celtic speaking peoples of Scotland and Wales and as the Brythonnic language retreated it became part of Welsh tradition. There is an understandable temptation to project known realities back into periods of which we have little knowledge. Thus Dark Age Britain is presented as being formed of a number of petty kingdoms. I suggest a more appropriate picture would be to look at them as tribal areas or tribal confederations. The reaction against the Roman invasion in both the north and south shows a capacity among the various tribes to unite in the face of a common adversary. In the south there were the revolts led by Boudicca and Cartimandua and in the north the Caledonian confederacy opposed the Roman general Julius Agricola at the battle of Mons Graupius, according to a Roman source. This pattern of behaviour is therefore not uncommon. Once any immediate threat was over, the warriors of the gathered clans or tribes would return to their own areas and people. War leaders, chosen for their ability not their lineage, would revert to their former status after such events. This pattern of behaviour survived to a considerable extent into 17th century Scotland amongst the Highland clans, Celtic-speaking warrior tribes whose life seems to have changed little for hundreds of years, perhaps at some levels even since the Dark Ages. The notion that there was some kind of feudal tie between a leader and his followers in this period is unsustainable – which has not stopped historians analysing them as if they were exactly like later kingship-based societies. The relationship between the warriors of a tribe and their chief is totally unlike that of feudal subjects and their king. This is borne out by what we know of late Scottish Highland Celtic society. An example of the relationship between tribesman and chief comes from Burt's *Letters of a Gentleman,* a collection of letters from the 1730s. He is telling us about the Highlanders' relationship with their chief:

> ... and as the meanest among them pretend to be his Relations by Consanguinity, they insist upon the Privilege of taking him by the Hand whenever they meet him. Concerning this last, I once saw a Number of very discontented Countenances when a certain Lord, one of the Chiefs, endeavoured to evade this Ceremony. It was in Presence of an English Gentleman in high station, from whom he would have willingly have concealed the Knowledge of such seeming Familiarity with slaves of so wretched Appearance, and thinking it, I suppose, as a kind of contradiction to what he had often boasted at other Times, viz., his despotic Power over his Clan. (2 p.109)

It was a clansman's right to shake his chief's hand. While this does not mean that the two were absolute equals it does show that the tribal/clan system was totally unlike that of post-feudal, hierarchic societies elsewhere in Britain and Europe with aristocracy, gentry, and those who were effectively serfs, or as Burt puts it 'slaves'. There is in clan societies a level of egalitarianism that not only contradicts but has no precursors in feudalism. Burt's eyewitness account bears this out. We also know that the Highland warriors were usually led into battle by the most able of their number, rather than the chief, and that chiefs could be, and sometimes were, replaced. This, allied with the well-attested elective aspect of chieftainship, and even kingship in tribal societies, in early Irish and Welsh sources, suggests strong levels of continuity within the social structure of the indigenous tribes.

The importance of kings and aristocrats in earlier societies has been consistently exaggerated. This can be explained to some extent because what we know of Dark Age British Society comes from sources which were not written down till the early Medieval Period, a time when the role of the king was much more important. Dark Age peoples seem to have been living in societies which were kinship- rather than kingship-based. This however does not diminish the centrality of warrior traditions in such societies.

Alfred P Smyth in his *Warlords and Holy Men*, dealing with Dark Age movements from Scotland to Wales writes:

> Welsh tradition asserted that Cuneda and eight of his sons migrated from Manaw to north Wales where they drove out Irish invaders who had settled there and founded in their turn various Welsh kingdoms and sub-kingdoms in Gwynedd. (p.16)

This shows the links between different Celtic-speaking areas of Britain at this period. We are dealing here with an ancient link between tribes whose descendants ended up speaking different languages, but who inherited some common traditions from when they were speaking the same, or closely related tongues. Such survivals are not surprising given similarities in economy, lifestyle and belief. To concentrate on linguistic differences as if they defined everything about these tribal peoples is to forget that language has never been a badge of ethnicity.

For most people, for much of human history, travel of more than a few miles from home was probably a rare event even though there were ongoing links between geographically diverse groups. My grandmother, for instance, lived in Dundee and her single trip to London, travelling by train, was a notable event in her life. However, though most people in the Dark Ages might travel rarely and for no great distance, there can be no doubt that communication between different societies in Britain and the Continent had been ongoing for millennia. Traders and fishermen were capable of travelling great distances. Travel by water had been normal from Megalithic times and provided a much easier alternative to overland travel, which involved passing through dense forests and vast areas of bog and marsh, particularly in the river valleys. In addition to river travel, the very existence of the megaliths along the Atlantic littoral of Europe, shows that the capacity for crossing the sea passages had been around for a very long time before the Dark Ages. Travelling by sea from central Scotland or further north to Ulster or Wales at certain times of the year would be eminently practicable.

Up until the early Middle Ages much of Britain and Europe consisted of self-sufficient, pastoral economies which had developed from tribal structures. Tribes are aggregates of family groups bound together within a shared environment, with a shared culture, beliefs and ancestry. Much scholarship has concentrated on the warrior and leadership aspects of such societies, reflecting the obsession with militarism and aristocratic dynastic structures. Such structures although arising from tribal societies do not define them. In the Highlands of Scotland the basic cattle economy warrior society survived at the very least from the Iron Age c.500BCE, to the 18th century. What existed before the Iron Age was probably also kinship-based. The term 'clan' means 'children', that is the children of the tribe. This concept is in no way feudal – it represents a fundamental attitude of communality among the Highland peoples, who were descended from both tribal Picts and tribal Scots. And between the Picts on the east and the Scots on the west, lay some of the lands of the Gododdin.

Manaw Gododdin, the land of the Gododdin, appears to have stretched from modern Stirling to Dunbar along the south side of the River Forth and included Edinburgh and all of East Lothian, and most likely going considerably further south. On the north-east, it adjoined Pictland and the Pictish tribespeople spoke a P-Celtic language closely related to that of the Brythonic tribes of Manaw. On the east it was bounded by what became known as the Kingdom of Strathclyde, whose people, the Britons, spoke the same language. The beliefs and oral traditions of these peoples would be similar – they lived in contiguous environments, had similar economies and technologies and spoke closely related if not identical languages. While we cannot definitely state that they shared precise religious practices, surviving evidence would suggest similar belief patterns. The tribes from Manaw, or at least some of them, are referred to in

Welsh tradition as the *Gwyr Y Gogledd*, the Men of the North and this points up that shared heritage of much of early British tribal life. One intriguing possibility is that the tales of Arthur, like those of Cu Chulainn or Finn Mac Cuill in Gaelic-speaking areas, might have in turn derived from some older mythology in a language predating any of the Celtic tongues. The 19th century Scottish scholar WF Skene went as far as to suggest that the tales of both Arthur and Cu Chulainn originated in the lands around Loch Lomond, possibly the western limit of Manaw Gododdin, and bordering the Q-Celtic speaking Scots of the west.

In Welsh tradition, we meet the goddess figure Cerridwen. Just as Bride's flame was tended by Nine Maidens at Kildare so Cerridwen's Cauldron of Poetry and Inspiration is said, in the poem *The Spoils of the Abyss*, to be attended by Nine Maidens. The poem is attributed to Taliesin and this translation is from Lewis Spence's *The Mysteries of Britain*:

> By the breath of nine damsels it is gently warmed. Is it not the cauldron of the chief of Annwn in its fashion With a ridge round its edge of pearls. (p.122)

In this poem King Arthur has gone into the Otherworld (*Annwn*) on a quest for a magical cauldron. As with so much mythological and legendary material, the story would be told in many places and in each would be an integral part of the traditions and beliefs of local society. Cerridwen's cauldron is, like many others in the various Celtic traditions, a singularly magic vessel. F Marian McNeill pointed out in *The Silver Bough* that such cauldrons have influenced later ideas:

> The legend of the Holy Grail is one of the most striking instances of the fusion of Druidical and Christian beliefs, for it derives in part from the Magic Cauldron of Celtic pre-Christianism and in part from the Sacred Chalice of Christianity . . . (2 p.164)

In one particular tale Cerridwen prepares a magic potion in her cauldron to give knowledge to her fearsomely ugly son Avagddu as compensation for his looks. A serving boy, Gwion Bach is set to watch over the brew. Cerridwen gives him explicit instructions not to touch the liquid, which has to brew for a full year when it will yield three drops of divine fluid which Cerridwen intends giving to her son. As the end of the year approaches, the three drops of the potion jump from the cauldron and land on Gwion Bach's finger which he immediately sticks in his mouth, thus becoming divinely inspired instead of Avagddu. Cerridwen immediately knows what is going on and rushes to the cauldron. In an endeavour to escape from her, Gwion becomes first a hare, then a fish and finally a grain of corn. Cerridwen chases him as a greyhound, then as an otter and finally, in the shape of a hen she pecks up the grain of corn. Nine months later she gives birth to the bard Taliesin, Shining Brow, whom she casts on a river in a small basket. He is rescued by Gwuiddno Garanhir and grows up to be the greatest bard of all time. MacCulloch in his *The Religion of the Ancient Celts* says of Cerridwen's Cauldron:

> Cerridwen was a deity of inspiration, like Brigit, though, like other Celtic Goddesses, her primary function may have been with fertility, of which the cauldron, supplying plenty and giving life, is a symbol. (p.112)

The similarity with Bride, given here as Brigit, is striking, but the point here is that we have a clearly portrayed group of nine females who can be interpreted as priestesses of the Goddess. They tend Cerridwen's Cauldron which is used for both inspiration and prophecy and this would appear to make their role as priestesses explicit. Divination, like the shape-shifting in the chase sequence of this story, is a common attribute of many Nine Maidens groups. Inspiration and divination are part of a complex layer of ideas associated with the Nine Maidens and the reference to shape-shifting stresses possible links to what we nowadays think of as shamanism. Many societies have seen poetry and music as being divinely inspired. It seems that in both Bride and Cerridwen we are seeing two different cultural manifestations of a Mother Goddess figure common to the Celtic-speaking peoples, perhaps a figure from what was remote antiquity even to the people of Dark Age Britain. MacCulloch suggests that Cerridwen had been a corn-goddess at an earlier stage and the association of the cauldron symbol with fertility would tend to support this.

Loomis in *Celtic Myth and Arthurian Romance* talks of the Caldron of Tyrnog (probably the same as the fabled Q-Celtic Tir-nan-Og, the land of perpetual youth, sometimes associated with Avalon) which was one of the fabled Thirteen Treasures of Britain in Welsh tradition:

> Of this caldron it is said that 'if meat were put in it to boil for a coward, it would never be boiled, but if meat were put in it for a brave man, it would be boiled forthwith'. It is obviously the same as the pearl-rimmed cauldron of the Head of Annwn, which would not boil the food of a coward or a perjurer. (p.233)

Both Welsh and Irish traditions have magical cauldrons which are in some ways similar. The Cauldron of the Dagda, a primaeval father god figure in Irish tradition, is undoubtedly also a symbol of fertility. This cauldron could feed a host, significantly nine at a time, and also could bring warriors back from the dead, though they could not speak. This is like the cauldron Arthur brings from Annwn, the Welsh Otherworld or Hades, and as we have seen this concept of the magical cauldron is believed by commentators to have been part of the original inspiration for the idea of the Holy Grail. As McCulloch writes:

> The three properties of the cauldron – inexhaustibility, inspiration and regeneration – may be summed up in one word, fertility; and it is significant that

> the god with whom such a cauldron was associated, Dagda was a god of fertility. But we have seen [the cauldron] associated with Goddesses – Cerridwen, Branwen, the woman from the lake – and perhaps this may point to an earlier cult of Goddesses of fertility, later transferred to gods. In this light the cauldron's power of restoring life is significant, since in early belief life is associated with what is feminine. Woman as the fruitful mother suggested the Earth, which produced and nourished, was also female. The cult of fertility was usually associated with orgiastic and indiscriminate lovemaking, and it is not impossible that the cauldron, like the Hindu yoni, was a symbol of fertility . . . (p.382)

McCulloch goes on to compare the concept of human food being interpreted as the food of the gods, (perhaps a bit like the wafer and wine in Christian communion?), with the idea of the actual family cauldron representing the cauldron of the gods. He suggests that myths then arose about the acquisition of magical cauldrons such as the Cauldron of Annwn sought by Arthur. Loomis makes the point that in Arthurian Romance the Grail has many aspects in common with such magical cauldrons saying,

> in the Grail there was a fusion of the magic cauldron of Celtic pre-Christianism and the Sacred Chalice of Christianity, with the product made mystic and glorious in a most wonderful manner. (ibid)

In *The Mabinogion* there are references to the same or similar cauldrons. In the story *Branwen, Daughter of Llyr*, King says to Matholwch:

> I will give thee a cauldron and the virtue of the cauldron is this: a man of thine slain today, cast him into the cauldron, and by tomorrow he will be as well as he was at the best, save that he will not have the power of speech. (p.124)

This is an exact match for the cauldron of the Dagda in Irish tradition. Also in the *Mabinogion* story *Peredur, Son of Efrawg*, there is reference to a similar vessel of healing:

> Peredur set out on his way thence, and he came to the court of the sons of the King of Suffering. And when he came to the court, he could see none but women. And the women rose before him and made him welcome. And at the beginning of their converse he could see a horse coming, and a saddle on him, and a corpse in the saddle. And one of the women rose up and took the corpse from the saddle, and bathed it in a tub that was below the door with warm water therein, and applied precious ointment to it. And the man rose up alive, and came to where Peredur was seated and saluted him and made him welcome. And two other men came in inside in their saddles, and the woman gave these two the same treatment as the one before ... (p.174)

There is also the Welsh tradition of Gwyddneu Long-shank's hamper which has some of the same attributes as the cauldron of the Dagda. In the *Tale of Culhwch and Olwen* the giant Yspadden sets Culhwch a series of tests before he will give him his daughter's hand in marriage. One of the tasks is to get this hamper:

> ... there is that thou will not get. The hamper of Gwyddneu Long-shank: if the whole world should come around it, thrice nine men at a time, the meat that every one wished for he would find therein, to his liking. I must eat therefrom the night my daughter sleeps with thee. (p.96)

This incidentally is the same Gwyddneu who found the baby Taliesin and raised him. This hamper, like the cauldron, is a deeply significant symbol. Cooking food in a cauldron suspended over a fire, which was generally at the centre of the house below a smoke hole, was widespread in much of the world. Not only did this put the cauldron at the centre of all family and social life but symbolically at the heart of the universe. In cultures where shamanism has survived, there are references to the shaman going on his spirit journey by climbing a tree. Such trees have been represented as linking the hearth to the centre of the sky through the smoke hole. Such symbolism is at one level quite mundane and at another remarkably intricate. It is a mistake to underestimate the potential for complex thought and communication in pre-literate societies. The cauldron is the cooking pot of the family and also a central mythic object at the same time. In votive deposits, materials deliberately cast into wells, lakes or rivers, cauldrons sometimes appear and there is a particularly striking one from Carlingwark Loch at Castle Douglas near Dumfries in Scotland which can be seen in the Museum of Scotland. The name of the loch, Carlingwark, contains the term Carlin, the Scots version of the Gaelic Cailleach, and a term used until very late to signify the Queen of the Witches in Scotland.

Among the Picts, we have direct evidence of the importance of the cauldron. Cauldrons are shown in a variety of forms on both Class I Pictish symbol stones which only have pre-Christian symbols, and on Class II stones where Christian crosses appear with pre-Christian symbols – generally on opposite sides of the symbol stone. The stone at Glamis Manse (there is a Nine Maidens Well nearby) has a particularly striking example of the cauldron with two pairs of legs protruding from it. This has been interpreted as showing some form of ritual execution. However, when we think of the respective cauldrons of the Dagda and Bendigeidfran in Irish and Welsh traditions there is a much more obvious explanation. This can be seen as a cauldron in which dead warriors are being brought back to life. The stated policy of the Christian church was to include pre-Christian ideas in their procedures and this is exactly what we see on some Pictish Class II stones – the combination of different sets of symbols reflecting different belief systems. Perhaps the most famous ancient cauldron, the Gundestrup Cauldron, found in Denmark, but believed to have originated in a Celtic-speaking area, shows in its motifs and symbols what seems to be an intricate and complex mythological series of scenes. It is made of silver, showing how important this artefact was. The powers associated with these cauldrons, fertility, regeneration and abundance, are fundamentally feminine and associated with Mother Goddess figures. The link to Cerridwen's cauldron is significant in that we can see here the Nine Maidens as the tenders of the sacred symbol of the cauldron. Later we will look at another group directly referred to as Druidesses, a rather vague term, but one which underlines this aspect of Nine Maidens groups as officiating priestesses in pre-Christian ritual.

The Christian use of pre-Christian temples, or ritual sites, to preach in, was meant to ensure a smooth transition to the new religion; the continuing use of known symbols would have been reassuring for people coming to terms with the new religion. This perhaps explains how so many remnants of pre-Christian thought survived into Christian times. It might also suggest why so many Pictish symbol stones have pre-Christian symbols on one side and Christian symbols on the other. The example of the Nine Maidens Well at Pittempton, where people came on the first Sunday in May, suggests that traditional practices which stemmed from pre-Christian times were deep-rooted in the minds of the people until surprisingly recently. It seems likely that this well would initially have been visited at Beltane, and that the day was moved to the first Sunday in May under the influence of the Christian church. There are several locations in Scotland where wells are still being visited.

Nine, the number, crops up time and again in folklore and mythology in many parts of the world. We will look at this in greater detail in a later chapter but meantime a couple of examples from *The Mabinogion* itself will serve to illustrate this. In the story of Culhwch and Olwen we have the following:

> Cei had this peculiarity, nine nights and nine days
> his breath lasted under water, nine nights and nine
> days would he be without sleep. (p.90)

Cei is of course one of the Arthurian warriors who later become Knights of the Round Table in popular romance. Another example from the same tale:

> She went to her chamber. They then arose to go
> after her to the fort, and slew nine gatemen who
> were at nine gates without a man crying out and
> nine mastiffs without one squealing. (pp.93-4)

In the poem *Cad Godeu*, Taliesin himself says he was created 'of nine-form faculties' (Skene 1988, p.137). It is clearly feasible to interpret the Nine Maidens associated with the Cauldron of Cerridwen as pre-Christian priestesses but there is another group who show up in *The Mabinogion* with a different aspect. Peredur in the story *Peredur, Son of Efrawg* is generally accepted to be the basis for the later Perceval in Arthurian literature. He is a hero on a quest who meets with many adventures. As Lewis Spence said of this material,

> the Peredur story was derived from a number of
> older British tales dealing with the figures of British
> myth, and it reveals 'the peculiarly weird and fantas-
> tic impress of Celtic mythic tradition'. (1995, p.171)

In time we will see that the motif of the Nine Maidens is indeed 'older' – but much, much older than any British tradition could possibly be.

In *The Mabinogion* story, Peredur comes to a castle. He hammers on the door of the castle with the butt of his spear and the door is opened by a powerfully-built, handsome, red-haired lad who leads Peredur into a hall. There a large handsome woman is sitting in a chair surrounded by her handmaidens. She welcomes him and offers him hospitality. The story continues:

> And when it was time to go to meat they went. And after meat, 'Twere well for thee chieftain,' said the woman,' to go elsewhere to sleep.' 'May I not sleep here?' 'Nine witches, friend,' said she, 'are there here, and their father and mother with them. They are the witches of Caer Lyow. And by daybreak we shall be no nearer to escaping than to being slain. And they have overrun and laid waste the dominion save for this house.'
>
> ' Aye,' said Peredur, 'here would I be tonight. And if trouble comes, if I can do good, that I will. Harm, however, I will not do.' They went to sleep. (p.164)

The following morning just after dawn Peredur is awakened by a dreadful screaming. Picking up his sword he rushes outside, still half-dressed, to see the castle watchman being chased by a witch. The watchman is screaming. Before the witch can harm the watchman, Peredur catches up with them and strikes the witch on her head with his sword, crushing her helmet.

The witch then pleads for mercy:

> Thy mercy, fair Peredur, son of Efrawg, and the mercy of God.' 'How knowest thou, hag, that I am Peredur?' 'It was fated and foreseen that I should suffer affliction from thee, and that thou shouldst take horse and arms from me. And thou shalt be with me awhile being taught to ride thy horse and handle thy weapons.' 'On these terms,' he replied, 'shalt thou have mercy: thy pledge that thou should never do hurt to this countess's dominion.' Peredur took assurance thereof, and by leave of the countess he set off with the witch to the Witches' Court. And he was there three weeks on end. And then Peredur took his choice of horse and arms, and set out on his way.' (ibid)

This episode with Peredur being trained and given arms by the witches is strikingly reminiscent of the Irish hero Cu Chulainn and his journey to receive training in arms from the female warrior Scathach. Although there are traditional tales of Scathach being on the Isle of Skye, off Scotland's west coast, Rees and Rees in their *Celtic Heritage* have the following:

> Then Domnall, king of Scotland told Cu Chulainn that he would not be fully trained until he came to Scathach [Shadow], at this [he] set out to the abode of this female champion in the East of Alba [Scotland]. (p.254)

The east and north of Scotland were, of course, the areas where the Picts lived; areas where we have seen there are many remnants of Nine Maidens traditions. Like Peredur, Cu Chulainn has to face many perils but like Peredur also, he is trained in arms under female supervision. As Ross points out in *Pre-Christian Celtic Britain*, Cu Chulainn is in fact trained by two warrior women:

> The warrior Goddess, who is also a mother figure, clearly underlies the two powerful women whom Cu Chulainn trains under in Britain. They are called Scathach 'The Shadowy One' and Buananna 'The Lasting One' . . . (p.291)

This motif is also present in the story of the arming of the Norse God Thor. Donald A Mackenzie writes in *Scottish Folklore and Folklife*:

> Heroes who fight against them [giants] are invariably assisted by dogs . . . and they are instructed by indispensable wise women who possess magic wands. What appears to be the oldest Thor story belongs to this class. When Thor sets out to visit Geirrod, he has neither hammer nor belt of strength. The Hag Grid, like the Scottish 'wise woman', warns and instructs him, and gives him her belt and magic wand. (xxxiii)

The wand/hammer is reminiscent of the great Scottish Mother Goddess in her winter aspect of the Cailleach who hammers frost into the ground with her hammer and might suggest that Thor is being made divine by the Goddess herself. Are we seeing something of this same idea in the tuition and bestowing of arms on both Cu Chulainn and Peredur? If so, this would strengthen the link that appears to exist between Nine Maidens groups and the Mother Goddess herself.

The Isle of Skye has been associated not only with Scathach but in ancient tradition with a fearsome nine-headed, half-serpent, half-human giant who is killed by a local hero after kidnapping Nine Maidens in order to eat them. It is from the body of this slain monster that the Long Island of the Hebrides – Lewis, Harris, North and South Uist and their associated islands are said to have been formed (see Chapter 6). Here again we have the motif of a monster and Nine Maidens though in this case the hero is successful in rescuing the group. Also we have a repetition of the lover-hero motif found in the Nine Maidens tales associated with Pittempton and Pitlsigo.

However, in the Peredur story, the nine witches – *gwiddonod* – of Caer Lyow are ambivalent in their nature – on the one hand they are devastating the land and on the other they give training and arms to the hero Peredur. Another group of Nine Maidens from Welsh tradition are also clearly malevolent, as recounted by Lewis Spence:

> In the life of the Welsh St Samson of Dol we are told that when he and a companion were passing through south Wales they had to traverse a vast forest. Suddenly they heard a series of shrieks so appalling that St Samson's companion took to his heels. The clamour arose from a forest-spirit which appeared in the shape of a very aged woman, with shaggy grey hair and wearing blood-red garments, who bore a large trident dripping with gore. She swiftly came up with the flying man and plunged her three-headed lance into his body. She addressed the saint abusively

> when he asked her to desist from attacking his comrade and seemed to revel in her wickedness. But she informed him that it was impossible for her to leave the wood, while in a more distant part of it there dwelt others of her species, her mother and her eight sisters. (1948, p.97)

Mont Dol is in Brittany, and this story continues the link to mountains and hills already noted. A Nine Maidens group there was associated with Belenus, generally seen as an early god among the Celtic-speaking peoples (Darrah, p.218). Robert Graves in *The Greek Myths* states that St Samson's acolyte was killed and eaten by this group of Nine Maidens, but this is possibly because Graves was thinking of his own interpretation of the Nine Dancing Maidens at Cogul, whom we will presently consider. I have found no other reference to cannibalism in this context.

The reference to her mother and eight sisters by this wild woman of the woods is possibly more reminiscent of the witches of *Caer Lyow* than either Bride or Cerridwen and their particular maidens. However, the tale seems to be a possible reference to sacrifice and recalls other tales in which the Nine Maidens are associated with a single male, though here a second male, St Samson himself, is spared to give us the tale. Just as Martin and Ochonochar are individually associated with groups of nine women so too are Arthur, the Norse god Heimdall, and the classical Apollo.

Potentially the oldest language spoken in Brittany is Breton, another P-Celtic tongue, related to Welsh. Breton traditions have references to yet another Nine Maidens group. Spence in his *Legends and Romances of Brittany* compares this being, the Korrigan, to the Welsh Cerridwen, telling us:

> Like Cerridwen, the Korrigan is associated with water, with the element which makes for vegetable growth. Christian belief would, of course, transform this discredited Goddess into an evil being whose one function was the destruction of souls. May we see a relation of the Korrigan and Cerridwen

> in Triduana, or St Triduana of Restalrig, near Edinburgh who presided over a certain well there, and at whose well-shrine offerings were made by sightless pilgrims for many centuries? (p.59)

He goes on to tell us about the traditions of the Korrigan abducting children and her habit of luring unwary travellers. She had the power, using her magic wand, to change the deep forest where she lived, into a magnificent castle, filled with delights, into which she would invite her chosen victim. There, seeing her surrounded by her nine attendant maidens he would fall deeply in love with her and abandon all that he had previously held dear, home, hearth, family, wife or lover. Then as the sun rose

> the charm was dissolved as the Korrigan became a hideous hag, as repulsive as before she had been lovely; the walls of her palace and the magnificence which had furnished it became once more tree and thicket, its carpets, moss, its tapestries, leaves, its silver cups wild roses and its dazzling mirrors, stagnant pools. (ibid)

Spence then recounts a specific tale concerning the mediaeval hero-knight Roland and his encounter with the Korrigan, from whom he was lucky to escape. There are several remarkable features in this story. We have a clear representation of what was once a goddess accompanied by Nine Maidens, but the switching from the beautiful, Bride-like figure to the Cailleach-like Hag is the opposite of many folktales in which the hero dares to kiss a loathly hag who then turns into a beautiful young woman. This could well be a sanitised, or Christianised version of an earlier tale. The underlying pre-Christian motif would seem to be that behind the duality of the Goddess lies the oldest duality of all, life and death. There is another similarity between the Korrigan and the Scottish Cailleach. The Cailleach has a hammer with which she pounds winter into the ground whereas the Korrigan has a wand that instantly changes her surroundings. The great

French folklorist Paul Sebillot saw clear similarities between the Korrigan and her maidens and an earlier Breton group of Nine Maidens – the Gallicenae, mentioned in classical sources, who are considered later. The vision of the Korrigan, surrounded by her beautiful maidens is also similar to a tale from Norse mythology where the central figure is the Goddess Menglod.

The generally accepted history of Brittany, at least in the British Isles, presents Celtic-speaking people migrating there from Cornwall in or around the 6th century, bringing with them mythology and legends which were originally British. If so this would strengthen the similarity Spence sees between Korrigan and Cerridwen. The suggestion of a link with St Triduana is not so clear but there are strong similarities in the stories of Triduana and Monenna, who also had nine female companions. Both are presented as having torn out their eyes to dissuade ardent suitors and both are associated with healing wells.

The association of Nine Maidens with Cerridwen, and also with the wild women of the wood that St Samson is said to have encountered, can be seen as supportive of my contention that what we are dealing with in these cases are stories about what were, at one time, actual groups of pre-Christian priestesses.

To return to Peredur: at the close of his story in *The Mabinogion* he is informed that the witches of Caer Lyow have killed his cousin and crippled his uncle:

> And Peredur and Gwalchmei [Gawain] resolved to send to Arthur and his war-band, to ask him to come against the witches. And they began to fight with the witches. And one of the witches slew a man of Arthur's before Peredur's eyes, and Peredur bade her desist. And a second time the witch slew a man before Peredur's eyes, and Peredur drew his sword and smote the witch on the crest of her helm, so that the helm and all the armour and the head were split in two. And she raised a shout, and bade the other witches flee and said that it was Peredur, the man who had been with them learning knighthood and

> who was destined to slay them. And then Arthur
> and his war-band fell upon the witches and the
> witches of Caer Lyow were all slain. (pp.187-8)

Just before this section, there is a statement which directly links the Gloucester witches to traditions of the Grail Quest. A yellow-haired youth tells Peredur he had appeared to him earlier as a black maiden at Arthur's court and then says,

> I came with the head all bloody on the salver, and
> with the spear that had the stream of blood from its
> tip to the hand grip of the spear. And the head was
> thy cousin's, and it was the witches of Caer Lyow
> that had slain him. And 'twas they that lamed thy
> uncle. And thy cousin am I, and it is prophesied that
> thou will avenge that. (p.187)

Here we are deep in mysticism. The head on the salver is reminiscent of the Grail itself, often carried on a silver tray; the blood-tipped spear is a recurring motif in Grail Romances and the lamed king is another version of the Fisher King who is central to later Grail legends. Additionally Peredur's cousin has already appeared to him as a maiden – a strong suggestion of shape-shifting. The colours yellow and black are also the colours associated individually with Bride and the Cailleach in Scottish tradition.

A similar situation to Peredur's occurs in Early Welsh literature. Loomis in his *Arthurian Literature in the Middle Ages* quotes a poem from *The Black Book of Carmarthen*, 'In the heights of Ystafngwn Cai pierced nine witches . . .' (p.14) Although we do not know where Ystafngwn was located it is notable here that the reference is to 'heights'. This suggests that as with the Dark Age sites associated with St Monenna we are dealing with a hilltop location. The witches with whom Peredur is involved are based at Caer Lyow and Caer generally refers to hilltop sites. That all hilltop structures are forts has been shown to be erroneous, the standard military and aristocratic interpretation which promoted this idea having ignored the fact that many hilltop sites were used for the great tribal fire festivals of Beltane and Samhain, and that hill and mountaintops have long been widely associated with Mother Goddess figures. Such sites were also likely to have been used in tribal society for a range of socio-political functions such as law-giving, land allocation, the inauguration of chiefs etc.

The motif of the *Caer Lyow* witches, like that of the wild women of the wood, seems likely to have come about through the necessity for a Christian explanation of these female groups who are so unlike the predominantly masculine Christian ideal, in which women are at best presented as meek and obedient and, at the worst, as the bearers of all sin. The wild women St Samson meets, like the nine witches of *Caer Lyow*, could hardly be further from the standard Christian ideal of womanhood. The Mother Goddess figure central to the old pre-Christian religion was herself subsumed to a certain extent in the person of the Virgin Mary (or in the case of Bride through extremely close association with Mary) but these groups of nine pre-Christian priestesses presented a different problem.

Whenever possible the Christian missionaries of the Dark and Early Middle Ages substituted Christ, Mary and a host of saints as figures to be worshipped in the place of pre-Christian gods and goddesses. As mentioned above (p.26) Bede's *Ecclesiastical History* quotes the letter, originally in Latin, from Pope Gregory to Bishop Mellitus in 605CE:

> I have come to the conclusion that the temples of the idols in England should not on any account be destroyed. Augustine must smash the idols, but the temples themselves should be sprinkled with holy water and altars set up in them in which relics are to be enclosed. For we ought to take advantage of well-built temples by purifying them from devil worship and dedicating them to the service of the true God. In this way, I hope that the people (seeing their temples are not destroyed) will leave their idolatry and

> yet continue to frequent the places as formerly, so coming to know and revere the true God. And since the sacrifice of many oxen to devils is their custom, some other rite ought to be solemnised in its place such as a Day of Dedication or Festivals for the holy martyrs whose relics are there enshrined. On such high days the people might well build themselves shelters of boughs round about the churches that were once temples and celebrate the occasion with pious feasting. They must no more sacrifice animals to the Devil, but they may kill them for food to the glory of God while giving thanks for his bounty to the provider of all gifts. (p.86-7)

So killing animals as a sacrifice to pre-Christian gods was not allowed but killing them for food and giving thanks for them to the Christian god was perfectly acceptable. For a religion that claims to be monotheistic it was very handy that the Christian missionaries had not only a supreme feminine figure but also a plethora of saints through whom to present their 'new' ideas. It would have been difficult to deal with the Nine Maidens in this way as they had no direct similarity within the Christian pantheon of saints. Within Pictish territory however this is what seems to have happened. In other instances we have seen them portrayed as dark and malignant pre-Christian figures. One Nine Maidens group was seen as Druidesses, in Brittany, and some Scandinavian sources portray them as brutal and sadistic. It is hard to avoid the comparison with the Christian propaganda spread about witches – those persecuted do seem on some occasions at least to have been women notable for their knowledge of traditional lore and healing skills. A reading of trial transcripts from Scotland or England soon shows that 'witches' were tortured into repeating the exact formulae that their torturers, good Christians all, wanted to hear. Whether the witches were intending to work good or evil was deemed irrelevant.

In discussing both the witches and the Nine Maidens groups we are largely reliant on early written sources that as far as we can tell were created exclusively by men – usually monks whose primary agenda was the propagation of their religion.

Another striking point about the witches of *Caer Lyow* is that they are fully armed and armoured. In this they resemble the Amazons, those shadowy female warriors of Classical lore. There are also scattered references to women warriors in Celtic sources and in Scandinavian legend we have the Valkyries who are clearly warrior women of some kind. We should be aware that the training of the hero and the granting of arms to him are apparently some sort of initiation and that this is not necessarily just military. We know that sexual activity at sacred sites was not unusual in pre-Christian times, and, given the references to sexual activity among different Nine Maidens groups, this may have been a component in such initiations. Most of what we know as history over the past few centuries, particularly in the dominant Western culture, has excluded the social importance of the feminine aspects of human existence, preferring to deal with military and masculine areas of human activity. Such an approach is not designed to recognise the situation in which the hero figure only reaches his potential because of feminine influence, whether directly from a goddess or through some sort of priestess, which may be the most significant point of such tales.

Another striking similarity among the different language groups of Dark Age Britain is the figure of the Sow which is associated with Cerridwen. In one Arthurian poem, *The Spoils of Annwn*, Arthur goes to the Underworld to seek out Tyrch Twylth, the sacred boar who has a comb and scissors between his ears. This boar is reminiscent of the magical boar of Ben Gulbain which brings about the death of the hero Diarmaid in an Irish tale of Finn McCoul. There are of course Ben Gulbains in various parts of Ireland and Scotland which are told of as the locale of the story. MacCulloch writes of this goddess/boar association thus:

> A bronze statuette represents the Goddess riding a
> wild boar, her symbol and, like herself, a creature
> of the forest, but at an earlier time itself a divinity

of whom the Goddess became an anthropomorphic form. (1992, p.42)

Further to this, the boar turns up on several Pictish symbol stones and the name Orc, meaning 'pig', is thought to have been the tribal name of the people from whom the Orkneys got their name. There is also the story of the sow which swam out from the Corryvreckan and then gave birth to nine piglets near Loch Craignish who were the progenitors of all the wild boars in Scotland. It is of direct interest that one of the islands in that loch is *Eilean na Nighean*, the Island of the Maidens, on which there is ancient structure, given on the Ordnance Survey map as a dun, or fort.

The association of the sow with the 'pot', or cauldron, of the Corryvreckan is reminiscent of Cerridwen. Perhaps what we have here is a veiled reference to a group of nine priestesses associated with the Corryvreckan. It might also be of some relevance that the shape the Corryvreckan whirlpool makes on the surface of the sea is the spiral that occurs on carved rocks at the prehistoric chambered cairn of New Grange in Ireland and in prehistoric locations in several parts of Scotland including some in the mainland area adjacent to the Corryvreckan itself. Here we have a cluster of ideas linking various prominent symbols and mythological motifs within an area that includes an Island of Maidens.

Before looking closer at the concept of Islands of Maidens or Islands of Women we should return briefly to the idea of the Grail. Many scholars have noted that the Grail seems to have developed from an earlier concept in the mythology of the Celtic-speaking peoples of Britain, and that the idea of the magic cauldron is the original of the Grail. It certainly seems to be a prime candidate. The Nine Maidens stories and other material points to the pre-Christian traditions of the British Isles having the idea of the Mother Goddess at their core. Later ideas of gods cannot be ignored, but are not relevant here. The point of mythology is to give an explanation of life and death, and the physical world, in human terms which are easily understood by all. The Corryvreckan itself could be interpreted as the original idea from which the Grail eventually developed. It appears as a physical cauldron at certain times of the year, is strongly associated with the Goddess, and its whirlpool creates a spiral effect on the surface of the sea whenever the tide runs. This spiral is sent out into the full force of the Atlantic tide due to a particular alignment of local tides caused by the geography of the islands. It is a truly awe-inspiring sight even in relatively calm weather and it is not difficult to imagine how such a remarkable, permanent, geophysical event could affect people whose idea of the Mother Goddess encompassed all existence. In Norse tradition, there is the motif of the roaring cauldron Hvergelmer, which is at the centre of the creation of the physical universe itself. There is also the Norse tale of the world being ground out on a giant mill, tended by Nine Maidens (see Chapter 7). Several scholars have drawn attention to the close links between deer and the Mother Goddess in several parts of Europe, including Scotland. Jura, the island on the south of the Gulf of Corryvreckan, means 'Deer Isle'. The wild boar has also been seen as a symbol of several goddess figures in the British Isles. Here at the Corryvreckan there is the Goddess herself, associations with animals and symbols linked to her and foundation mythology explaining the onset of winter. It is a rich mythological mix indeed. And in nearby Loch Craignish there is that ancient structure, interpreted as a dun, or fort, on *Eilean na Nighean*, the Island of Maidens. The Seannachie of Clann Arthur, Hugh McArthur has suggested that the action in the early Welsh poem *The Spoils of Annwn*, previously referred to, took place at, or close to the Corryvreckan whirlpool. (McArthur 2010)

In Cerridwen, we have a figure that is more like Bride than the Cailleach but it is within Welsh tradition we have the clearest and most explicit ideas of the Grail as they developed in a Christian context. As we have seen, there are explicit continuities between Scottish and Welsh traditions and it is conceivable that these continuities result from the central importance of the Mother Goddess figure in pre-Christian religion. And, time and again, with the Goddess, we find the Nine Maidens.

CHAPTER 4

The Nine Maidens in Irish Tradition

IRELAND DOES NOT appear to have the same extent of Nine Maidens material as Scotland, though the links with Bridget and the earlier Bride appear to have been strong in both countries, though some traditions have St Bridget's sacred fire at Kildare being tended by Nine Maidens. However, in one of the early 12th century Irish texts which have survived, *Accalamh na Senorach* or *The Colloquoy of the Ancients*, there are some intriguing references. The document itself is the longest of the early medieval Irish texts and contains a considerable amount of material regarding Finn MacCoul and the Fianna, stories of which were widespread amongst all the Q-Celtic speaking groups.

In one excerpt from Standish O'Grady's 1892 translation, referring to Eochaid, a king who has married Dairne we have this:

> In this place for a year she was by him, but he loved her not; one night therefore in his bed he framed within himself a snare and artifice, which was this: to carry the king of Ireland's daughter into mid-forest, to fell it round about her and, nine foster-sisters that she had being with her, to construct for her a secret and secluded house; then to say that she was dead (pp.109-100)

Following on from this, in a section concerning the renowned warrior, mac Lughach, who was one of the Fianna, there is this:

> Mal mac Aiel, three hundred *óglaechs* strong, went to hunt *sliabh mór monaidh* in Scotland; who being gone the lady in her bower framed a design: to take with her over to Ireland nine own foster-sisters that she had; and such nine women accordingly came over the 'sea's mane' [i.e. wave-crests] to Ben-Edar, where the nine women, the queen, tenth, landed. (p.117)

Shortly after there is this:

> Far and wide on every side the youngster looked about him and there before him saw a vessel that took the haven's beach, there being in her after part a modest-eyed queenly lady with nine women in her company. (ibid)

In these cases we have women who are presented as being of high status, accompanied by nine companions. Many commentators have seen much of this material, particularly that concerning the Fianna, as having originated in the First Millennium, while others have even suggested that they could go back to the dawn of the Iron Age, circa 800BCE. However we must remember that oral tradition's roots can be very deep indeed and in the references to the Nine Maidens themselves we are almost certainly seeing remnants of cultural ideas that are even older than that. We can never know the actual antiquity of the material the monks wrote down in the early Irish manuscripts but the association with queens and kings may well be monkish interpretations of pre-Christian material that had originated at a more mythological level. This is itself illustrated by a later quote from O'Grady's translation,

> It was nine sisters of the *tuatha dé danann's* women that hither came to meet nine warriors of the Fianna; but they being come thus far the children of Morna spied them out as they kept their tryst, and slew them: from whom this spot has the name

> of *líos na mban*. There then they passed that night; on the morrow they took leave and bequeathed a blessing. (p.159)

The Tuatha de Danaan are generally interpreted as being derived from very early material and have been seen by many commentators as essentially supernatural, their name meaning interpreted as Children of the Goddess Danu. Here they are associated with the Fianna whose leader Finn McCoul has many striking similarities with the figure of Arthur amongst the P-Celtic speaking peoples. This section may also have echoes of the meeting of Brendan, and earlier Mael Duin, with twice nine women (see p.135). This is followed by:

> They reached *carn na finghaile* or 'the cairn of fratricide,' now called *dumha na con* or 'the mound of wolf-dogs,' where as they stepped up the *tulach* they saw nine lovely women that with a queen of excellent form in their midst awaited them. A smock of royal silk she had next to her skin; over that an outer tunic of soft silk, and around her a hooded mantle of crimson fastened on her breast with a golden brooch. Upon seeing Caeilte the lady rose and gave him three kisses; then he asked: 'maiden, who art thou?' She replied: 'I am Echna daughter of Muiredach mac Finnachta, the king of Connacht's daughter that is to say.' (ibid)

Here again we have nine women at a putatively mythological level and another reference to them directly associated with royalty. This royal association seems peculiarly Irish but we must remember that there is a considerable amount of Irish material that underlines the inherent sacral role of kingship and that to a Christian the idea of groups of women as religious practitioners would likely have been abhorrent.

Previous to this O'Grady gives us a precis of parts of the text in which he writes of

> *tobar Pátraic* or 'Patrick's well'; the Saint's banishment of the nine goblins into *inis scríne* or 'shrine island' in loch Carra (p.247)

In Harmon's more recent translation of the *Colloquoy* (2001) this story is given in detail:

> Then the entire host and Patrick continued westward to the Witches' Thicket, now called Patrick's Well. The king of the country, Conn Cumachlach, came to see Patrick.
>
> 'Tell us,' said Cailte, 'why is this place called the Witches' Thicket?'
>
> 'Nine women were practising witchcraft,' said the king. 'They did not allow woman or man to go away without killing them. For twenty years they have been destroying the heritage and the land.'
>
> Con then said to Patrick, 'Holy cleric, drive these witches away from us and the distress that is ruining the country and the earth.'
>
> Then Patrick said, 'Where is the acolyte?'
>
> 'I am here' he replied.
>
> 'See if there is water near us.'
>
> 'I see none here.'
>
> Then Patrick raised his hand and stuck his staff into the ground from which a clear bright well broke out. Patrick blessed the water.
>
> 'The water we have here,' said the sinless Patrick, 'will be famous for all. This well of shining water.'
>
> 'I grant,' said Patrick, 'protection for three days and three nights and help and assistance for anyone on distress who drink from it.'
>
> They were not long there before they saw the nine dark, repulsive witches approaching them. If the dead were accustomed to rising from the ground they would have uttered such shrieks as these made on all sides. Patrick took the holy water and sprinkled it on the witches and they fled from him until they reached the Island of Tears, now called the Isle

> of the Shrine, in Loch Carra. There they heard their wailing at the end.
>
> The host sat down afterwards on the mound of sods and the king of Connaught said, 'You have given the demons good cleric's hunting.' (p.156)

Here it is quite specific that the nine women are witches, which in this context can clearly be understood as representatives of pre-Christian beliefs, and practices. This encounter can be compared with both Peredur and St Samson encountering witches, and perhaps also with one of the groups of nine women that the Icelander Thidrandi came across, whom we will meet later.

Regarding the process by which such originally oral material became literature in Ireland, McCrone tells us:

> ... it can confidently be asserted that medieval Irish literati were quite unaware of their Celtic and Indo-European roots, whereas the Bible and other Christian works played a central and indispensable role in monastic life and letters. Once it is conceded that monastic writers were capable of moulding their material creatively, it must be regarded as highly likely that ecclesiastical literature in general and the Bible in particular provided vital conceptual and narrative models capable of modifying inherited patterns where necessary or appropriate. At the very least, such scribes would have been very much alive to parallels from the Bible that they studied so intensively. (p.18)

While this is fine in so far as it goes, like so much other commentary it suffers from an under-appreciation of the actual culture that gave rise to these particular tales. It is as if commentators seek to validate their own culture by reference to ancient cultural roots from elsewhere, and thus the constant emphasis - driven partially by linguistic theory developed in the eighteenth century, which effectively created the modern concept of 'Celtic' culture - on supposed Indo-European roots. I say supposed as the whole concept of the Indo-European language tree is itself theoretical, no matter how often it is repeated, and will remain theoretical, the testing of which rests on the most blatant circular logic. What in fact is valuable and worthy of study in the culture behind the early Irish sagas, as elsewhere, is the fact that culture develops over time, through a process of localisation. Just as megaliths were obviously part of a wider culture but are always unique to their own location, so it is with stories, legendary or mythological, that have been handed down orally. They belong to the communities that told them and each localised variation is as culturally valuable as any other. The idea that the literati of Ireland, monks all, were unaware of their own history is patronising. Certainly they would not have recognised anything in the terminology of either Celtic or Indo-European, these are much later constructs, but as Isaacs showed in Australia, the capacity of oral tradition to pass on provable material is undeniable. I have noted elsewhere that there are some grounds for seeing part of the 1320 Declaration of Arbroath as referring back to truly ancient reality that could only have survived through oral transmission (McHardy 2015, p.87). Once turned into literature, by monkish scribes who were raised with the idea of a canon of acceptable literature (remember the lists of books banned by the church), they attain a level of respectability that to a certain extent is reliant on downgrading or ignoring the realities of the culture from which they had sprung. While the monks who first wrote this material down can be understood as being dominated by their religion, I find it unfortunate that so much interpretation is focused on interpreting ancient tales, and the ideas behind them, through the prism of a theoretical model of how human languages are supposed to have developed. I would suggest that for too long the process of classifying language within an established framework to achieve a form of academic regularity may have led to ignoring the forest for the trees. The fact that the widespread provenance of the Nine Maidens cultural motif, spread well beyond the assumed boundaries of putative Indo-European cultures, has not been accorded much notice in the past is an illustration of this, and though we do not have the same amount of material in Ireland as we have in Scotland, what we do have does suggest it is of significant cultural value.

In his *Traces of the Elder Faiths of Ireland*, published in 1901, Wood-Martin, describing Manannan mac Lir, a sea god and one of the mythical Tuatha de Dannan, tells us this:

> . . . and is now best known from having left nine daughters, who bequeathed their names to nine lakes. Of these only five are remembered by the peasantry — they are Gill, Erne, Labe, Arrow, and Key. Gill, from whom, in current tradition, Lough Gill, near Sligo, takes its name, is said to be often seen in the vicinity of the lake, over the waters of which she skims in her fleet rolling chariot. This banshee, or rather fairy queen, possesses an acknowledged pre-eminence over her other sisters (p.315)

Gill here is apparently very like Morgan, who is predominant over her sisters on the Isle of Avalon, and who has been seen by many as being akin to a fairy queen. The *Tuatha de Danaan* are generally understood as being part of some of the oldest traditions of Ireland and thus of considerable antiquity. The idea of a sea-god with nine daughters is one that also occurs in Norse material as we shall see later and there is another Irish group of Nine Maidens who strengthen this link with Norse belief.

We should remember that from the 8th to the 12th centuries Ireland was very much part of the Norse-influenced world, as were the islands and parts of the west coast of Scotland. The so-called Celtic Revival of the 19th century, driven by a perhaps justifiably Anglophobic rejection of all things 'Germanic', has tended to obscure this important part of Ireland's history and thus culture. Cork, Dublin, Limerick, Waterford and Wexford were all founded by the Vikings and became major trading ports, a process that incidentally, did not occur in Scotland.

One of the most interesting sections of Early Irish texts are known as Dindshenchas, which has been translated as 'lore of places' and they contain old traditions that are particularly interesting in that they are site specific, even if nowadays we cannot always be certain to which locale they were originally applied.

In the *Metrical Dindshenchas* there is a story relating to the place-name *Inber n-Albine* about one Ruad, son of Rigdonn. He sails off on a voyage to Norway in a company of three ships. The vessels come to a stop and will go no further despite a favourable wind. Ruad decides to investigate and dives into the sea. He discovers there are three giant maidens hanging from each of his ships, stopping them from going on. The Nine Maidens take him to their realm below the sea. This is the translation:

> Nine women of them excellent and strong
> hard it was to approach them;
> He slept nine nights with the women
> without gloom, without fearful lament
> under the sea free from waves
> on nine beds of bronze.
>
> Though a woman of them was with child by him
> it was a disfigurement of a little space
> he separated from them without wrongful offence
> on condition he should come back again.
> (Dindshenchas URL)

Although Ruad promised to return to the nine women he in fact went straight back to Ireland after trading in Norway. The women pursue him and the poem continues:

> Nine of them, fierce, radiant and bright
> to high Inber Ailbine
> an evil deed then wrought;
> a woman of them, with no unconscious burden
> even the slaying of the son of Ruad strong and good
> and her very own son
> [She made] a cast with her son, worse than any crime
> it was a stain on his house for him in earth;

> She hurled [him] out in fair combat
> so that he died the death. (ibid)

Although this is rather obscure, the motif of sacrifice seems clear, and the reason for the death of the child is apparently because Ruad has broken his word to return to the Nine Maidens. There are echoes here of the visits of men to Islands of Women (Chapter 6) for sexual purposes and though it is never explicit, it seems at least possible that tales like this refer to situations where the role of the man was to father a new member of an insular community of nine women. Although many of the Nine Maidens groups do seem to be primarily mythological, we have seen enough references to specific sites and activities for us to be relatively certain there were actual groups of them functioning as priestesses in some way. There is only one other obvious mention of a child among the Nine Maiden groups, in the story of St Monenna. The actual priestess groups would have had to replace their members as they died off, to keep up their numbers. Their separation from day-to-day society would require some sort of process through which sexual intercourse could be arranged with a man for one of them to conceive a child. Other possibilities do exist – there could have been candidates in waiting to replace a lost group member – but the ongoing association with a single man, with overtones of sexual congress, does at least raise such a possibility.

Perhaps in the story of Ruad, with the Nine Maidens no longer presented as the mothers of a god, but as brutal and sadistic semi-supernatural beings, we are seeing the influence of Christianity. However Mother Goddess figures in many societies are portrayed as capable of brutality, or what seems to us as brutality. This may merely reflect their overall control of both life and death, as giver and taker-away. As we shall see when we consider the Norse material, there are other groups of nine 'sea-maidens' and Mannanan is directly paralleled by the sea god Ran, who also has nine daughters.

Elsewhere in the *Metrical Dindshenchas* we have the following reference associated with the place name *Cell Chorbbain*:

> There are nine women, fair to see; yonder beside the Cross rest their remains: Sadb and Etain, not meek of mood, Medb and Deccair Der Choisse; Aillend and Aine in one tomb, Ailbe and full-modest Aife, Uasal óen-gel, wife of Faelan - many a noble desired her! (p.343)

Here, as in other examples, we have the nine given names, and it is perhaps significant that amongst them is Medb, who in other contexts has been interpreted as an aspect of a sovereignty goddess, representative of the land of Ireland itself.

In Bonwick's *Irish Druids and Old Irish Religions* he makes mention of the nuns of Tuam who, while not nine are said to number nine-score, though the following description finds many echoes in Nine Maidens groupings:

> The well-known Tuam . . . the Cluan-Feart, or sacred Retreat for Druidical nuns. It was decidedly dangerous for any one to meddle with those ladies, since they could raise storms, cause diseases, or strike with death. (pp.15-16)

In what appears to be a faded echo of a Nine Maidens story there is a tale told of the Nine Daughters' Hole at Ballybunnion in County Kerry on Ireland's west coast. The story is that a local king threw his nine daughters into the open roof of the cave here either to save them from Viking raiders or because they had taken up with nine Norsemen. It seems the original story has not survived intact but, as with several of the Irish sources, the link to royalty is strong.

The Nine Maidens' Rocks is the name of a set of dangerous rocks off Belfast Harbour but as yet I have found no traditions to explain the name.

CHAPTER 5

Sisters of Avalon

IN HIS *VITA MERLINI*, the Life of Merlin, written in the 12th century, Geoffrey of Monmouth relates that after the final, fateful battle of Camlaan, the mortally-wounded King Arthur is taken away to the mystic isle of Avalon by Morgan, a mysterious and magical figure, similar to other mythological figures in the Celtic-speaking world. As Loomis puts it in his *Celtic Myth and Arthurian Romance*:

> [Geoffrey] tells of the nine sisters who dwell there, of whom Morgan is the fairest. She teaches them how to use healing herbs, and herself knows how to change her form and how to fly through the air. (p.191)

These attributes of healing and shape-shifting link the sisters of Avalon to other groups of nine women and also to the later traditions associated with witchcraft. Healing and shape-shifting are also associated with shamanism and we should bear in mind that shamans are not always male, even today. Shape-shifting, taking the shape of various animals, is found in many traditions.

The Isle of Avalon is in many ways like that other mythical Celtic Otherworld – *Tir nan Og,* the land of eternal youth and is itself a form of Paradise. Jean Markale tells us in *Women of the Celts*:

> it was also called the Fortunate Isle, because all the vegetation there grew naturally with no need of

cultivation. The harvests were rich and the forests thick with apples and grapes, nine sisters ruled over it ... It is the island of the apple trees, as Eden was the apple orchard and the Garden of the Hesperides contained the golden apples. The name Avalon became the Celtic word for apples (Breton and Welsh aval, English apple and Latin malum). In Irish legend, the Island of Women, towards which the hero Bran sailed, was known as Emain Ablach, and poets praised the apple trees that grew there and the beauty of their fruit. (p.79f)

Here we are dealing with an ancient and widespread motif indeed. Rolleston in his *Celtic Myths and Legends* says that Caliburn (Excalibur) was made on such an island, telling us:

Avalon, a word which seems to imply some kind of fairyland, a Land of the Dead, and may be related to the Norse Valhalla. It was not until later times that Avalon came to be identified with an actual site in Britain (Glastonbury). (p.138)

There are several important points here. The connection with the idea of the Land of the Dead links us back to the ideas of ancestor worship which is central to so much pre-Christian belief and ritual. The suggestion of a similarity to Valhalla is striking in that, as we shall see, the Valkyries of Norse tradition can be interpreted as a Nine Maidens group. The suggestion that it is only in later times that Avalon became identified with a particular locale however goes against the idea I have put forward that such mythological material would be naturally sited in many different locales.

Avalon is an idealised concept and would thus be located in more than one place. In *Pre-Christianism in Arthurian Romance* Darrah makes this point when he writes, 'There were several cult sites of the same type, of which Avalon is merely a well-publicised example' (p.217). Such cult sites, however far apart in space or time, share common characteristics suggesting that there is continuity in their being the focus of ritual activity. Such activity I believe was widespread and in which the figure of the Mother Goddess was understood as the unifying symbol of all life itself. Behind this concept is the physical reality that we all come from our mothers. This gives the idea of the Mother Goddess a very strong psychological resonance. The significance of the Nine Maidens accompanying Arthur to Avalon has been diminished because of models for interpreting the past which emphasise the masculine, military and hierarchic aspects of human existence. This is perhaps why so many commentators have not realised how widespread the motif of the Nine Maidens is. Their role as healers would appear to be central to the notion of Avalon, just as they are at the heart of so much other mythological and legendary material in other areas.

It is arguable that the motif of nine women involved in ritual activity, and therefore priestesses, comes from the Stone Age as we shall see. It is therefore possible that the sanctity of Avalon and other similar locations originates from the physical presence of such groups. It is worth considering the possibility that Arthur also inherited his original mythological significance from being associated with them. This could also apply to the other male figures associated with the Nine Maidens groups. The putative historical Arthur is a somewhat different case and, as with the Nine Maidens, he is just as at home in Scotland as in Wales or England, perhaps even more so. It is quite common in societies dependent on oral transmission that heroes can be given the names of gods and can perhaps become gods themselves. The key point would be whether such developments would give the resultant stories more benefit for contemporary society, i.e. they made the tales themselves work better.

In *The Celts*, Professor Jean Markale gives us the following:

> Morgan's kingdom is the Isle of Avalon, the mythical isle somewhere in the sea, the island in the middle of the world, a kind of navel but also a matrix,

> an inexhaustible store of energy. There Arthur stays
> until he can be reborn and return to the world.
> There Queen Morgan reigns . . . (p.285)

The 'inexhaustible store' is reminiscent of the magical cauldrons of Celtic tradition, and at a more fundamental level signifies fertility and perhaps the womb, hence the recurrence of sexual motifs in this material. Despite the inability of the Christian and other male-dominated religions to come to terms with human sexuality, such ideas will not go away. This perhaps also explains why so much originally pre-Christian material has had to be disguised while being assimilated, and why we get such divergent interpretations of the Nine Maidens – saints in Abernethy, witches in Gloucester, Druidesses in Brittany etc. Markale goes on to make a similar point:

> As mistress of Avalon, Morgan must be the Mother
> of the Gods, or at least a transposition of a Mother
> Goddess myth into medieval times. Psychoanalytically speaking, the journey to Avalon is the *regressus ad uterum*, which appears to motivate most human activity and which finds its most poetical expression in Celtic legends. (ibid)

Without accepting this Freudian view of mythological and legendary material, it is clear that we are dealing with material that has a strong hold on human thought. It is also interesting that Markale suggests Morgan may represent the Mother Goddess. This seems somewhat different from other Nine Maidens groups associated with figures like Cerridwen, Bride and perhaps Monnena, where there is a clear goddess figure to whom the nine are attached. Female fertility figures in mythology and folklore are often interpreted as direct representations of the Mother Goddess herself. However in situations where the Nine are presented as a priestess group then perhaps their chief priestess could herself be seen as a direct representative of the Mother Goddess. There has been a widespread assumption that belief in a Mother Goddess, which many scholars now accept played a significant part in early human development, disappeared completely with the rise of patriarchal religions like Judaism, Christianity and Islam. The widespread and late existence of so many variants of the Nine Maidens motif suggests the inheritance of old ideas concerning supernatural females has never totally disappeared. I will be exploring the reality of this in a forthcoming work which, while primarily focussing on Scottish traditions will consider other material. And of course many magical or 'superstitious' rituals in folklore have long been considered as possible remnants of actual earlier worship.

In the *Vita Merlini*, Morgan is the leader and teacher of the rest of the group, being the most skilled in the healing and magical arts. In the development of Arthurian traditions she takes on a variety of roles. Some Arthurian romance tales like the French *Estoire de Merlin* have her as Arthur's sister, others like the Latin *Vulgate Merlin* and the French *Huth-Merlin* have her as his niece and daughter of Lot, King of the Lothians, in Scotland. Lot's supposed capital was Traprain Law, historically manned by the British tribe the Gododdin, known to Ptolemy in the 2nd century CE as the Votadini, and the site of one of St Monenna's chapels. Traprain Law is some 20 miles east of Edinburgh. As we have seen, the first recorded mention of Arthur is in the Early British poem, *The Gododdin*, written in Scotland in the 6th century CE and describing a warrior raid, supposedly into England by the Votadini or Gododdin. Traprain Law, like Edinburgh Castle, can be interpreted as a Castle of the Maidens, particularly through the association with St Monenna. On top of the hill is a cleft rock known as the Maiden Stone which is associated with fairies in local lore. The importance of this motif, and of Lot and his sons Modred and Gawain within the Arthurian material is quite obvious. Arthur, as a mythological figure, or as a figure derived from a particular heroic character, had an important role in the traditions of the Gododdin, next-door neighbours to the Picts on one side and the Scots of Dalriada on the other. Arthur's association with the Nine Maidens is echoed by other heroic and god figures in other traditions and appears to suggest a stratum of belief underpinning such material, which harks back to the notion of the Mother Goddess material previously discussed.

In Arthurian literature as it developed in Europe, particularly in France, Morgan became known as Morgan le Fay. Markale in *Women of the Celts*, gives us a description of Morgan:

> She was the sister of King Arthur, very gay and playful; she sang most agreeably; though dark in the face, very well made, neither too fat nor too thin, with beautiful hands, perfect shoulders, skin softer than silk, engaging of manner, long and straight in the body: altogether wonderfully seductive and, beside all that, the warmest and most sensual woman in Britain. Merlin had taught her astronomy and many other things, and she studied them so well that she became an excellent scholar and was later called Morgan la Fée because of the marvels she wrought. (p.137)

This idealised female figure is perhaps a specific representation of the original Mother Goddess. The reference to her overt sexuality make her the complete opposite of the idealised Virgin Mother of the Christian Church. There is an ongoing awareness and appreciation of such female sexuality within the oral and song traditions of most European rural populations, harking back to pre-Christian times and recognising the importance of sexuality in human existence. In Malory's 15th century *Morte D'Arthur* this perfect goddess figure has transmogrified into a devious plotter set on usurping Arthur by stealing Excalibur to give to her lovers, most notably Accolon of Gaul whom Arthur eventually kills in combat. This suggests that the magical sword itself was symbolic of power. The opposite portrayals of Morgan sit very well with the idea of the Mother Goddess as both giver of life and bringer of death.

Loomis draws attention to the possible link between Morgan and Modron, a goddess who was known in ancient Gaul. He tells us in *Celtic Myth and Arthurian Romance*:

> Celtic scholars are agreed that Modron is the old
> Gallo-Roman Goddess Matrona, who gave her
> name to the river Marne and to that extent at east
> was associated with the waters. But of course she
> [Morgan] was originally entirely distinct from the
> nine island priestesses, of whom she later became
> the chief. (p.193)

The reference to the association with the waters is significant, reminding us of the sanctity of wells in particular. The suggestion that Modron derives from Matrona seems to be made on the usual grounds that because the Romans were writing things down before the rest of Europe (except Greece), their ideas must take precedence over all others, but Loomis here reinforces the possibility that a chief priestess could be seen as the direct representation of the Goddess herself. And as we shall see, Morgan and her sisters are not the only Nine Maidens to inhabit an island.

Many scholars have commented upon the similarity between Morgan and the Irish goddess, the Morrigan. The Morrigan and her sisters Badb and Mach, sinister and destructive beings said to haunt battlefields, are like the tripartite goddess figures which occur all over Europe. The sisters often appeared as crows or ravens, carrion birds traditionally associated with the dead in battle and, in the portrayal of the three sisters as Furies, there is some similarity with the Norse concept of the Valkyries. They in turn are closely associated with the Norse god Odin who had two ravens, Thumin and Mummin, representing Memory and Thought. In the late medieval Scottish ballad, *The Twa Corbies*, two ravens talk over the corpse of a dead knight, intriguingly linking these themes and reflecting how the Germanic and Celtic traditions, far from being separate, are interwoven at many levels. The appearance of Morgan, with or without her sisters, on the battlefield of Camlaan where Arthur lies mortally wounded would appear to derive from the same idea as the Irish battle goddesses and the Norse battle maidens and there are clear parallels between the taking of Arthur to the Paradise

Island of Avalon and the Valkyries convoying the dead warriors to the Norse warrior heaven of Valhalla. This reinforces the point made by Rolleston that there are similarities between Avalon and Valhalla.

In the Irish saga the *Tain Bo Cualnge*, the Cattle raid of Cooley, the Morrigan gives direct assistance to the great hero Cu Chulainn who, like the later Finn Mac Cuill, is in some ways similar to the figure of Arthur in P-Celtic tradition. Initially Morrigan offers Cu Chulainn counsel which he is glad to take but later when she offers him love, he spurns her, always a dangerous course of action, and later they actually fight each other. In this light, it is interesting that when Cu Chulainn dies, having tied himself to a standing stone so he would die on his feet facing his enemies, a crow comes and settles on his shoulder. This can be construed as the Morrigan coming to claim him, either from revenge or in her role as a battle goddess carrying off the dead hero. Again in this classic Irish saga, we see two sides to the Goddess.

Darrah mentions that:

> Avalon has already been mentioned in this book in the story of the dying raven which changed into a beautiful young woman and was carried off through the air by her raven companions to recover in Avalon. (p.216)

Here we have a strong similarity to both the Morrigan and possibly the Valkyries, though here the crow figure is injured after a battle. The crow is a maiden who has shape-shifted and is one of a group from Avalon. This motif of groups of women living on islands and capable of shape-shifting is known elsewhere and it is not stretching a point to see this raven-woman as one of a group of Nine Maidens.

Morgan has been interpreted, then, as the leader and teacher of the sisters of Avalon and also as a version of the Mother Goddess herself. Thus it seems feasible to see Morgan as a

High-priestess and as such, a living representation of the divinity herself. This idea survives in Christianity with the notion of the Pope being God's representative on earth and, as such, infallible. Whatever her dominant role, as goddess or priestess, the figure of Morgan has continued to fascinate. Ideas and motifs, like myths and legends, survive because they continue to have relevance to the societies in which they function.

In the *Vita Merlini* Geoffrey of Monmouth gives the names of seven of the other maidens who inhabited Avalon with Morgan. Most scholars have seen these as a hotchpotch of references from classical sources. However there are possible links to other Celtic and Germanic sources. The names as given by Geoffrey are Moronoe, Mazoe, Gliten, Glitonea, Gliton, Tyronoe, Thiten, though the latter is given as 'Thiten, cithara notissima Thiten'. Geoffrey speaks of nine sisters so we must accept the possibility that two of these women were called Thiten, one of them being the noted exponent of the lyre. Parry in his notes on the *Vita Merlini* says:

> The personal element in Geoffrey's names may here frustrate permanently a conventional solution about sources. Allowing for this, some suitable classical allusions may after all be present. Otherwise there is only a tenuous hint of acquaintance with Irish names. This added to the more likely link in the case of Morgan may mean that Geoffrey possibly saw some Irish material or was shown it by visitors or returned travellers and had it explained. Assuming Geoffrey was based at Llandaff at a suitable period of his life, contacts between that part of south Wales and Ireland were old, and sea access, by the evidence of the Llantwit Major breakwater, was still easier in the twelfth century than later. (p.208)

Sea transport was of major importance in communications from the earliest times till relatively recently and can be seen as the medium by which the commonalties we have noticed within separate language-based traditions were developed and maintained. Trade alone, if continuous over generations, will foster extended cultural contact and communication.

The names of Morgan's sisters on Avalon are perhaps somewhat less obscure than Parry suggests.

Moronoe: other than its slight similarity to Morgan, or to Morrigan, this seems to convey little else. However if one takes note of how many names of goddesses or supernatural females have names beginning with Ma or Mo, we perhaps here have a reference to something other than the Q-Celtic *mor* meaning 'great' or 'big'. This, however, is purely speculative. Some scholars have suggested that the *mor-* prefix could have derived in names from a word like *muir* meaning 'sea'. As we will see, the idea of the great sea goddess is not obscure.

Mazoe: This name is very like Mazota, the eldest of the nine daughters of St Donevald (Donald) and a saint in her own right according to the *Aberdeen Breviary* and Forbes' *Kalendar of Scottish Saints*. Mazota or Mayota is given as the original dedication of the church at Drumoak on Deeside and it is an intriguing thought that she might be behind the name Portmoak at Loch Leven, given the plethora of antiquities in the area which include place-names referring to St Serf, tutor of St Mungo (Kentigern), the natural stone tower known as Carlin Maggie, Carlin being the Scots equivalent of Cailleach, and Gruoch's Well on Benarty, a name taken by some to be Arthurian. There is also the place-name Navitie Hill, at the east end of Benarty, which derives originally from *nemeton* meaning a sacred enclosure or area. Mazota is said to have talked to geese eating corn and convinced them to desist suggesting a possible remnant of a belief that the Goddess, or her priestesses had power of animals. It is also notable that her saint's day, according to the *Aberdeen Breviary* is 22 December – the Midwinter solstice. Mazota is the most clearly distinguished of the Nine Maidens from Glen Ogilvy and seems to stand in the same sort of relationship to her sisters as Morgan does to the other eight inhabitants of Avalon.

Gliten, Glitonea, Gliton: these three are clearly linked and a possible comparison exists with Cliodhna's wave, mentioned in the early Irish text *Acallamh na Senorach*. It was a term given to every ninth wave, supposedly the strongest. The references there are in the forms Clidna, Cliodhna and Cliodna within a few lines. This is possibly an example of the common motif of three linked goddesses so common in the ancient world. The reference to waves brings to mind the daughters of the Norse sea goddess Ran (see p.148), who are often portrayed in Norse material as the waves themselves. One old Irish text refers to 'the seven daughters of the sea who fashion the threads of long life' (Miscellany, p.231) which could be taken to be a degraded reference to the Nine Maidens of the Mill (see p.150), another Norse group of Nine Maidens. It is worth also thinking here of the tale of Ruad, Son of Rigdonn (see p.100), who is stopped at sea by nine sea-maidens. His journey seems to have been from Ireland to Scandinavia. linking the Irish and Norse material. Parry also tells of Kleite who appears as the wife of King Cyzicus, who clashed with the Argonauts seeking the Golden Fleece (Graves 1958, 1 p.227), and on whose death by suicide had a fountain of nymph's tears named after her. This at least continues the link with water.

Thiten: this name has been seen as deriving from Thetis, herself an ocean nymph and mother of Achilles. However, another similar name with an equally marine connection is Tethys who in Ovid's *Fasti* was the wife of Ocean and herself a mother of sea-nymphs and river gods. Parry tells us that Teite's wave was, like Cliodhna's wave, a common expression in Cork on Ireland's west coast. He quotes the story of Teite, daughter of Ragamain, who was drowned along with many girlfriends while out surf-riding! One interesting similarity, though not really close enough to suggest an absolute identification with Thiten is Thenew, the legendary daughter of King Lot of the Lothians who had his capital on Traprain Law in East Lothian, already mentioned as a Nine Maidens site. Lot is also the father of Modred and Gawain in Arthurian legend. Thenew converted to Christianity, was cruelly seduced and made pregnant, then, on refusing to marry, was first thrown off the citadel in a chariot which floated to the earth, then set adrift in the Forth estuary in an oarless boat. She drifted to the Isle of May, an important pre-Christian and early Christian site, the name of which means the Island of the Maiden(s). It is perhaps not stretching a point to see that this could have been seen as Avalon within local tradition in the Forth valley. From here, accompanied by a shoal of fishes, she went upstream where she landed at Culross on the north shore and gave birth to St Kentigern. Here Kentigern was raised by St Serf, a character associated with dragon lore and that long-surviving remnant of the Celtic Church, the Culdees. Kentigern went on to fame himself at the court of the King of Strathclyde. He later became the patron saint of Glasgow under the name given him by St Serf – Mungo. In some Arthurian material Morgan herself is given as the wife of King Lot. Again there are strong marine references in Thenew's story as well as links to pre-Christian and Christian sites. JS Glennie in *Arthurian Localities in Scotland* (p.54) suggested that Thenew was one of the maidens accompanying St Monenna (see p.53), who were nine in number.

Tyronoe: Parry tells us this is like the Tyro whom Odysseus meets in Hades (Od. II 235) and who is said to be the daughter of Ocean. This is explicit and very similar to the notion of the daughters of Ran mentioned above. It is tempting to see a link with the Irish place-name Tyrone and WJ Watson in his *Celtic Place-Names of Scotland* mentions a female name Turanais occurring in an Ogham inscription. Ogham, line or notch writing, primarily surviving on standing stones, occurs both in Ireland and in the Pictish areas, although in highly differentiated forms and apparently in different languages. Oghams in Scotland mainly occur on Pictish symbol stones.

Because of the truly ancient provenance of our earliest source, a Magdelanian cave painting in Catalonia, it seems highly probable that the Classical, Celtic and Germanic sources are waters from the same well. By the time Geoffrey of

Monmouth was alive there were probably some literary sources available, as Parry noted – and he may even have had access to oral material regarding the priestesses on the Isle of Sena. Oral tradition also preserved some of the relevant material within the islands of Britain. Given the ongoing survival of such traditions as those at the Nine Maidens Well at Pittempton and the ritual at Bride's Well at Sanquhar, more than half a millennium after Geoffrey was writing, it would appear folly to argue against such a possibility.

In Malory's *Morte D'Arthur* the hero is spirited away after his final battle to the Isle of Avalon having ensured the return of his magic sword Excalibur to the Otherworld. The story of the return of the sword to a lake, or loch, has survived in folklore in out-of-the-way places such as Loch Moan in Galloway in south-west Scotland, an area long inhabited by people speaking a P-Celtic language. Similarly, in Dorset, Loe Pool is said to be the location for the return of Excalibur. In this case, a further connection is the source of the river Loe which feeds the Loe Pool basin. This rises to the north on the Nine Maidens' Downs. We are close to Cornwall here and Cornish like Welsh, Breton and Pictish is a P-Celtic language, currently undergoing a revival. As we have seen, similar societies, with closely related languages are likely to have closely linked sets of beliefs, myths and legends. Such beliefs are the psychological glue of any given society. Striking similarities in mythology and folklore, originally passed down through storytelling, exist in significantly different human societies. One such motif closely linked to the Nine Maidens themselves is the notion of the Island of Women.

CHAPTER 6

Islands of Women

WE HAVE ALREADY seen that Avalon was inhabited by Nine Maidens. The concept of Islands of Women is quite widespread in early Irish and other European sources. The concept of men, or in a number of instances, a single man, visiting an island to make love to the isolated women there, is also widespread. Talking of the motif within the Celtic-speaking world, Rees and Rees tell us that, 'The Island of Women is . . . the quintessence of femininity and erotic pleasure' (ibid p.323). This is quite explicit and we should remember the importance of fertility within what we know of pre-Christian thinking. In Arthurian legend, Avalon is the home of healers. It is linked to the concept of *Emhain Abhlach*, the Island of Apples, which has often been interpreted as a Celtic Paradise. Markale identifies *Emhain Abhlach* as an Island of Women and compares it to Abalum in the Baltic, an important prehistoric centre of the amber trade. Amber was sometimes described as the tears of the Goddess. He suggests that the Celtic Paradise island was non-patriarchal and suggests that such manifestations might be relics from an earlier time. To support this idea of older origins Markale then gives two classical sources which are of fundamental importance to the search for the Nine Maidens.

The first he quotes is Pomponius Mela, a Romanised Iberian geographer writing in the 1st century CE, and giving an account Markale sees as tallying very closely with Geoffrey of Monmouth's account of Avalon:

> Facing the Celtic coast lie a group of islands which takes the collective name Cassiterides because they are very rich in tin. [Britain] Sena in the British Sea [English Channel], facing the coast of Osimi [North Finistere] was renowned for its Gallic oracle, whose priestesses, sacred for their everlasting virginity, were said to be nine in number. They were called 'gallicias' [Gallicenae] and were reputed to have the power to unleash the winds and storms by their spells, to metamorphose into any animal according to their whim, to cure all disease said to be incurable, and finally, to know and predict the future. But they reserved their remedies and predictions exclusively for those who had travelled over the sea expressly to consult them. (1986, p,81)

These Breton Druidesses, as they are referred to elsewhere, are in many ways similar to Morgan and her sisters. Shape-shifting, weather working and divination also link these women to that much later, and much-maligned group, the witches. Elton, in his *Origins of British History*, says that there was another similar group on the Isle of Ushant, to the west of the Isle du Sein (p.25). Markale draws attention to a similar account from Strabo, the same Roman geographer as Elton quotes:

> In the ocean, not right out in the open sea, but just facing the mouth of the Loire, Posidonius pointed out to us a rather narrow island inhabited by the so-called Namnete women, who were possessed by Bacchic passion. They tried by means of mysteries and other religious ceremonies to appease and disarm the god who tormented them. No man ever set foot on their island: it was they who crossed to the mainland every time they wished to do business with their husbands. (ibid)

He informs us that Pomponius Mela in his 1st century CE work *De Situ Orbis*, seems to have perceived these island groups of women as being like the Roman Vestal Virgins who were priestesses and goes on to differentiate Morgan and her sisters from this idea:

> Judging from the various accounts of King Arthur's sister, 'the hottest and most lustful woman in all Great Britain', as the author of the *Lancelot en prose* described her, Morgan and her sisters were more like bacchantes. (ibid)

Bacchantes were the female followers of the god Bacchus and were known for drunken orgiastic behaviour. Markale notes that ancient writers interpreted the term virgin differently from today. The term could be used of a woman with a child or a married woman without a child, that is a female who is not a matron, i.e. married with at least one child. They did not use the term to mean *virgo intacta*, a female who has not had sexual intercourse. This is a later meaning, developed in Christian society where women are understood as being fundamentally the property of men, as in all patriarchal religions.

Several earlier writers made the connection between Morgan of Avalon and the *Gallicenae* of Sena. Darrah mentions the similarities between the Isle de Sein and Avalon and raises another interesting link:

> There is a close parallel to Sein in the ancient Welsh epic Preiddeu Annwn which describes Arthur's raid on an Otherworld Island surmised to have been Grassholm, off the east of Pembrokeshire where there was a cauldron tended by nine virgins. The cauldron evidently had an oracular function for it was warmed by their breaths to provide inspired utterances. Nine priestesses on an island is a feature common to Avalon, Sein and Grassholm, and there is a remarkable similarity in the situation of two of them, Sein and Grassholm. Both are some miles off extreme west-pointing peninsulas, and both are offshore from megalithic holy places, in the case of

> Sein, from the south of Brittany leading to Carnac in the east; and of Grassholm, not far from the source of the bluestones [of Stonehenge] at nearby Prescelli. (p.216)

He comes very close to anticipating the proposition presented here, which is that ancient ritual practice, possibly rooted as far back as the Stone Age, survived through an institution of nine priestly women existing over a wide geographical area. He goes on to say:

> To have several recollections of this cult, again in three entirely different literatures, Latin, Welsh and French, gives some idea of its original power, but it does not lead directly to the location of Avalon. Glastonbury certainly fits, but at this stage only because it was once surrounded by water. On the other hand, the three recollections, of three different places of similar characteristics, two of them identifiable and far apart indicate that Avalon was not unique. There were several cult sites of the same type, of which Avalon is merely a well-publicised example. (ibid)

Although these locations are distant from each other, the journey from Grassholm to Sena is practicable by sea through much of the year and similarly, Glastonbury would have been accessible by water while it retained its island form, an annual occurrence till the area was extensively drained. Glastonbury has often been suggested as the site of Avalon and is certainly a very important sacred site. However, so far, I am unaware of any direct association there with Nine Maidens. And as has been noted, wherever the idea of Avalon was rooted in local cultural tradition, there would be a 'localised' island site.

JF Campbell in his great work *Popular Tales of the West Highlands*, written in 1860, mentions the maidens of Sena when discussing the Gaelic term *gruagach* which he said generally meant a maiden and that

> this may be the same word as Groac'h or Grac'h, a
> name given to the Druidesses, who had colleges in
> an island near the coasts of Brittany. (p.10)

The Isle of Sena lies a few miles off the north-west coast of Brittany. It is known today as the Isle of the Druidesses and is something of a tourist attraction. Campbell also mentions a '*Greogaca*' that had Druidic connections and haunted the island of Insch near Easdale (p.61). Lewis Spence in his speculative and entertaining *History of Druidism*, commented on the widespread occurrence of Islands of Women. A section of his book is devoted to Insular Communities of Women. Here Spence talks of the *Gallicenae* and tells the story of the contemporary Namnete Women with their annual rebuilding of their temple, which was originally reported by Strabo in the 2nd century CE:

> Each woman brought a bundle of building material to the work, but should any of them permit her burden to fall to the ground, she was instantly torn to pieces by her companions. It is noteworthy that later Norse lays retain memories of such cults in the Channel Islands, allusions being made in the Helgi lays to the existence of sibyls or hags such as Mela mentions in Guernsey and other adjoining insular localities. (p.63)

Both the description of the killing of one of the women and the choice of the word hag are significant here. This passage could be a memory of some sacrificial rite. Spence goes on to mention similarities to Circe in the *Odyssey*, suggesting a link with the lost account of the travels of Pytheas to north-western Europe and then mentions Campbell's reference to *gruagach* and *grac'h*. He continues:

> We find a parallel to the priestesses of Sein, perhaps in the legend of the sorceresses or fairies of Gloucester, who guarded the thermal waters of that

> city. One of them indeed appears in the legend of
> Peredur, who, it was prophesied, should overcome
> her and her sisters. (ibid)

Somehow he does not make the connection to Morgan and the sisterhood of Avalon. The Breton term *grac'h*, whether or not related to *gruagach*, undoubtedly has something of the same meaning as the Welsh *gwrach*, meaning 'hag', or 'witch' – Breton and Welsh are after all related P-Celtic languages. The Welsh term survived at least into the 19th century in Pembrokeshire where the last sheaf of the harvest was called *Gwrach*, exactly as the last sheaf in Scotland was called the Cailleach in Gaelic-speaking areas. The association with the harvest and the exact match of the words leads to the conclusion that this was initially in the far distant past a term for the Mother Goddess herself which had perhaps been transposed to her devotees by Celtic-speaking times.

Some similar ideas from Breton lore are mentioned in Anson's *Fisher Folk Lore*:

> On the intensely Catholic Isle-de-Sein, there used to
> be the conviction that certain women had what was
> known as '*le don de vouer*', i.e. the power of com-
> municating with the Devil or his emissaries, in other
> words, that they were witches. Fishermen alleged
> that they had seen these women on dark nights
> launching mysterious boats (*bag-sorcérs*) to enable
> them to take part in a witches' Sabbath or coven
> known as *groach'hed*. (p.30)

These women are clearly believed to have been witches but their location and the name of their meeting is a tantalising link with previous inhabitants. In fisher communities around the coast of Britain, many witches were reputed to be able to raise the wind – an attribute of the *Gallicenae*, according to the early accounts. Such beliefs lasted in different parts of Scotland till at least the 19th century.

Robert Graves in his highly speculative *The White Goddess*, which he subtitles *A Historical Grammar of Poetic Myth* tells us this:

> The Island of Sein, which is not far from the great religious centre of Carnac and must have had a ritual connexion with it, retained its magical reputation very late. It was the last place in Europe to be Christianized: by seventeenth-century Jesuits. (p.111)

In the late 17th century church leaders on the Castennec peninsula in southern Brittany were worried by an upsurge of what appeared to be pre-Christian worship of a goddess figure. The idol was called *Groa-hourn*, Breton for 'old woman' or 'sorceress', a title that is like *grac'h* and *gwrach* with the same sense as Cailleach in Gaelic or Carlin in Scots. It seems that the figure was possibly something like a sheila-na-gig, the naked females found carved on churches in England, Ireland and Scotland, holding their labia open to display their sex. The statue was thrown in the River Blavet by outraged priests but 30 years later was rescued by a local aristocrat. The local people were disappointed to hear he was to keep her locked up on his estate and eventually he commissioned a mason to clean her up. In trying to do this the statue was destroyed and the count ordered a new, more respectable one which he considered fit to be seen by the general public. This still exists, known as the Venus of Quiniply. Although it was possibly nothing like the original *Grou-hoaurn*, the locals took the new 'Venus' to their hearts and began to pray to her. This suggests a transference of belief that is hardly to be wondered at, if we are indeed dealing with a pattern of belief originating thousands of years ago.

Another author who noticed links between Arthurian tradition and the *Gallicenae* of Sena was Robert Sherman Loomis. In his *Celtic Myth and Arthurian Romance,* he says:

> This name, according to some medieval writers was either due to the many apples to be found there or

ISLANDS OF WOMEN

> to a certain Avalloc, who is said to have lived there with his daughters because of the secrecy of the place. Rhys also quotes an anonymous Latin description which mentions not only the eternal spring, the abundance of flowers, the absence of age or disease, but also a royal virgin, most beautiful, surrounded by her maids. She bears the wounded Arthur to the hall of King Avallo, and heals him. It goes without saying that the relation of this *regia virgo* to *rex Avallo* is that of daughter to father. Geoffrey of Monmouth in his *Vita Merlini* gives another description of the fairy isle under the name Isle of Apples. He tells of the nine sisters who dwell there, of whom Morgan is the fairest. She teaches them how to use healing herbs, and herself knows how to change her form and how to fly through the air, so that when she will, she is at Bristol, Chartres or Pavia. After the battle of Camlaan, the wounded Arthur is brought across the seas by Telegesinus and Barinthus (in whom have been recognised the mythical bard Taliesin and a sea-god) to Morgan, who undertakes to cure him if he is left with her long enough. De la Rue has justly pointed out how strikingly this story of nine women, skilled in healing and shape-shifting, who live on an island, ministering to those who come, bears to the account which Pomponius Mela gives of an island, Sena off the coast of Brittany, the modern Sein, which modern tradition connects with Merlin. (p.191)

Loomis did not think that Geoffrey had access to Pomponius Mela's *De Situ Orbis* in which the *Gallicenae* were described. Nor does he notice the widespread occurrence of the Nine Maidens motif. The presence of a king, Avallo, is an example of how the past has been interpreted through masculine and hierarchic models – such an important island would simply have to be ruled by a king! He does mention that several medieval texts refer to Morgan as a goddess and that she was called *Modron* in an early Welsh source. This he connects to the old

Romano-Gallo goddess *Matrona* as others have done. It is also significant that he has Morgan as the teacher of the other sisters on the Isle of Avalon, underlining her possible original function as a goddess, or at least her role as chief priestess directly representing the Goddess. Discussing the fundamental role of Mother Goddess in providing fertility, Loomis says:

> According to the vulgar traditions of the Bretons Arthur was borne away to the Isle of Avalon in order that his wounds, annually reopening, may be cured by the Fay Morgan with her healing applications. Now I venture to say that the immortal hero, whose wounds break out afresh every year, must be like the Maimed King, in sympathetic tune with the vital forces of the earth, with the ripening and rotting grain, with the greening and withering trees, with the waxing and waning solar heat. (p.194)

One of several possible instances of the Islands of Women motif within Scotland is Innishail in Loch Awe. In Mackinlay's *Ancient Church Dedications in Scotland* it is described thus:

> Its church, of which some remains are still to be seen in an ancient burying-ground, was under the invocation of St Fyndoca, whose name appears in a shortened form in that of Findo-Gask . . . in the Strathearn district of Perthshire, where the church is believed to have had the saint as its titular. (p.488)

This St Fyndoca is one of the Pictish Nine Maidens referred to in Chapter One as being at Glen Ogilvy and Abernethy. Nigel Tranter in *Argyll and Bute* refers to a tradition of there being a nunnery on Innishail. He further says that, '. . . it was renowned as being tainted by the evils which were apt to beset such places' (p.168). This is possibly a reference to tales of illicit sexual activities. There is no evidence of a nunnery on the island but this again may possibly be a faded memory of a group of pre-Christian priestesses.

Priory Island in Loch Tay is a crannog or artificial island which was also supposedly the site of a nunnery. We have already seen that the memory of these women survived in the *Feill nam Ban Naomh* – the Fair of the Holy Women (see p.31) which they reputedly started and which took place on 26 July at Kenmore till the turn of the 20th century, having moved there from its original site at nearby Inchadney where there was an early Christian site.

Heather Wheater in *Kenmore and Loch Tay*, tells us:

> It is said too, that they did emerge once a year to go to the market, but not to sell their wares. To have, instead a rollicking good time one day of the year and then return to their celibate cloister for the next 364 days. (p.3)

Tradition tells us that they were eventually expelled and crossed by the ferry at Kingharry to Portbane on the south side of the loch. Above nearby Acharn is a hillock called *Faire nam Ban*, the Nun's Watch, where it is said they looked for the last time on their former home before tramping away across the hills forever. Strictly speaking, we might translate *Faire nam Ban* as the Woman's, rather than the Nun's, Watch, and the name of the Holy Women, *Ban Naomha*, crops up in other locations in Scotland. John Christie in his *The Lairds and Lands of Tayside* gives a reason for the expulsion of the nuns from the community:

> According to local tradition, the Priory . . . [was] occupied by nuns who, breaking their vows of celibacy, were summarily expelled from the island, which was never again templed by a religious body. (p.32)

A charter known as the Chronicle of Fothergill, long kept in nearby Taymouth Castle, and published in *The Black Book of Taymouth*, tells us:

> The year of God 1615 on the Nine Virgin's day the procession and market was held and begun at Kenmore on Loch Tay, and there was no market nor fair held at Inchadin where it was wont to be held.
> (trans p.324)

The Chronicle does not mention the presence of any nuns. Perhaps the nuns are themselves a late development in this story of Nine Maidens or virgins. These local traditions present a picture of what appears to be a Nine Maidens group living on an island late into the Christian era and taking an active part in the social life of the community by organising an annual fair. We also have a tradition that stresses the disruption of the 'nunnery' because of sexual activity. This is echoed in the story of monk killing an errant nun on Inchcailloch in Loch Lomond. It is an intriguing aspect of the Nine Maidens that in their role as priestesses of some kind, several of their stories have such strong erotic overtones. A society which worshipped the Mother Goddess might well have been free of coyness and repression when dealing with female sexuality. However, the possibility cannot be totally discounted that the story of the banished nuns was Protestant propaganda after the Reformation. Even so, it would still leave us with what appears to be an Island of Women.

Innishail and Priory Island are not the only possible Islands of Women in Scotland. *Eilean Nighean* (Island of Maidens) in Loch Craignish has already been mentioned but there are others, suggesting the Nine Maidens' link with islands is very strong and very ancient. Tradition has it that the island of Inchcailloch, the Island of the Cailleach in Loch Lomond, had a nunnery though there is no other evidence available for this. While this may be another instance of the confusion between the idea of the Cailleach and nuns, it is notable that the prominent mound on the island is known as Tom na Nigheanan, the round hillock of the maidens. A similar tradition exists concerning Nuntown on the Hebridean island of Benbecula. This story intriguingly involves a woman called *Cailleach nam Mogan* or the Old Woman of the Footless Stocking who elsewhere (MacLeod, p.248), occurs as one of the principal witches of the Gaelic world. Whether this is a misreading of an original reference to Morgan is impossible to say, but as the founder of this nunnery was said to have been an Irish princess, there may be a connection with the Morrigan. The idea of Islands of Women is particularly strong in Hebridean tradition as are associations with Bride.

In her book *The Inner Hebrides and their Legends,* Otta Swire tells of the island of Eigg being called *Eilean nam Ban More,* the Island of the Big Women. JG Mackay mentions that there is a loch on the island known as the Loch nam Ban Mora and that it contains a crannog. He says that the women of the place were 'of such unique proportions that the stepping stones by which they gained their home were set so far apart as to be useless to anyone else.'

This finds an echo in the tale of Mac Iain Direach in Campbell's *Popular Tales of the West Highlands*, (Campbell v2, p.90 ff) in which the hero works for the Seven Big Women of Jura in order to gain their Glave [sword] of Light to help in his quest to find a particular blue falcon. These women are clearly supernatural and may represent another ancient grouping of pre-Christian priestesses. I believe they were probably originally nine. Whether the women were giantesses or not, they clearly fit into this motif of Islands of Women. Just as there is an *Eilean Ban* (Island of Women) off the isle of Iona, sacred before Christian times, there is mention of something similar in Ireland. Borthwick in his *Irish Druids and Old Irish Religions* says:

> . . . in the Bog of Monaincha are two islands. On one was a monastery for men, their wives occupying the neighbouring Woman's Isle. Giraldus Cambrensis, who wrote of the Community of Monaincha in the twelfth century, called it the church of the old religion, and politely designated as Demons all who belonged to that former church. (p.285)

It is also interesting that another well-known group of forceful women – the Amazons were said to live on a lake in Libya. Graves in *The Greek Myths* writes that they 'once inhabited Hespera, an island in Lake Tritonis which was so rich in fruit-bearing trees, sheep and goats, that they found no need to grow corn' (1 p.147). This fertility is very much like the idea of Avalon and the name Hespera seems linked to the Hesperides the female guardians of the golden apples of the goddess Hera on Mount Atlas, who may have numbered nine. Another similar Greek idea is mentioned by Graves. Elysium is a Paradise island where it is perpetual day, always pleasantly warm, and where there are constant games and revels. Graves also points out that 'Elysium seems to mean apple land – as does the Arthurian Avalon.' (ibid, p.123)

We have already seen that Avalon was inhabited by Nine Maidens and that the concept of Islands of Women existed in early Irish and European experience, the best known possibly being the Island of Women in the *Odyssey*. Odysseus manages to pass the notorious island of the Sirens without his crew being lured to their deaths by the Sirens' singing. This is because he had been advised to fill his crew's ears with wax by Circe, an enchantress who also lived on an island.

In the Gaelic story type known as *Imrama*, journey tales, there is one strikingly relevant example. This is in the *Imrama Mael Duin*, generally thought to have originated in 8th century Ireland and surviving in a text from the 10th century. Mael Duin sets off on a journey to locate the slayer of his father. On the advice of a Druid he takes 17 companions who with himself comprise 18 souls. Rees and Rees in their *Celtic Heritage* tell us:

> An Island of Women. Here Mael Duin and his seventeen men are received by a queen and her seventeen daughters [two groups of Nine Maidens?] The women feast them, consort with them and try to induce them to remain there to live a life of perpetual pleasure and eternal youth. (p.321)

A later, more generally known version of the tale is the Voyage of Bran or Brendan. St Brendan is considered as being specifically Irish. However it is interesting that one of the wells above Abernethy was dedicated to the saint as mentioned by Butler, in *The Ancient Church and Parish of Abernethy*:

> A well in this parish, adjacent to the Gattaway stream, was known to the old inhabitants as Brendan, and the name still survives in the corrupted form Brendi Well . . . Tradition states that St Brendan died and was buried at Glamis in Forfarshire, and an ancient cairn there was known as Brendi's cairn . . . it seems beyond doubt that he did visit this district, it is more than likely that he must have been at the early Abernethy church. (p.102)

As we have seen, Glamis was associated with the Nine Maidens and perhaps in this association with Brendan, who also visited an Island of Women, we may be seeing some remnant of belief linking him directly with the Nine Maidens. The motif of a single man, or a group of men visiting an island to make love to the socially isolated women there frequently recurs, raising the possibility that Brendan's voyage is a Christianised, sanitised, version of this motif.

Folklorist and storyteller Dr Sheila Douglas gives a tale collected from storyteller John Stewart of Blairgowrie in her book *King of the Black Art and other folk tales*. John Stewart was illiterate and all his stories came to him through oral transmission. It is likely that none of his direct ancestors had been literate. It is only fairly recently that the children of the travelling people in Scotland generally learned to read and write. Remembering that the Australian material earlier referred to showed how long data can survive within the oral tradition, perhaps the similarities in the following with the Imram of Mael Duin are not so surprising. In the tale Jack and his companions are setting off in pursuit of pirates who killed his father 18 years before. After preparing for all of two months they are just about to set off when Jack is asked by an old man if he has the right number of men. He tells the old man, who happens to be a druid, he has six companions making a total of seven. They set off and were rowing past a castle when two young princes came out and asked to accompany them. Jack tells them that the druid said it would be unlucky to take more than seven. Despite this, the two young princes threaten to jump in the sea and swim out to the boat until Jack agrees to take them along. The company now numbers nine. After about a week they come to an island with a big castle. They go ashore and approach the castle but seeing a big crowd of people gathered there, they decide to bide their time and sit down. Soon a splendid lady on horseback approaches, but rides straight past them without a word, and on up to the castle. Soon a woman comes down from the castle and says the queen wants them to visit her.

The story goes on:

> So Jack an his men were ushered into this great big hall, an there were seven cups a sittin down this long table an decanters o wine, an bread an fruit, an a long sofa. So Jack counts the seats an says, Seven seats. She must hae known we were common! But she doesnae know there's two extra. But we'll try an roll them in an they'll maybe no notice . . . So they stayed and they wandered about the island, hunting an havin fun wi the girls till they'd been there a month. (p.56)

The last comment clearly hints at sexual escapades. In the end, despite the tricks and remonstrations of the queen and her daughters, Jack and his companions escape. There are no specific mentions of a woman for each of the sailors but this does seem to be an Island of Women: the erotic motif is not explicit, but there are nine sailors so we can perhaps assume there were originally Nine Maidens in this tale. The story continued to be told within Irish and Scottish traveller communities well into the 20th century having survived the social upheavals resulting from the major industrial and urbanising developments of Western society.

In the story of MacPhie's Black Dog in Campbell's *Superstitions* (1900, p.109), MacPhie, a famous hunter, is hired by a group of seventeen men to take them hunting on Jura. In the evening while they are resting in a big cave they are joined by a group of 18 beautiful women and it is only MacPhie's dog that allows him to escape from the clutches of these evil spirits, the rest of his companions being killed by them. This has faint echoes of the Isle of Women that Brendan visited. Colonsay where this story starts also has an ancient structure on its eastern shore called *Dun na Nighean*, translated as Fort of the Maidens. Jura also has a tale of a MacPhie, it may well be the same one originally, who escaped the clutches of the Cailleach on Beinn an Oir, one of the Paps of Jura, in much the same way as Brendan and his 17 companions got away from the Isle of Women. In Brendan's case he cut off the hand of one of his companions which was stuck fast through magic to a thread thrown by the Queen of the Isle of Women, while McPhie used the Cailleach's own axe to cut her magic thread which was attached to his boat. This latter tale is linked to a large scar on the western side of Benn an Oir, known as *Scgriob na Cailleach*, The Cailleach's Scrape, or Score, and this is also where the Seven Big Women of Jura were said to have met their end.

The tale of the Hebrides being created by the Cailleach dropping an apron full of material she had intended using to help build Scotland was mentioned earlier. Here is an ancient tale from the Skye also mentioned by Otta Swire in her *The Legends of the Outer Hebrides*:

> Long ago, before the Outer Hebrides had come into being, before the Druids or their ancestors had raised the stone circles of Scotland, a fierce giant lived in a great castle on the only island beyond the Inner Hebrides, Stack Rock. This giant was half human, half serpent and had nine heads with appetites to match. He favoured the flesh of young girls and was

constantly raiding the Inner Hebridean islands like Skye, Eigg and Rum, taking nine maidens at a time. One day he raided Skye and made off with his nine captives. One of these lasses was betrothed to a local lad who on hearing the news, refused to mourn for her. He decided to try and rescue her. He headed off for a remote mountain loch he knew of. There he spoke to the kelpie, or water-horse, of the loch, and enlisted his help. Together they headed off for Stack Rock and went straight into battle with the giant. After a long, fierce struggle the young man and his kelpie assistant overcame the giant and killed him, cutting off eight of his nine heads. He then freed his betrothed and her friends. His assistant, back in the shape of a horse, wanted to return to Skye immediately. But the young hero wanted to bury the giant. There was no land big enough. They tried to sink his great body in the sea with rocks, but this proved fruitless. So they gave up and returned to Skye, all ten of them fitting on the horse's back.

Swire finishes the tale:

> Mighty is the sea, able to cope even with a monster. The birds of the air came in their flocks, called by the murmuring of the sea waves, the fishes came in their shoals and soon all that remained were bare bones, but even the skeleton was too large to be sunk completely below the water, so it lay, buffeted by the wind and waves, a shelter for birds and fish, until at last its bones turned to rocks and cliffs, earth formed from the flotsam and jetsam of the sea and the sea-wrack [seaweed], and the Long Island [Harris and Lewis], the two Uists, Benbecula and Barra grew from the skeleton. If you look at it from above you can still see a vague outline of his bones, with his one remaining head the Butt of Lewis and his soles, the cliffs of South Bernera rising some 600 feet above the sea. The monster's other eight heads

which had been cut off, floated round him like marker buoys and soon they too grew into islands. Bernera, Eriskay, Mingulay, Vallay, Gramsay, Taransay, Pabbay and Killegray though they do seem to have varied rather in size. Thus came the Outer Isles into being. (p.2)

This account of the creation of the Outer Hebrides recalls a Norse legend of the formation of the world. There the original world is formed from the bodies of the ice giants, led by Ymir, who were defeated and killed by the Norse gods (see p.149). It also bears some similarity with the story of Martin and the Nine Maidens at Pittempton, in that the tale carries the recurring motif of the nine females, the single man and a fearsome beast preying on women, though here the hero is successful in saving his intended bride and her companions. There are traditions of nunneries on the Hebridean islands of South Bernera and Benbecula and far out in the Atlantic on Heisgeir near St Kilda though none of these can be substantiated through early church records. It would be ironic if the liking of Columban monks for islands and out of the way places was preceded by a tradition of isolated pre-Christian female communities when learned opinion sees this Christian tradition as undoubtedly having been inspired by the isolation in the desert of Middle Eastern monks in the early centuries of Christianity.

That the Hebridean tradition of insular communities of Women was widespread is reflected in place-names such as *Sgurr nam Ban Naomha* on Eigg, *Rubha Sgor nam Ban-naomha* on Canna, *Eilean nam Ban* off Colonsay, *Eilean ban-leac* off Insh near Easdale, *Eilean Ban* at the Kyle of Lochalsh and *Eilean nam Ban* between Iona and Mull. *Ban* can mean 'woman' or 'women' and *Ban-naohma*, 'holy woman' or 'women'. If *Eilean nam Ban* off Iona refers to an actual island of pre-Christian priestesses, it would shed a different kind of light on the early, supposedly Druidic, history of that island.

Within the widespread traditions of Islands of Women, one worth looking at is the island off the Dutch coast called

Walcheren. A shrine there in the 3rd century CE was dedicated to the goddess Nehalennia, a fertility goddess related to the common European goddess grouping, the Mothers, of whom there were usually three. There is some similarity here with the Danish goddess Nerthus who travelled among her people in a sealed wagon, into which only her priest was allowed to look or enter. HRE Davidson describes the practice in *Gods and Myths of Northern Europe*:

> When the wagon was not in use, it was kept in a grove on an island. When the Goddess returned to her sanctuary, the wagon, the cloth that covered it, and some symbol which it contained were all cleansed in a sacred lake by slaves who were drowned when their task was over. (p.95)

A further link can be seen when she writes:

> in the Roman period, the Goddess Nehalennia, whose shrine stood on the island of Walcheren, was depicted as a woman, sitting in a chair with a bowl of what appears to be apples beside her ... (p.166)

Here the symbol of the apples as a symbol of fertility leads us back to the idea of Avalon as *Emain Abhlach* and, as Davidson points out, the apple as a symbol of youth and regeneration is common to Celtic and Scandinavian traditions. The link between female sanctity and islands is also present in both of these instances. McCulloch made a telling point about such islands within the traditions of the Celtic-speaking peoples in *The Mythology of All Races*:

> The tradition of the Isle of Women still exists in Celtic folklore. Such an island was only part of the divine land and may have originated in myth from actual custom – women living upon or going at certain periods to small islands to perform rites generally tabu to men ... (3 p.117)

It may well be the case that the Nine Maidens entered tradition from actual practice, and that the practice continued in some areas even after they had been assumed into myth. However or wherever the cult of the Nine Maidens originated it has at some point in the pre-Christian past been closely linked to islands, healing and divination. The significance of the island motif – land surrounded by water – might spring from a reverence for water among pre-Christian people, water representing, or being seen as the very blood of the Mother Goddess. The notion of the inherent sanctity of water – after all life itself depends on water – was common to many ancient societies at one level or another. There is also the fact that, as on mountaintops, such island groups would be separate from the day-to-day existence of the rest of contemporary society.

Another version of the Island of Women from the same source reflects the widespread existence of the motif. This example comes from the island of Raratonga in Oceania:

> In the Raratonga tale there are various dangers to be encountered, chief of them is the island or land of fierce women, all of whom wish to marry a rash intruder. (9 p.66)

There is no mention of the women being nine in number but the reference to a rash intruder perhaps echoes those instances already noted in which a single male visits an Island of Women for sexual purposes.

We started this chapter looking at Avalon, the home of Morgan and her sisters. Geoffrey of Monmouth in the *Vita Merlini* relates that these nine sisters took the wounded Arthur off to their island home after the fateful battle of Camlaan. As I have argued in *The Quest for Arthur*, the Battle of Camlaan is well-attested in early sources. We know that each tribal community would tell the matter of their mythological and legendary traditions within the known environment of the tribe and as it has been argued that Camlaan was in fact fought at, or near, modern Camelon, now a suburb of Falkirk on the southern shore of the River Forth, we can perhaps locate a specific local site for Avalon. Most commentators to date have always seen Avalon as being in the west, but as we know that the Lothians on the south of the Forth, and in all probability the lands of Fife on the north of the river, were inhabited by P-Celtic speaking peoples who knew of Arthur, surely there should be a local candidate for Avalon. Out in the Firth of Forth a few miles off Fife Ness there is the Isle of May which as noted above, means the Island of the Maiden, or Maidens. The Isle of May is known to have been a site of early Christian activity and excavations in the 1990s suggest that it could have been used as a burial site in the pre-Christian period, supporting the possibility that it had previously been an already-established ritual site. While the idea of Avalon has been generally seen as primarily a mythological concept, it is an intriguing thought that if Geoffrey of Monmouth in the *Vita Merlini* was writing of a specific event after a historical battle, then Arthur, or perhaps the warrior who had taken a powerful name from his people's traditions to bolster his own influence, could have been buried on the Isle of May. We saw that the Isle of May was traditionally visited by Thenew, before she gave birth to St Kentigern, a significant figure in the history of Christianity in Scotland and Thenew herself was supposedly the niece of Arthur. In this respect is worth recalling that JS Glennie referred to Thenew as perhaps being one of the maidens accompanying St Monenna whom as we have seen, numbered nine. However, why would a group of pre-Christian priestesses have taken the dying Christian warrior to a pre-Christian site? Perhaps we are seeing here a tale that survived as part of ongoing pre-Christian belief within an ostensibly Christianised society. Many pre-Christian practices, often designated as superstitions, continued in Scotland, as elsewhere, well into the 20th century, and, as we have seen, ancient tales likewise survived.

CHAPTER 7
Sagas and Sea Spirits

THE WRITTEN SOURCES on the subject of pre-Christian beliefs from Scandinavia are comparatively late and fragmentary. What we know, as elsewhere, comes to us mainly through the writings of Christian scribes. Scandinavia became completely Christianised relatively late in the 12th century though pre-Christian rites and beliefs survived long afterwards there as elsewhere. The problem of the written material is exactly the same as in the Celtic-speaking countries. It isn't just the issue of the influence of Christian beliefs on the texts, it is also that Christian scribes were trained in a strictly classical fashion and were thus heavily influenced by the models from which they had learned. We have to rely on sources such as Snorri Sturlusson's *Heimskringla*, a chronicle of early Norse kings, the collections of poetry and story known as the *Eddas* and various surviving sagas that have survived in literary form. Ultimately though, they derive from oral tradition. However, the use of rhyme, rhythm, alliteration, assonance and all the other mnemonic tricks of the poets and storytellers are virtually absent from these stories which are arranged for presentation on the page, as literature. However, just because the scribes were writing the stories down in this way does not mean that the myths and legends were no longer being told, and listened to. In Scotland, as we have seen, the storytelling tradition of the travelling peoples, as within many localised communities, both Scots and Gaelic speaking survived into the late 20th century and much of what has been described as 'folklore' or 'superstition' can now be seen to contain useful information about ancient belief and practice, much more so than had been previously realised. Sometimes ancient motifs have been transformed and survive as stories, or even jokes, in urban environments. This is true everywhere. It is easy to forget that near-universal literacy and the widespread availability of books are relatively recent phenomena, even in the Western world. Just 300 years ago, books, apart from the Bible were very scarce, and in the scale of human existence that is a short time indeed. It is an especially short time when we are dealing with beliefs and institutions that are potentially thousands of years old.

There are many instances of the importance of the number nine in Norse tradition but perhaps none more intriguing than that of the god Heimdall, watcher of the gates of Asgard, who was said to have been born to nine mothers. In the poem the *Rigspula,* which is part of the *Poetic Edda,* one of the great core collections of Norse myth and lore, Heimdall is said to have fathered the ancestors of the thralls, the farmers and the earls, i.e. all of humanity. The tale of a wandering god travelling from house to house and fathering children is also told of the Celtic god of the sea, Manannan. This link with the sea is very significant.

In the ancient text the *Heimdallargaldar* the god is quoted as saying, 'I am the child of nine mothers, I am the son of nine sisters'. This is reinforced by an ancient poem from the *Shorter Voluspa,* quoted by Davidson in *Gods and Myths of Northern Europe*:

> One was born in olden days,
> of strength surpassing, kin to the Powers.
> He, nail-resplendent, was born to nine
> giant maids, on the edge of the earth. (p.175)

In Norse mythology these nine females were the daughters of the sea god Aegir and his wife, the sea goddess Ran. As in so many other instances of Nine Maidens groups there is the motif

SAGAS AND SEA SPIRITS

of their relationship with a single male. This apparently strange idea of the Nine Maidens being mother to one son is a motif that we have seen in the Irish saga of Ruad, son of Rigdonn (see p.100). Heimdall is a complex figure. He is the watcher at the gate, the father of the people and, variously, a sun god, a god of the moon, a ram god, the spirit of the rainbow, and the personification of the spirit of the World Tree itself. Heimdall, as the watcher, sits on guard on the rainbow bridge Bifrost, needing no sleep, seeing as well by night as by day and constantly listening for the slightest sound of threat to Asgard, the home of the Norse gods. It is his great horn, Gjallahorn, that sounds to waken the gods before the final battle of Ragnarok. Such a diversity of aspects in one figure demonstrates his great importance in Scandinavian mythology.

The nine sisters who are said to be Heimdall's common mother have been interpreted as the personification of the sea. As we discussed earlier the ninth wave is believed in various countries to be the strongest; in Welsh folklore fishermen are said to have called the ninth wave the ram of Gwenhiddy with the other eight waves being her sheep, reminding us that one of Heimdall's aspects is that of a ram god. Another similarity with Welsh tradition concerns Aegir, father of the nine sea maidens. He has a great cauldron in which he brews mead for his feasts, recalling Cerridwen's cauldron of poetry and inspiration, which was tended by Nine Maidens. Mead inspires poetry and it was for the mead of poetry that Odin seduced the giant Suttung's daughter, by reciting her nine poems.

The association of these Nine Maidens with Odin, the chief of the Norse gods is precise. In *The Norsemen*, HA Guerber tells us:

> In the course of a walk along the seashore, he once beheld nine beautiful giantesses, the wave maidens Gjalp, Greip, Egiea, Augeia, Ulfrun, Argiafa, Sindur, Atla and Iarnsaxa sound asleep on the white sand. The god of the sky was so charmed with these

beautiful creatures, the Eddas relate, he wedded
all nine of them, and they combined at the same
moment, to bring forth a son, who received the
name of Heimdall . . . The nine mothers proceeded
to nourish their babe on the strength of the earth,
the moisture of the sea, and the heat of the sun,
which singular diet proved so strengthening that the
new god acquired his full growth in a remarkably
short space of time and hastened to Asgard to join
his father. (p.146)

The mothers of Heimdall seem to be closely related to the Nine
Maidens who at the beginning of the world in Norse mythology,
ground the body of the great giant Ymir on the great World-
Mill. Ymir was the first being, formed from the primaeval universe and the world was formed from his body. The Nine Maidens of the Mill appear to be the same as the Daughters of Ran,
the sea goddess who was Aegir's wife. As Donald Mackenzie in
Teutonic Myth and Legend says:

> The great World-mill of the gods was under the
> care of Mundilfore. Nine giant maids turned it with
> much violence, and the grinding of the stones made
> such fearsome clamour that the loudest tempests
> could not be heard. The great mill is larger than is
> the whole world, for out of it the mould of the earth
> was ground. (p.4)

Mackenzie goes on to provide more detail of the creation of the
world by the Nine Mill-maids:

> When Ymir was dead, the gods took counsel among
> themselves, and set forth to frame the world. They
> laid the body of the clay-giant in the mill, and the
> maids ground it. The stones were smeared with
> blood, and the dark flesh came out as mould. Thus
> was earth produced, and the gods shaped it to their
> desire. From Ymir's bones were made the rocks

> and the mountains; his teeth and jaws were broken asunder, and as they went round at their labour, the giant maids flung the fragments hither and thither, and these are the pebbles and boulders. The ice-blood of the giant became the waters of the vast engulfing sea. Nor did the giant maids cease their labours when the body of Ymir was completely ground, and the earth was framed and set in order by the gods. The body of giant after giant was laid upon the mill, which stands beneath the floor of the Ocean, and the flesh-grist is the sand which is ever washed up round the shores of the world. Where the waters are sucked thorough the whirling eye of the millstone is a fearsome maelstrom and the sea ebbs and flows as it is drawn down to *Hvergelmer*, 'the roaring cauldron', in *Nifelheim* and thrown forth again. The very heavens are made to swing by the great World-mill round *Veraldar Nagli*, 'the world spike', which is the Polar Star. (p.5)

The idea of the roaring cauldron, *Hvergelmer*, echoes the physical reality of the Corryvreckan whirlpool. Here we have a description not only of the origin of the physical earth but perhaps also an account of the precession of the equinoxes – the circling of the stars over any particular point which takes 25,800 years to come back to its original position. This basic idea is very like that of the well-known motif of the Axis Mundi – literally the axis of the world, the fixed centre point around which the heavens revolve. Such ideas were known in ancient Egypt and elsewhere and underpin the notions of astrological 'houses'. In his remarkable book on this phenomenon, *Hamlet's Mill*, Georges de Santillana tells us:

> Medieval writers, and after them Athansius Kircher located the gurgus mirabilis, the wondrous eddy, somewhere off the coast of Norway, or of Great Britain. It was the Maelstrom, plus probably a memory of the Pentland Firth. (p.91)

The Pentland Firth, initially *Pjettaland*, the Firth of the Picts, is off Scotland's north coast and the sea there can be horrendous but this 'wondrous eddy' appears to me more like a reference to the Corryvreckan though it is on the west, not north of Scotland. There is though, something similar in the Pentland Firth. Here it described by F Burton in *Wonderful Curios*:

> Between the coast of Caithness and Orkney is a dreadful Frith or Gulf, in the north end of which by reason of the meeting of 9 contrary Tides or Currents is a Male Stream or great Whirlpool. (p.22)

Again we come across the number nine. In the *Revue Celtique* of 1885, Whitley Stokes wrote in a similar vein:

> A great whirlpool there is between Ireland and Scotland on the North. It is the meeting of many seas – it resembles an open cauldron which casts the draught down and up, and its roaring is heard like far-off thunder. (p.16)

The idea of *Hvergelmer*, the roaring cauldron, and Stokes' description of the whirlpool could hardly be better suited as descriptions of the Corryvreckan. One intriguing aspect of this is Santillana's reference to the World Spike. In the Gulf of Corryvreckan, there is a great underwater pillar of rock, or spike, around which the waters are forced by the powerful tides to create the whirlpool. The spike is known as the Cailleach and as noted before, the whirlpool is said to be the breath of the Goddess under the waves.

One of the earliest referents to the Maelstrom motif comes from an ancient fragment of poetry attributed to a Norwegian *skald*, or poet, Snæbjörn who wrote:

> Men say that the nine maidens of the island-mill are moving the host-fierce mill of the skerries out beyond the skirts of the earth, they who long ago ground *Amlodi's* meal. (Hansen, p.129)

Amlodi is the original of Hamlet in Scandinavian mythology. Mackenzie's account of these remarkable mythological beings in *Teutonic Myth and Legend* continues:

> These giant maids at the beginning ground Ymir's body on the World Mill. And ever do they turn the great mill at the sea bottom. Angeyja and Eyrgjafa grind mould; Jarnsaxa is the crusher of the iron which comes from clay and the sea; Imder, Gjalp, and Greip are fire-maids, for whom the world-mill is fire sparked forth and there is fire in the sea; Eistla, Eyrgjafa, and Ulfrun are also at work like the others. (p.99)

Here we have the Nine Maidens at the very start of creation, portrayed as the agency by which the world is brought into being and by which the universe keeps on turning. Jarnsaxa in some tales is said to have been the first wife of the great god Thor.

Other names for the Nine Maidens given by Snorri Sturlusson in the *Skaldasparmal* are Himingglaeva ('the heaven-shining one'), Blodughadda ('bloody hair'), Dufa, Udr, Hronn, Bygla, Bra and Kola ('the cold one'). It is probable that these names were derived from descriptive appellations of waves in the tradition of the Norse poetic technique of kennings. A kenning is a metaphor; thus a boat can be a cleaver of the waves, a spade, the sword of the soil or the ladle of the earth, and gold the fire of the serpent or sun of the sea.

The description of the Nine Maidens in the story of Ruad, son of Rigdonn, as 'fierce, radiant and bright' would also fit the most famous of the female figures in Norse mythology, the Valkyries, the hand-maidens of Odin. They are variously given the capacity to decide victory, select which warriors would die on the battlefield and then choose which warriors were worthy of being taken to partake of the joys of Valhalla, the Norse warriors' Paradise. Their presence on the battlefield is akin to that of the Morrigan in Irish mythology.

The Valkyries occur in different numbers in Norse mythology but Grimm in his *Teutonic Mythology* makes the following point:

> Usually nine *valkyjrur* ride out together . . . their lances, helmets and shields glitter . . . This nineness is also found in the story of Thidrandi to whom nine *disir* [sorceresses] appear first in white raiment then nine others in black . . . Nine, as the favourite number of the valkyrs, is confirmed by *Saemunddredda* 228, where one of them speaks of [having] *atta systra* (eight sisters). To our surprise, a hero Granmar turns *valkyra* in Asgard, and bears nine wolves to Sinfiotli . . . (p.421)

Asgard is the home of the gods and Sinfiotli was one of the heroic family of the Volsungs, who along with his father the hero Sigmund, became a werewolf for nine nights.

Guerber, in *The Norsemen*, tells of the Valkyries in Valhalla:

> These maidens, nine in number according to some authorities, brought the heroes great horns full of delicious mead, and set before them huge portions of boar's flesh, upon which they feasted heartily . . . (p.19)

And further:

> The numbers of the Valkyrs differ greatly according to various mythologists, Ranging from three to sixteen, most authorities, however, naming only nine. (p.174)

The significance of boar's flesh as the meat of heroes again links us to the Celtic traditions wherein the hunting and eating of the boar is a recurring motif. We should also remember the association of swine with several goddess figures.

In the saga poem *Helgakvida Hundingsbana II*, the hero Helgi is the lover of a Valkyrie, Sigrun and just before a sea battle we have these lines:

> Helgi drew together a great fleet and sailed to Freka Stone. At sea, a fearful storm arose. Flashes of lightning shone about them and struck the ships. They saw nine valkyries ride aloft and knew again Sigrún.
> (Helgi URL)

Here the nine Valkyries have apparently arrived to help the hero, and this repeats the motif of the nine and a single male.

Guerber gives the names of the Valkyries as Skuld, Skaugul, Gunnr, Hildr, Gaundul, Geir-skaugul, Olrun, Alvit and Svanhvit (p.175). Geir-skaugul is suggestive of the Scots Gyre-Carlin. The Gyre-Carlin in Scots tradition was often called the queen of the witches, and was clearly at one time a goddess figure. Gyre in this context is usually interpreted as meaning 'biting' but can also mean a ring, spiral or even vortex. Which, in the light of the spiral as a symbol, as well as the living manifestation of the Corryvreckan whirlpool, perhaps illustrates the complex cross-referencing of ideas in pre-Christian symbolism. Svanhvit suggests another aspect of the Valkyries – their ability to change into swans. This returns us to the theme of shape-shifting so common amongst Nine Maiden groups.

The Valkyries did occasionally appear in the form of swan-maidens, as in the tale where the Valkyrie Brynhild, heroine of Wagner's musical drama, incurred the wrath of Odin. One day when she and eight of her sisters were flying from Valhalla, they landed on earth and removed their plumage. Unseen by them King Agnar approached, seized the discarded apparel and hid it under an oak. From then on the nine Valkyries were in his power.

Agnar forced Brynhild to counteract Odin's wishes in battle and as a result she was banished to earth and could only be married to a hero who would ride through flames for her.

In time Siegfried appeared as this hero. Here again we have a shape-shifting motif and it is significant that the king hid the swan plumage below an oak tree, a sacred tree in so many cultures. Like other Nine Maidens groups, there is also a relationship with mountaintops.

Grimm in *Teutonic Mythology* tells us,

> it is conceivable, why Brynhilde, the valkyr dwelling on her mountain, had *lif med laekning* (*pharmaca cum medela*) ascribed to her . . . she is a wise woman skilled in magic, a pharmaceutria, herberia and moreover understands the binding up of wounds . . . At medicinal springs, by mineral waters, appears the white lady with the snake. (p.1149)

This medical knowledge is like that of Morgan and her sisters and the Gallicenae of the Isle of Sena, while the association with the well and the snake reminds us specifically of Bride. That these similarities exist between the Germanic and Celtic belief patterns suggests a much closer inter-relationship between these different language groups in terms of mythology and culture than has generally been appreciated. The extent of the common ideas suggests that their origin lay long before the influx of Scandinavian settlement and consequent extensive cross-fertilisation, following the Viking raids that began in the late 7th century. The similarities in the descriptions of so many of the Nine Maidens groups and their activities underlines this.

Grimm links the Valkyrie with other Norse wise women and tells us,

> Skuld and Heid are, like Hulda and Berhta, purely pre-Christian half-Goddesses, round whom gathers the magic ring-dance; they stir up storm and tempest, they make invulnerable, they prophesy . . . (p.1044)

Again this is remarkably like the *Gallicenae* and the storm-raising is reminiscent of the Cailleach as Mother Goddess; the power of raising the wind was widely accredited to witches into relatively modern times. The ring dance and the tempest-raising are also suggestive of both *Hvergelmer* and the Corryvreckan. The reference to making invulnerable takes us again to the motif of the teaching and arming of heroes like Peredur and Cu Chullain.

Grimm comments further that,

> sorceresses have at their command, a bird's shape, a feather garment, especially that of the goose, which stands for the more ancient swan, and they are like swan-wives, valkyrs, who traverse the breezes and troop to the battle. (p.1045)

Mazota, the eldest of the Pittempton Nine Maidens group, is said to have been able to stop geese from eating the corn she and her sisters had planted. Did she have powers over birds? And if so, is this power a faded memory of a connection with bird-priestesses of some kind? Shape-shifting into the form of swans is also given as an attribute of the Greek Muses, another group of nine females. Grimm makes an interesting comparison between the witches in Shakespeare's Macbeth and the wise-women of Norse tradition:

> In Macbeth three witches – but they are weird sisters too.. – meet on a heath and in a cave to boil their cauldron. They are not so much enchantresses in league with the Devil, as fate-announcing wise-women or priestesses, who prophesy by their cauldron. (p.1046)

As they danced around their cauldron the weird sisters in the play sing, 'Thrice to thine, And thrice to mine, and thrice again to make up nine'. It is likely that Shakespeare found this chant in contemporary folklore. He would have known that the king, James I of England and VI of Scotland had a strong interest in witchcraft, believing he had been the subject of a plot by witches to sink his ship by raising a storm in the river Forth in 1590. AD Hope, in *A Midsummer Eve's Dream*, suggests the existence of a 'fairy cult' in 15th century Scotland; this would have been based on ancient pre-Christian belief. It is quite likely that such beliefs continued into the later years of the 16th century. As we have seen some such survivals lasted well into the 20th century. Although there is no mention that the North Berwick witches, led by a single male, were nine in number they have certain things in common with the Nine Maidens groups. They are involved specifically with weather-working, Devil worship, which probably refers to pre-Christian ritual behaviour, and at North Berwick itself, there is a very prominent hill called North Berwick Law, one of the Paps of Lothian, the other being Arthur's Seat. Many such sites have been the locations for ritual activity in pre-Christian times, and several different groups of Nine Maidens have been associated with prominent hills and mountains as we have seen.

The Valkyries are nine in number and shape-shift, sometimes into swans. Grimm notes that they are also involved in storm-raising and prophecy like so many other Nine Maidens groups. They are also close to the most important of the pre-Christian Norse gods, Odin. All this places them firmly within the Nine Maidens type. They were though, not the only such groups in Scandinavian lore.

HR Ellis Davidson tells us in *Gods and Myths of Northern Europe*, 'Human princesses are said to become Valkyries, as though they were priestesses of some cult.' (p.61) She also tells us of wise women prophesying in the *Flateyjarbok*, another compilation of Scandinavian lore, and quotes the use of the term 'spae-wife', a term that has survived in Scots, meaning a medium, or one who can get in touch with the spirits of the dead. Here again we have a modern remnant of an ancient belief. Davidson describes an act of divination by a wise woman known as a *volva* and says:

> The volva in Greenland was described in detail, was said to be the last survivor of a company of nine

women and the sagas elsewhere represent the seeresses as going about in groups. (p.120)

In the mythology of the Scandinavian peoples there is another particularly interesting group of Nine Maidens associated with the goddess figure Menglod. Her name means 'necklace-glad' which links her to the goddess figure Freyja, who had a famous necklace Brisingamen. Freyja is a Norse goddess of fertility and thus akin to the Mother Goddess figures we have already considered. Interestingly she often appears with her twin brother Frey, a different kind of duality than the one previously considered. In the *Svipdagsmal*, a poem in the *Elder Edda*, we meet Menglod. She is the object of a search by Svipdag whose mother, the seeress Groa, has come from beyond the grave to help him in his quest. She sings nine charms over him. Svipdag then searches through nine worlds before he finds Menglod on a mountaintop in her magic hall, Lyr, the Holder of Heat. Lyr had originally been created by Loki, the Norse Trickster god, with the help of nine dwarves. These nine dwarves are called Uri, Iri, Bari, Jari, Var, Vegdrasil, Dori, Ori and Delling. Like other nine name lists, this has something of the sense of a chant about it and may reflect some old ritual. The recurrence of nine in this tale is remarkable.

Menglod's hall is on *Lyfiaberg*, the Hill of Healing. There Svipdag sees her surrounded by Nine Maidens sitting at her knee, Hlif the Helper, Hlifthrasa, Thjodvara, shining Bjort, Bleik the white, Blid, Frid, kindly Eir and the gold-giving Aurboaa. The names again have a ring of poetry about them. Crossley-Holland says, '... they soon help all those who make offerings on the high altars' (p.122), which is reminiscent of supplicants approaching the *Gallicenae*.

Speaking of Freyja, Guerber tells us that:

Although Goddess of love, Freyja was not soft and
pleasure-loving only, for the ancient Northern races
believed that she had very martial tastes, and that

> as Valfreyja she often led the Valkyrs down to the battlefields, choosing and claiming half the heroes slain. She was therefore often represented with corselet and helmet, shield and spear, the lower part of her body only being clad in the usual flowing feminine garb. (p.131)

Here Freyja relates to the Valkyries just as Bride, Cerridwen, Monenna and Morgan relate to their different Nine Maidens groups. One of Freyja's other names was Vanabride which is, to say the least, tantalising. Within Scottish mythology, we have the embodiment of vicious winter in the Cailleach or Carlin. However, we also have tales that tell of the Cailleach becoming Bride at Beltane by drinking from a magic well, Bride, the goddess of Summer who is beautiful and kind and clearly a fertility goddess. (McNeill, 2 p.21) In this double aspect we can discern an ancient dual Goddess. Freyja seems here to contain something of the same duality and as Valfreyja she is clearly linked to the Nine Maidens motif, as is the Cailleach in Scotland. Freyja, like Bride, is often referred to as being golden-haired. Menglod herself is a supernatural female being with nine attendants, is associated with healing and to whom prayers are made. The Valkyries and volvas and Menglod's companions are all apparently Nine Maidens groups.

The father of the twins Frey and Freyja was Njord, who like Aegir was linked with the sea. He is also said to have had nine daughters. This is from the poem Solarljod:

> Here are runes which have engraven Njord's daughters nine,
> Radvor the eldest, and the youngest Kreppvor, and their seven sisters. (Njord URL)

Davidson suggests (Davidson 1990, p.106) that though associated with the sea, Njord may have been initially a fertility figure and suggests close links to Nerthus, the Germanic fertility goddess mentioned by Tacitus (Tacitus, p.133), mentioned above (p.96).

We now turn to the Icelandic tale already mentioned. This is the story of *Thidrandi whom the Goddesses Slew*. He was a handsome, brave and intelligent young Icelander but his father's friend Thorhall Seer feared for his future. One night at a harvest feast held at the start of winter in Thidrandi's father's house, Thorhall told everyone not to go outdoors that night, no matter what happened. Thidrandi had given up his own bed to a guest and slept in the main hall. Late that night when all but Thidrandi were asleep a knock came at the door. Three times the knock came and Thidrandi, forgetting Thorhall's words thought it must be more guests arriving. This is the story from Gwyn Jones' *Erik the Red and other Icelandic sagas*:

> He picked up his sword and went outside, but he could not see a soul. Then it occurred to him that some of the guests must have ridden on ahead to the house and then have turned back to meet those who were coming along more slowly. So he walked under the woodpile and heard the noise of riding from the north into the home-field. He saw that there were nine women there, all in dark raiment, and they held drawn swords in their hands. He heard likewise the noise of riding from the south into the home-field, and there too were nine women all in bright raiment, and on white horses. Thidrandi now wanted to get back indoors and tell them of this sight, but the dark-clad women came up with him first and set upon him; and he defended himself well and bravely.
>
> A long while after Thorhall awoke and asked whether Thidrandi was awake too. He got no answer. They had slept too long, cried Thorhall.
>
> They went outside. It was moonlight and frosty weather. They found Thidrandi lying wounded, he was carried indoors, and when they got word of him he told them all that had appeared to him. He died the same morning at daybreak and was laid in a howe after the old heathen fashion. (p.161)

Wanting to understand the events of the previous night Thidrandi's father, Hall asks his friend, Thorhall the Seer, what it all meant. Thorhall tells him that the two groups of nine women were wraiths of Hall's kinsfolk. He then comes out with what must be one of the most blatant manipulations of traditional lore by a Christian scribe, saying the event must mean that a new faith is coming to Iceland, the dark nine being spirits who followed the old faith and, knowing they would be rejected once the new faith took hold, determined to exact some price for this betrayal by taking Thidrandi. The white nine were good spirits who had arrived too late to help him. The new faith of course would be a good thing for Hall, his kinfolk and their descendants.

This tale seems to be a post-Christian attempt to give credence to the new religion by claiming it had been foretold. The idea of the black, bad spirits, and the white, good spirits is plainly Christian with the emphasis on the battle between good and evil. The use of the Nine Maidens motif in such a way would suggest they were widely known in Iceland at the time the story was composed and were perhaps based upon the idea of the volvas or seeresses. The slaying of Thidrandi himself is, as in some other tales of the Nine Maidens, suggestive of some sort of sacrificial rite. The tale also conforms to the motif of the single male and the nine females though here the females appear in two separate, and opposite, groups.

These various stories are evidence of the existence of groups of nine women with some sort of sacred or divinatory function among the Scandinavian and Icelandic peoples, echoing tales of Morgan and her sisters and the Gallicenae, and there are links to North Eurasian shamanistic practices in the references to prophesying and shape-shifting. The point has already been made that the Islands of Women motif is particularly widespread and we should keep in mind that the pre-Christian Norsemen were expert sailors. As Iceland was the last part of Europe to be Christianised there are perhaps stronger clues as to pre-Christian practice in their traditions than elsewhere.

Although the link between the Nine Maidens and Heimdall is obvious, we should remember that Odin was his father as they were his mother. The motif of the nine women and the one man can therefore perhaps be seen twice here, once with Odin and once with Heimdall. This, and the function of the Nine Maidens of the Mill grinding out the physical universe from the corpses of the Frost Giants, shows them to have been very close to the heart of pre-Christian Norse mythology and this must strengthen the possibility that they have an origin in the very far distant past indeed.

Another group of nine occur in Bard's Saga, set in western Iceland. The giant Bard has nine daughters who live with him in a cave and young men come to the cave to receive instruction in law and one of them marries the eldest daughter Helga. Davidson suggests that

> the relationship between the giant's nine daughters and the young men who visit them is similar to that between the shamans and their spirit wives. (1976, p.298)

As we shall see in at least one shamanic tradition, the god Solboni has nine daughters (see p.228) with whom the aspiring shaman must sleep in a remarkable echo of the exploits of Ruad, son of Rigdonn (see p.100). Davidson also mentions other tales relating to a King Gudmund who has many daughters as fitting the same general pattern. Such similarities amongst sub-Arctic cultures echoes the idea presented by the Pictish Art expert Isobel Henderson when she drew attention to similarities between the symbols used in Pictish carving and what she described as Eurasian Hunter Art stretching from Scotland as far as Siberia. Such cultural linkages stretch well-beyond linguistic commonalities.

What is abundantly clear is that Norse tradition, like so much Irish material, makes great use of the number nine from the cosmological symbolism of the Nine Worlds through to magical practice and much more mundane areas. As Soltysiak tells us:

> The distinguished number was used for definition of various symbolical values, often not related to the cosmology at all. The second aspect of the Norse symbolism of nine refers to Odin and his Valkyries – here number nine associates with initiation, the cycles of life and death, as well as magic. An analagous symbolic complex can be found in the Orphic tradition of ancient Greece . . . (p.241)

I hope I have shown that in Norse tradition there were many more nines than the Valkyries and that, as we shall see, these groups of often mystical or sacral women find echoes far beyond Europe.

CHAPTER 8

Muses, Maenads and beyond

THE MOTIF OF the Nine Maidens occurs in many different societies and locations. Perhaps the most widely known example in Europe is that of the Nine Muses, attendants on the god Apollo. This arises from the influence of classical learning on the education systems of Europe. The theory which interprets Europe – and eventually the world – being civilised by the spread of influence from the Mediterranean nation-states of Greece and Rome, borders on racism. The obsession with the classical world has determined the perspective of teaching at most European universities, particularly since the Renaissance. Even now, as the limitations of such classically-centred ideas are being appreciated, their influence still lingers. Over many years, archaeological investigation in Scotland has been all too often focused on Roman sites, despite the fact that the Romans were only in Scotland on a handful of occasions and their longest period of, limited, occupation was manning the Antonine Wall, created in the early 140s and abandoned, for good, around 167. Despite this, archaeologists and historians have treated the Romans, little more than visitors, as being of more importance than, say, the Picts, the people whose direct ancestors, the Caledonians, had fought off the Romans. Within indigenous oral tradition, the Picts can be construed as essentially the ancestor people, and their importance in the development of what became Scotland, one of the oldest nation states in Europe has still to be totally understood. Thankfully the balance is beginning to be, slowly, redressed. Our museums are still overly full of Roman antiquities, which tell us more about the mindset of the establishment than about our own past. After all how many times is it necessary to dig up a Roman marching camp when we already know all there is to know about them? Surely we would be better off devoting our limited resources to finding out more about our own ancestors?

The ongoing search into the Nine Maidens is part of my attempt to try and redress this balance by finding out more about my own culture, but I have been taken far beyond Scotland in the search. Several authors have noticed similarities between different groups of Nine Maidens, but the very idea of the pre-Christian peoples of north-west Europe having significant, long-term and highly developed sacred institutions of their own does not sit easily with the emphasis on the classical world; the Greeks and Romans, and subsequent classically-dominated scholarship, have seen most other peoples as barbarians – which the *Oxford English Dictionary* gives as meaning:

a. one not Greek;
b. one living outside the pale of the Roman empire and its civilization, applied especially to the northern nations that overthrew them;
c. one outside the pale of Christian civilization.

Out of this essentially imperialist insularity comes the stereotype of the barbarian or outsider peoples as being brutal, ignorant and bent on wilful destruction. It is particularly regrettable that such stereotypes have occurred so often here in the British Isles. Millennia before the Greek cities or the Roman state developed, the inhabitants of Britain were, in a presumably illiterate society, erecting such sophisticated and magnificent structures as Avebury, Calanais, Maes Howe, Stonehenge and the Ness of Brodgar, one of the most striking monuments of which is Maes Howe – the Maiden's, or Maidens' Mound.

Without hard evidence to the contrary, I see no reason to assume other than that the majority of the population of

Scotland one or two thousand years ago was descended directly from the people who raised the megaliths. There was a continuity of culture and thus belief even if it seems clear the skills of the Maes Howe builders disappeared. It is my contention that the Nine Maidens existed within that continuity of belief in a mythological sense and also as extant groups. There is also evidence to suggest the Nine Maidens existed elsewhere while the ice still covered Britain over 10,000 years ago, long before the rise of Greek civilisation.

Because European literacy developed in Greece before the advent of Christianity we have many literary sources from there to draw upon. For the purposes of this study we will concentrate on Robert Graves' *The Greek Myths* which drew upon his lifetime's study and contemplation of this material. There are many instances of priestess groups in classical mythology and some of them, while not reported as being groups of nine have many aspects in common with Nine Maidens groupings. Classical mythology itself developed directly from pre-Christian ideas and motifs in earlier societies in and around the Mediterranean. In Greek mythology, after the Olympians had defeated the Titans, they asked Zeus to create divinities who were capable of celebrating their victory. Zeus then went to Pieria, where he slept with the nymph Mnemosyne for nine consecutive nights. Mnemosyne gave birth to nine daughters who became the choir of the Muses. According to Graves, the Muses had initially numbered three but developed into nine.

The Muses are clearly significant in their own right but they show many similarities with other Nine Maidens groups. They are the personification of the creative arts, and this is a close parallel with the Nine Maidens who tended Cerridwen's cauldron of poetry and inspiration in Welsh tradition. They were the companions of the inspirational god Apollo and were seen as patrons of poetry themselves as well as being the guardians of the oracle at Delphi. They also possessed the gift of prophecy and were known to teach others the arts of divination. This is reminiscent of other Nine Maidens groups like the Druidesses of Gallicenae, the sisters of Avalon and the volva of Iceland, who also foretold the future. The Muses were associated with Mount Helicon and also with the mountains of Olympus and Parnassus and various Nine Maidens groups are associated with mountain or hilltops, including the companions of Menglod in Scandinavia and St Monenna in Scotland. Mount Helicon was the site of fragrant plants which provided an antidote to snake venom, which suggests the Muses had knowledge of healing, another attribute of these groups. We might also remember that snakes are a recurrent symbol of the Goddess. Helicon was a site of many springs and the Muses are strongly associated with the spring of Castalia at Parnassus which suggests possible parallels with the Nine Maidens wells in Scotland. At Delphi, the officiating priestess was known as the Pythoness, reminiscent of the goddess Bride and her symbol, the adder, which figures so often on Pictish symbol stones. This is truly ancient symbolism as noted by Marija Gimbutas talking of the 4th millennium BC in *The Goddesses and Gods of Old Europe*:

> The presence of the Bird and Snake Goddess is felt everywhere – on earth, in the skies and beyond the clouds, where primordial waters lie. Her abode is beyond the upper waters, i.e. beyond meandrous labyrinths. She rules over the life-giving force of water, and her image is consequently associated with water containers. The Snake Goddess and the Bird Goddess appear as separate figures and as a single divinity. (p.182)

The symbolism of water and the snake are implicit in many of the variants of the Nine Maidens groups; an example already given is the ritual at St Bride's well at Sanquhar in south-west Scotland where nine white stones were placed in the well by local lasses into the 20th century.

These similarities between the Muses and other Nine Maiden groups are apparently not a result of classical influence on northern Europe, but derive from a truly ancient source.

That this is so, seems clear from the existence of Nine Maidens material from well beyond Europe, and as we shall see, potentially beginning in Africa.

The Muses themselves are:

Clio, who represents History and is associated with the trumpet and clepsydra, a form of lute;

Euterpe, who is associated with the flute and its music;

Thalia, who represents Comedy;

Melpomene, representing Tragedy and who carried the club of Hercules;

Terpsichore, who represents Lyric Poetry and Dance, and is linked with the cithara, a form of harp;

Erato, the nymph of Love Poetry;

Polyhymnia, who initially represented Heroic Hymns, then Mime;

Urania, who represents Astronomy and is symbolised by a globe and compass; and

Calliope, the leader of the Muses, who represents Epic Poetry and Eloquence, shown by a stylus and tablets.

The wide range of subject matter the Muses are associated with can not only be seen echoing the Nine Maidens who tended Cerridwen's cauldron of poetry and inspiration, but also Irish tradition wherein Bride was seen as a goddess of poetry and poets. Many springs were dedicated to the Muses, which were presumably the locations of rites in their honour. It is possible that these groups performed a role as officiating priestesses at such wells. This perhaps makes sense, in that though we have many mythological sources for the Nine Maidens, there do seem to have been many sites where at some point in the distant past they carried out actual rituals as priestesses. This suggests a role as both remote divine beings and humans participating in everyday life.

The Muses are said to have been priestesses of Apollo, who, like the other groups we have looked at, operated in groups of nine. The Dramatist Thomas Heywood (1570-1641), discusses the number of the Muses in *Gunaikieon*:

> But there are nine received and allowed amongst us, and that for diverse reasons; as first because the number nine is held to be vertuall and perfect; being an even foure, arising from a first odde, and then oddlie to an odde; it is likewise divided into three equal oddes; then it consists of Triangulors etc.; Besides Mnemosine, who is said to be the mother of the muses, her name consists of nine letters. Fulgentius saith, that the nine muses, with their brother Apollo, import nothing else than the tenne modulations of man's voyce, therefore is Apollo's harpe represented with ten strings. (p.59)

This is somewhat obscure but the passage shows that within the ideas of his time the number nine was seen as significant, underlined by the use of the word of 'vertuall', meaning 'virtuous'. He gives a list of places associated with the Muses:

> I will onlie speak brieflie from what places they took their generall denominations, and so precede to every particular person. They were called Pierides of the mountain Pierus, or as some will have it Pierius, who had nine daughters; Likewise, Caameanae, a Canendo of singing; Heliconides, of the fountain called Helicon, that flowed from a mountain in Boetia; Pernasides, of the Pernassus, situate in the region of Phocis; Aonides, of the Aonian mountain; Pegasides from a spring or well so called, first discovered by the hooffe of Pegasus; Citheirides, of Citheron, a hill near to Thebes; Libethrides, from a mountain in Magnesia; Pimpleades, from a place in Macedonia; Ilissiades, from a flood near Athens; Thespiades, from the Thespians; Ligyae, of a people of Larissina, who ayded Xerxes Against the Greeks; Castalides, of the fountain so called; Corycides, of a hill or rather a cave amongst the Delpheans; Pateides, of a well in Macedonia; Oilimpiades, of the mount Olimpus; Ardalides, of Ardalus, the sonne of Vulcan; (p.61)

It is striking that many of the locations given are at wells or on mountains, so often where we find other Nine Maidens groups. This spread of locations, some of which, like Parnassus and Olympus, are particularly important sacred mountains, strongly suggests that the Muses, either originally or at some point in the development of Greek religious experience, existed as separate groups. Their geographical spread is what one would expect if there were diverse groups of nine priestesses originally honouring the Mother Goddess and perhaps later, the god Apollo. The links with Parnassus and Olympus suggest, like the locations of St Monenna at significant Dark Age locales in Scotland, an important role, close to the heart of contemporary society. The Oracle of Delphi on Parnassus was the most ancient and sacred site in Greece, while Olympus became known subsequently as the home of the gods. Heywood's earlier comments on the relationship to music are fitting for a group that is so associated with the arts, but the location of different groups in such significant locations suggests that they had earlier had a more central role than simply as the inspirers of the Arts. Given that some groups of Nine Maidens, like the Maenads, were involved in bloody and orgiastic rituals, the arts may be more related to ancient and visceral notions of religion than is realised, though it is generally accepted that drama as an art form arose directly from religious ritual. Within the activities of 'orgiastic priestesses' there were perhaps rituals that eventually gave rise to other artistic activities.

Apollo is a fascinating figure in his own right. In *The Greek Myths* Graves says '[Apollo] . . . brought the Muses down from their home on Mount Helicon to Delphi, tamed their wild frenzy, and led them in formal and decorous dances.' The frenzy here seems like that of the Namnetes, who rebuilt their temple every year and tore to pieces any of their number who dropped thatch during the annual re-roofing of their temple. Graves continues:

> Every ninth year a hut representing a king's dwelling was built on the threshing floor at Delphi and a

> night attack made on it. The table of first fruits was overturned, the hut set on fire, and the torch-men fled from the sanctuary without looking behind them. (p.82)

This ceremony is called the Septerias (veneration) and the hut is said to symbolise 'the dragon's lair'. This takes us back to the dragon at Strathmartine; also it was every nine years that the great Norse pre-Christian festival took place at Uppsala. Apollo and his mother Leto are also associated with Hyperborea – the land beyond the North Wind and every year at the end of autumn Apollo went away north, beyond the Rhipraei mountains towards the mysterious land of the Hyperboreans. It was also said that Leto herself was a native of this blessed land.

Some commentators have surmised that Apollo originated in Asia and Arabia while, others, because of his close relations with the Hyperboreans, think he was originally a Nordic divinity, brought to the Greeks from the north in the course of their migrations. The most obvious Nordic link, apart from the link with Nine Maidens, would be with Heimdall who was also a god of light.

Leto, Apollo's mother was said to have been in labour with him for nine days and nine nights. Apollo has powers of healing and divination, giving us another link to Nine Maidens groups like Morgan and her sisters, and the *Gallicenae*. A more tentative correlation can be made between the Pythoness, Apollo's priestess at the Oracle of Delphi and the snake (adder) in Scottish mythology; the serpent is an ancient symbol of chthonic power, the regenerative force of the earth itself which allows the annual growth of plant life.

In *The Greek Myths* Graves gives another interesting Apollonian association, with swans:

> When Apollo appears in ancient works of art riding on swanback, or in a chariot drawn by swans on a visit to the Hyperboreans, this is a polite way of

depicting his representative's annual death at midsummer. Singing swans then fly north to their breeding grounds in the Arctic Circle, and utter trumpet-like notes as they go; which is why Pausanius says that swans are versed in the Muses' craft. Swans sing before they die: the sacred king's soul departs to the sound of music. (2 p.294)

Here Graves is talking of the idea of the sacrifice of the sacred king to ensure fertility – a rite many scholars believe used to take place and which provided the thematic background for James Frazer's influential *The Golden Bough*. We should keep in mind that such sacrifice, if it did take place, may have been symbolic. The association of Muses with swans is an intriguing one as it is very like that between the Valkyries and swans. This is not to suggest that the northern versions of the Nine Maidens are ultimately derived from the Greek ones. The opposite might be worth considering given the references to Apollo as coming from the north. Humans only occupied northern Europe after the retreat of the last Ice Age some 12,000 years ago but the concept of the Nine Maidens predates this as we shall see. What this relationship with swans does show is that the symbolic associations with different Nine Maidens groups are remarkably similar over great distances and periods.

The relationship of the single male with Nine Maidens groups varies considerably – Apollo is presented as being supreme over the Muses, Arthur is nursed by the Nine Sisters of Avalon, Heimdall is the son of Nine Maidens, Ruad is effectively wooed by Nine Sea Maidens, Peredur is at first aided by then attacks the Nine Witches of Caer Lyow, St Monenna is accompanied by nine women and a baby boy and the Strathmartine tale has Martin as the suitor of the eldest of the Nine. There are other Nines that conform to some extent to this pattern. In the story of St Samson of Dol, a representative of the Nine kills a single male, though the Wild Woman, while claiming eight sisters, is herself alone. There are also strong hints of sexual intercourse with a single male in Islands of Women such as Sena, Priory Island and others.

However the Muses are not the only group of Nine Maidens in Greek mythology and it seems possible that the different locations they appear at might disguise separate groupings of Nine, just as we see elsewhere. Whether all such groups were priestesses of Apollo like the Muses, or whether the Muses have come to represent a wide variety of different Nine Maidens is probably impossible to adduce. There are however many different names and locales associated with the Muses.

Pierides

This group of Nine Maidens were said to have been the daughters of Pierus, a king of Macedonia. It is said he had nine daughters whom he named after the Muses. Another version of the tale is that these maidens presumptuously challenged the Muses to a poetry contest and predictably were defeated. Their punishment was to be turned into birds, in some cases magpies, by Apollo, or into other birds by the Muses themselves. The names of the Pierides are given as Acalanthis, Cenchris, Chloris, Cissa, Colymbas, Dracontis, Lynx, Nessa and Pipo, all Greek bird names. The Muses are also sometimes referred to as Pierides after the place where Zeus is supposed to have fathered them. Here we have a clear suggestion of the recurring motif of Nine Maidens on a hilltop.

The Sirens

The Sirens in Greek mythology were a group of supernatural beings who lured sailors to their deaths, so entrancing them with the beauty of their song that the ships crashed into rocks and were wrecked. The Sirens were turned into birds with women's faces by Aphrodite because they refused to give up their maidenheads to either gods or men. This might be a reference to the changeover from Goddess worship to a patriarchal religion – other Nine Maidens groups are noted for being free of patriarchal influence. Sometimes as with St Samson of Dol, they actually kill a male; the Witches of Caer Lyow are equally aggressive, and as we have seen in our discussion of Islands of Women, Nine Maidens groups in several instances are certainly not submissive in sexual matters. Another version of their origin has the Sirens being deprived of the power of flight after being beaten by the Muses in a musical contest. This strongly suggests that they too, like the Pierides, were nine in number. They are said to have inhabited Cape Pelonus, Capri, the isle of Anthemusa and the Siren Isles which further links them to the motif of Islands of Women.

The Sirens eventually lost their power of luring sailors to their deaths when the Argo passed their island with Orpheus on board. His singing was more magical than theirs and they lost their power forever and were changed into rocks. Orpheus eventually died at the hands of the orgiastic Maenads who were also nine in number. A further possible link is that the Sirens have been presented as daughters of Melpomene, herself one of the Muses.

Graves believed that the Sirens were a pre-Olympian cult inhabiting the island of Paestum off Capri and draws a parallel between their island home and the Island of Avalon. He further thought that the Muses superseded them as part of the new Olympian religion, and that this was the origin of the supposed singing contest between the two groups. All of this suggests great antiquity.

The Hydra

The Hydra was a mythical serpent with nine heads, which came out from its lair in a marsh, near Lerna in the Peloponnese, to ravage the countryside.

Graves tells us in *The Greek Myths*:

> The number of heads given the Hydra varies; as a college of priestesses it had fifty heads; as the sacred cuttle-fish, a disguise adopted by Thetis – who also

> had a college of fifty priestesses – it had eight snaky
> arms, and one head on its trunk, together making
> nine in honour of the Moon-Goddess. (2 p.110)

Here again we have the number nine, goddess figures and in this case the moon. It is also worth noting here that Geoffrey of Monmouth in the *Vita Merlini* gives one of the names of Morgan's sisters as Thiten which may be a possible reference to Thetis, who is strongly associated with the sea. Graves (1 p.27) tells us of an incident in which Thetis was involved in an episode of shape-shifting. She had retreated into a cave on an islet of Thessaly where she was pounced upon by Peleus, chosen by the gods to be her husband. As she struggled to get away from him, she changed into fire, water, a lion, a serpent and lastly a giant cuttle-fish. Despite her shape-shifting and having been burned, clawed, stung and drenched in ink, Peleus held on to her and at last she succumbed and gave herself to him. At their wedding feast, the Apple of Discord was thrown into the company by the goddess Eris. The incident is said to have led in time to the Trojan War. Shape-shifting occurs in many different Nine Maidens scenarios and it may be that this is an essential part of their original identity. It might even be a reference to some sort of hallucinogenic-induced trance used in prophecy. The Apple reference here is reminiscent of Avalon.

The Maenads

The Maenads were the followers of the god Dionysus or Bacchus who ordered them to tear Orpheus limb from limb when that hero failed to honour the god as he thought was his due. The Maenads are generally presented as being in an ecstatic fury which some scholars consider was the result of eating hallucinogenic mushrooms, rather than drinking alcohol which is more commonly associated with Dionysus/Bacchus. Graves commented on the possible links between the Muses and the Maenads in *Mammon and the Black Goddess* telling us:

> At some time before the 8th century BC, the god Apollo took over the Muse worship and calling himself 'leader of the Muses', transformed the cult to his own sacred precincts. This meant more than self-identification with the lyre-plucking danced leader of a nine-woman Maenad company; he was asserting his authority over the Muse herself. (pp.145-6)

Dionysus is also associated with the Muses who, with the Maenads, helped to educate him. Both are potentially Nine Maidens groups and here, in their teaching of Dionysus, we have yet another correspondence with the role of Morgan as teacher of her sisters, and perhaps even more closely with the role of the Nine Witches of Caer Lyow teaching Peredur. The many references to shape-shifting might find some support in the concept of inspiration by hallucinogenic substances. The flight of witches may well derive from subjective descriptions of drug-induced experiences which seemed like flying. This has been extensively commented on in writings on shamanism where the shaman's spirit flight is frequently described as being preceded by the ingestion of such substances. Dionysus was said to have passed his childhood on the fabulous mountain Nysa where he was sent by his father Zeus to escape the wrath of his maternal grandfather Cadmus. Dionysus was handed over to the nymphs of Nysa – and given their location on a mountain and their association with Dionysus it is worth considering whether there were nine of them too.

Telchines

A strange group of nine that occurs in Greek myth are the Telchines, described by Graves in *The Greek Myths*:

> That the Telchines were Children of the Sea, acted as the hounds of Artemis created magic mists, and founded the cities named after the three Danaids, Cameira, Ialysa, and Linda suggests that they were

originally emanations of the moon Goddess Danaë: each of her three persons in triad. 'Telchin' was derived by Greek grammarians from *thelgein*, to enchant . . . They were, it seems, worshipped by an early matriarchal people in Greece, Crete and Lydia and the Aegean Islands, whom the invading patriarchal Hellenes persecuted, absorbed or forced to emigrate westward. Their origin may have been East African. (1 p.189)

The Telchines are children of the sea, like the daughters of Ran, and their ability to create magic mists is reminiscent of the tradition of weather-working we have seen with other Nine Maidens groups. The suggestion of an East African origin chimes with the story of the origin of the Kikuyu people of Kenya, as we shall see. Graves also tells us that devotees of the Telchines occupied the nearby Mount Nonacris, meaning nine peaks, which was at one time the chief religious centre of Greece. Nonacris was the origin of the river Styx, the river over which the dead were ferried to the Otherworld by Charon, and which plays such a strong role in Greek mythology. In *The White Goddess* Graves expands on Nonacris as a goddess in the story of Lycaon the Pelasgian, son of the bear-goddess Callisto:

His clan used the wolf-totem and Lycaon as wolf-king (or werewolf) reigned until the ninth year. The choice of King was settled at a cannibalistic feast. His wife Nonacris was clearly the Ninefold Goddess, and he is described as the first man to civilise Arcadia . . . Above Nonacris are the Aroanian mountains and in them is a cave to which the Daughters of Proteus are said to have run when the madness overtook them. (pp.367-8)

Although the madness of the Daughters of Proteus might link them to the Maenads, they are generally presented as having been three, not nine. Proteus himself is both a shapeshifter and an oracular prophet – attributes common to the Nine Maidens groups. Graves mentions a depiction of Proteus on a vase as fish-tailed, with a lion, a snake and a stag emerging from his body. He was buried on an island and Graves links this to the Island of the Hesperides and Heracles' Quest for the Golden Apples. In *The White Goddess,* he specifically compares Proteus' island of Pharos, off Alexandria and home of a legendary lighthouse, with the Isle of Avalon (p.276). The serpent, the island location and the Avalon-like Garden of the Hesperides are all motifs suggestive of Nine Maidens groups.

This is not the place to go into an extended analysis of how and when the Mother Goddess was superseded by a masculine-dominated pantheon of gods and goddesses in Greece or elsewhere, however it is highly likely that any god-like figures replacing earlier goddesses would take on some of their attributes, much in the same way as the Christians deliberately took over heathen temples and celebrations.

The reference to the goddess Artemis, the huntress, brings us back to the association of deer with priestess groups. The link between goddess figures and deer is widespread. Many Greek priestess groups were, like Nine Maidens groups, strongly linked to the moon, a motif associated with goddesses in many different societies. Given the recurrence of the theme of divination, the derivation of the name Telchines from a term for enchantment is significant. There are other instances in Greek mythology which although not directly concerned with groups of Nine Maidens do seem to carry traces of beliefs that might have been associated with them. These often involve the number nine in magical rites and symbols like the serpent.

The Cumaen Sibyl

The Cumaean Sibyl, or priestess of Apollo, is said to have offered nine books of prophecy to King Tarquin of Rome in the 5th century. He thought the price too high and refused to pay it. The Sibyl threw three books on the fire and demanded the original price for the six remaining books. Again Tarquin refused and the priestess threw another three volumes on the fire asking the original price for the remaining three books. At this, the king gave in and paid the full price for the remaining three books. These Sibylline Books were long kept in the temple on Rome's Capitol. They were said to contain details of how to gain the favours of foreign deities which might mean that they were instructions for particular religious rites. Yet again we have the number nine associated with significant religious knowledge.

Another intriguing story is given by Graves in *The Greek Myths*:

> At Aulis, while Agamemnon was sacrificing to Zeus and Apollo, a blue serpent with blood-red markings on its back darted from beneath the altar, and made straight for a fine plane tree which grew nearby. On the highest branch lay a sparrow's nest, containing eight young birds and their mother: the serpent devoured them all and then, still coiled around the branch, was turned to stone by Zeus. Calchis explained this portent as strengthening Aius' prophecy: nine years must pass before Troy can be taken, but taken it would be. (2 pp.283-4)

Here we have the serpent, with its associations with the chthonic powers of the Mother Goddess, and nine birds being interpreted as a prophecy concerning Troy. Even in ancient Greece such ideas and symbols had perhaps lost their primary meaning. We should remember that Schliemman the German amateur archaeologist who located the site of Troy was dismissed by contemporary professional archaeologists as a dreamer. They were convinced that Troy was either purely mythological or a literary creation based on originally oral stories and that there was no factual basis to Homer's *Iliad*. It has been suggested that the story of Troy had originally come to Homer by word of mouth from earlier Greek tradition. The suggestion in this work, that we can learn a great deal about earlier societies from the oral tradition is not that new!

In *The Greek Myths* Graves also writes of Semele, daughter of Cadmus:

> Semele was worshipped at Athens during the Lenaea, the Festival of the Wild Women, when a yearly bull, representing Dionysus, was cut into nine pieces and sacrificed to her, one piece being burned, the remainder eaten raw by the worshippers. Semele is usually explained as a form of Selene ('moon'), and nine was the traditional number of orgiastic moon-priestesses who took part in such feasts, nine such are shown dancing round the sacred king in a cave painting at Cogul, and nine more killed and devoured St Samson of Dol's acolyte in medieval times. (I p.58)

Whether or not cannibalism formed part of such rites, the reference to nine as the traditional number of moon-priestesses is significant. Nine is particularly significant in lunar terms, and in many societies the moon has been associated with the Mother Goddess. The moon's effect on the motion of fluids on the earth, including tides and the menstrual cycle of women, was well known in the ancient world and the moon was thought to influence female fertility. As already noted, worshippers of the Mother Goddess might have seen water itself as analogous to the blood of the Goddess. If, as Graves suggests, nine was the standard number of priestess groups in Greece, this might encompass the priestesses of Artemis, Circe, Demeter, Diana, Hecate and Selene. Certainly Greek mythology includes a variety of instances of Nine Maidens. Until recently the orthodox interpretation of this material would have been that all the Nine Maidens groups we have been looking at must have derived from such classical sources. However, contact between peoples is a two-way process and, as we have seen, there are grounds for considering Apollo as originating in the north. Given that we know the culture of megalith construction spread over the area from north Africa to the British Isles and encompassed parts of the Mediterranean, this is certainly not beyond possibility. The growing acceptance of the relative importance of folklore and the retreat from absolute adherence to the classical interpretations of our history will probably lead to new and fresh interpretations of this evidence. The notion of the barbarian northerners being enlightened by the more 'civilised' peoples of Greece and Rome is not one that we need accept.

Before the rise of the Greek city-states and classical Greek society in the 1st millennium BCE the islands of the Aegean were flourishing and their influence on later Greek development was considerable. The people of the Aegean worshipped a Mother Goddess. She was the Great Goddess, the Universal Mother, in whom were united all the attributes and functions of divinity. She symbolised fertility above all else, and her influence extended over plants and animals as well as humans. The entire universe was her domain and as the celestial Goddess she regulated the course of the heavenly bodies and controlled the alternating seasons. Here we have an echo of the Scottish Cailleach with her power over the winter weather. The Aegean Great Goddess caused the products of the soils to flourish, gave men riches, protected them in battle and at sea guided them on their adventurous voyages. She also reigned over the underworld and, as mistress of life, she was also sovereign of death.

This duality is akin to that of the Goddess in Scottish mythology, personified in the Cailleach and Bride. In Greek mythology the Mother Goddess is given as Gaea who coupled with her son Uranus to give birth to the Greek pantheon of gods and goddesses. Even in the supposedly patriarchal pantheon of the Greek gods, Gaea is central as the mother of all life. Belief in the dual Goddess figure, even if it did not come with the first settlers to northern Europe after the retreat of the last Ice Age, appears to be one of the oldest human belief systems known. It has survived, if only faintly, in folklore and what is called superstition, through the overlay of later pre-Christian thought and the propaganda and education of subsequent religions. Such survivals demonstrate the power of oral transmission as this is the means by which this material has been passed on in an increasingly literate world. An example of the tenacity of this type of belief can perhaps be seen in modern ecologists adopting the idea of Gaea as an all-encompassing single-system vision of life on the planet. At a time when we are facing widespread environmental destruction and pollution born of the blinkered pursuit of short-term profit, this idea makes a lot of sense. It is significant in this light, that the Oracle at Delphi, was devoted to Gaea before being taken over by worshippers of Apollo.

Demeter was the Greek goddess of Agriculture, Fertility, Sacred Law and the Harvest, a combination of attributes that suggests she was of considerable antiquity even in the Classical Greek period, and she too is associated with nine maidens. A collection of ancient documents known as the *Oxyrhynchus Papyri* was found in Egypt around the beginning of the 20th century. Written in a variety of languages including Greek, Arabic and Hebrew many of these documents still await translation. One of them has a section with the following lines:

> We came to great Demeter's fane, we nine
> All maidens, all in goodly raiment clad:
> In goodly raiment clad, with necklets bright
> Of carven ivory, that shone like snow (Grenfell & Hunt, 1 p.13)

A fane is a temple, and this appears to be a group of, if not priestesses, certainly ritual participants of some kind. The references to necklets is also intriguing in that it is reminiscent of the Norse goddess figures of Freyja and Menglod. (see p.160)

Concluding this look at classical sources, here is another quote from *The White Goddess*:

> At Athens the . . . Festival called the Lenaea, [Festival of the Wild Women] was held at the winter solstice, and the death and rebirth of the harvest infant

> Dionysus were . . . dramatised. In the original myth
> it was not the Titans but the Wild Women, the nine
> representatives of the Moon-Goddess Hera, who
> tore the child into pieces and ate him. (p.399)

This link to the winter solstice, one of the most significant points of the pre-Christian year, still celebrated as Christmas in many parts of the world, has already been discussed. The eldest of the Nine Maidens who were remembered as Pictish Saints in Scotland was Mayota, and her saint's day was 22 December, the winter solstice.

Graves accepted that societal change, in this case from a matriarchal pre-Hellenic religion to the Greek male-dominated pantheon, came about because of an invasion. The inference is that such changes result from the defeat of one people by another, militarily superior one. How then if people are so totally subjugated do their ideas continue? Do they lie quiet for a period and then resurface later? Or is it that while ruling elites come and go, the ideas of the common people continue relatively unchanged? Or could it be that this militaristic approach to human history misses the point about human development? The obsession with invasion and conquest was quite natural within the British Empire – historical empires were built on slaughter and conquest - but now that the Empire has fallen we should no longer be restricted by its hidebound, and blinkered, attitudes and analyses. In societies across the world some aspects of older beliefs continue to be practised even after they have been replaced in public ritual by new concepts and ideas. There is also the well-attested fact that many religions have adopted what they could not change in local societies, and made it their own, as was the case with Christianity.

Beyond Europe

There is evidence from the southern side of the Mediterranean which suggests that groups of nine supernatural beings also existed among the Egyptians. Mackenzie, in *Egyptian Myth and Legend* tells us that:

> Representatives of the groups of Egyptian spirits called the Fathers are found at Memphis, where Ptah, assisted by eight earth gnomes called Khnumu, was believed to have made the universe with his hammer by beating out the copper sky and shaping the hills and valleys ... But Ptah never lost his elfin character, even after he was merged with deities of different origins. He was the chief of nine earth spirits (that is eight and himself added) called Khnumu, the modellers. (p.80)

He later explains:

> As the theology of the sun worshippers developed at Heliopolis, other gods, which were imported or had their origin in Egypt, were included in the divine family. The number three and its multiple evidently had magical significance. Ra, Kephera, and Tum formed the sun triad. The sun god and his children and descendants: Nut, the heavens, Shu, the air, Seb, the earth, with the lioness-headed Tefnut, the spitter, Osiris, the deified king and corn spirit, Isis, the Delta Great Mother, and her sister Nephthys, and the Semitic Set, formed Ennead of Heliopolis. The group of Nine Gods varied at different periods. (p.161)

Another tantalising Egyptian reference is made by Diodorus Siculus, a 1st century BCE Greek historian. He tells us,

> For Osiris was laughter-loving and fond of music and the dance; consequently he took with him a multitude of musicians, among whom were nine maidens who could sing and were trained in the other arts, these maidens being those who among the Greeks are called the Muses; and their leader (hegetes), as the account goes, was Apollo, who was for that reason also given the name Musegetes. (Diodorus URL 18,4)

Osiris as the god of the dead was of considerable importance in the Egyptian pantheon, and his cult retained its importance throughout the flourishing of ancient Egyptian culture. The statement that 'these maidens being those who among the Greeks are called the Muses', is remarkably explicit and underlines the influence of Egyptian, and thus African, culture in the development of Greek culture.

Further south in Africa, a story is told that is even closer to our subject. This version is from the pen of the late President of Kenya, Jomo Kenyatta, in his *Facing Mount Kenya, The Traditional Life of the Gikuyu*:

> According to tribal legend we are told that in the beginning of things, when mankind started to populate the earth, the man Gikuyu, the founder of the tribe was called by the Mogai (the Divider of the Universe), and was given as his share, the land with ravines, the rivers, the forests, the game and all the gifts that the Lord of Nature (Mogai) had bestowed on mankind. At the same time Mogai made a big mountain which he called Kire-Nyaga (Mount Kenya), as his resting place when on inspection tours, and as a sign of his wonders. He then took the man Gikuyu to the top of the mountain of mystery, and showed him the beauty of the country that Mogai had given him. While still on the top of the mountain, the Mogai pointed out to the Gikuyu, a spot full of fig trees, right in the centre of the country. After the Mogai had shown the Gikuyu the panorama of the wonderful land he had been given, he commanded him to descend and establish his homestead on the selected place which he named Mokorwe wa Gathanya. Before they parted Mogai told Gikuyu that, whenever he was in need, he should make a sacrifice and raise his hands towards Kire-Nyanga, and the Lord of Nature will come to his assistance. Gikuyu did as he was commanded by the Mogai, and when he reached the

> spot, he found that Mogai had provided him with a beautiful wife whom Gikuyu named Moombi (creator or moulder). Both lived happily and had nine daughters and no sons. Gikuyu was very disturbed at not having a male heir. In his despair he called upon the Mogai to advise him on the situation. He responded quickly and told Gikuyu not to be perturbed and everything would be done according to his wish, then commanded him saying, 'Go and take one lamb and one kid from your flock. Kill them under the big fig tree near your homestead. Pour the blood and the fat of the animals on the bark of the tree. Then you and your family make a big fire under the tree and burn the meat as a sacrifice to me, your benefactor. When you have done this, take home your wife and daughters. After that go back to the sacred tree, and you will find nine handsome young men who are willing to marry your daughters under any condition that will please you and your family . . . Gikuyu told the young men that if they wished to marry his daughters he could give his consent only if they agreed to live on his homestead under a matriarchal system . . . (p.3)

Though this tale is not a precise match with any of our European material it is striking that the Kikuyu people are said to have descended from nine sisters and that the original system of the tribes was matriarchal. Here we have an idea stemming from a period before the establishment of a patriarchal society, being used to explain that society. Could this be along the same lines as Christianity taking over the pre-Christian temples to maintain some form of continuity? Intriguingly this version of a Nine Maidens tale comes from that part of our planet where human life is believed to have originated.

If the idea of the Nine Maidens did originate in the heart of Africa we should find other aspects of it beyond Europe. Later we shall consider the survival of modern shamanistic beliefs in Siberia but there are Oriental examples worth considering.

In India the Hindu goddess Durga is celebrated at the festival of Navaratri, in September or October, which lasts for nine nights, each night being dedicated to a particular one of her nine manifestations, namely Shailaputra, Brahmacharini, Chandrghanta, Kushmanda, Skandamata, Katyayani, Kalaratri, Mahagauri and Siddhidatri (Navaratri URL). This is strikingly similar to other supernatural figures in Western traditions like Cerridwen, Korrigan and Menglod having nine females linked to them. In Korea, the goddess figure of Gaeyang Halmi, an aspect of the Taoist goddess Mago, or Magu, has nine attendants (Gaeyang URL). Whether these religious figures find echo in more localised, folklore traditions pertaining to groups of nine women is a tantalising possibility.

To return to Europe there is one particular Nine Maidens locale which may provide the link between an African origin and the widespread appearance of the motif in Celtic, Germanic and Romance-speaking countries. This is the painted cave at Cogul, near Lerida in Catalonia. The painting is generally believed to have been created in the Magdelanian period which is defined as between 12,000 and 17,000 BCE. It clearly shows nine women dancing around a startlingly obvious male figure. Included within the group is the figure of a deer. Robert Graves interpreted this as a representation of an orgiastic ceremony which culminated in the physical dismemberment of the male by the females in an erotic frenzy. He noted that the male figure at Cogul was priapic – possessed of an outsize penis, symbolic of fertility – which it is, but the male organ is not erect in the painting, which one might expect if this is a direct representation of a basically erotic ritual. Nevertheless, the grouping can surely be interpreted as being some kind of fertility rite. However, in the context of this work, the most important point about the cave painting at Cogul is its age. If this group is indeed an example of the Nine Maidens motif (and the association with the single male strengthens this), we are dealing with something extremely ancient, though we cannot be sure that the Stone Age artist in Catalonia thought of his nine women in the same way as the Norse storytellers thought of the Maidens of the Mill or their Welsh counterparts thought of Morgan and her sisters. It is worth reiterating that we have evidence for cultural contact over wide areas, particularly along the eastern littoral of the Atlantic Ocean, the existence of megalithic monuments from north-west Africa to north-west Europe in the fourth millennium being a particular example. One of those particular monuments, Calanais, on the Scottish Isle of Lewis, is said in local tradition to have been originally built by black men. We now know that the first settlement of Europe after the last Ice Age originated from the inhabitants of the refugium that was located in northern Iberia. And people settling, or even resettling, new areas, bring their culture with them.

CHAPTER 9

The Number Nine in Folklore, Literature and Ritual

THE OCCURRENCE OF the number nine in traditional cultural material is widespread, the idea of their being nine worlds for instance being found in both Scandinavia and China. Several of the mythological figures we have looked at illustrate that the number nine itself was apparently of importance within pre-Christian belief, and survives within a wide variety of folkloric beliefs and superstitious practices. Odin hung for nine nights on the World Tree, Yggdrasil; Apollo's mother was in labour for nine days and nights before he was born; the Dagda had a cauldron that fed warriors nine at a time. Other striking instances of the importance of the number nine include the spell of the witches in Macbeth and the placing of nine white stones in Bride's Well at Sanquhar. This latter case is interesting in that it has been said that the nine stones were specifically in honour of the Nine Maidens. The Sanquhar rite also raises the question of whether the groups we are looking at number nine because of the magical/pre-Christian importance of the number or, whether the significance of the number might arise from the Nine Maidens groups themselves. The repetition of actions nine times within folklore ritual certainly appears to have descended from earlier pre-Christian practice and belief.

The widespread belief that every ninth wave is stronger than the rest has been noted and could possibly be linked to such Nine Maidens groups as the daughters of the sea goddess Ran, the Nine Sea Maidens encountered by Ruad and the Maidens of The Mill who grind out the physical universe in Norse mythology. The fact that the ninth wave is also named after goddess figures in different traditions might be seen as a further example of this association. Several commentators have noted that the names of the daughters of Ran are all names that echo the sea itself.

Bessie Smith when she was on trial for witchcraft before the Presbytery of Lesmahagow in west central Scotland in 1623, admitted that she had been guilty of 'charming the heart fevers' by recommending 'the waybore [plantain] leaf to be eaten nyne mornings' while the patient was kneeling and chanting the following spell or charm, as given in *The Silver Bough*:

> For Godes sak
> For Sanct Spirit
> For Sanct Arkit
> For the Nine Maidens that dyed
> Into the Bourtrie in the Ladywellbank
> This charm to be beuk and bell to me
> And that sua [shall] be. (2 p.148)

This, spell like so many that survive in folklore, combines a certain amount of Christianity with older beliefs. The Sanct Spirit might be a reference to the Holy Ghost but the Sanct Arkit is obscure. The reference to the Nine Maidens could be specifically to the group at Abernethy who are said all to have been buried at the foot of an oak tree there. Bourtrie is generally used for the elder, which was used in witchcraft, both black and white. The spell itself suggests some sort of continuity into later practice from a time when the reference to the Nine Maidens would have been clearly understood. On this point the folklorist Eleanor Hull comments in *Folklore of the British Isles*:

> [T]here is no break between the ancient magical formulae chanted by the Druids and the later incantations of the wizard and the wise woman. They both arose in the Veda-like sacred hymns which formed the repository of the learning professed by the body of Druidical teachers and diviners and taught orally in the Druidic schools. Most of them were never written down, and the fragments we possess in writing are probably only the remains of a considerable body of oral literature. In course of time, these forms became antiquated and were unintelligible even to the bards themselves. (p.173)

The Druids are said to have taught by memory and considered it sacrilegious to write down their teachings. This type of belief is incredibly tenacious. For instance the mother of James Hogg, the 19th century Scottish novelist and poet, knew a great many stories and ballads and is on record as saying that, if written down, such material would lose its power. Oral transmission was not a haphazard process in pre-literate societies and even today many storytellers have a clear set of ideas of what is and what is not permissible. The role of the storyteller has always been central to human society and the modern term, tradition-bearer, reflects this.

Scottish folklore is full of instances of the use of the number nine in magical activity, much of it directly associated with witches. In the great Middle Scots epic *The Flyting betwixt Montgomerie and Polwarth* we have the following:

> Thir venerable virgins, whom ye wald call witches
> In the time of their triumph tirr'd me the taide,
> Some backward rade on brodsowes and some on black bitches,
> Some in steid of staig over a stark monk straid.
> Fra the how to the hight some hobles, some hitches.
> With their mouthes to the moon murgeons they maid

> Some be force, in effect the foure windes fetches
> And nyne times, withershins, about the thorne raid.
> (Bawcutt and Riddy, 1 p.285)

To 'tir the taid' is to strip a toad, a 'staig' is a horse and to go 'widdershins' is to circle something anti-clockwise. Going with the sun or *deasail* is the positive direction, *withershins* definitely negative. Flyting was a standard form of poetic combat based on creative insult, and in the quoted section Montgomerie is claiming Polwarth to be witch-born and effectively a practitioner of the Black Arts. Hope (1970) points out there is evidence for some kind of organised fairy cult in Scotland in the Middle Ages. In the poem Montgomerie describes NicNiven, the Queen of the Witches, perhaps herself a degraded form of the Mother Goddess, her companions and their magical practices. The detail implies he knew what he was talking about, and that his audience did too. The point here is that they went against the sun, nine times to work harm, just as we shall see nine times *with* the sun was used for benefit. Earlier we looked at the witches in *Macbeth*; it seems probable that Shakespeare drew upon contemporary folklore for his portrayal of witch activity in the early years of the 17th century.

Within the Gaelic-speaking parts of Scotland, nine also occurs widely in folklore. The following is from *Carmina Gadelica* a collection of traditional Gaelic prayers, hymns, charms, incantations, blessings, poems and songs, proverbs, historical anecdotes, natural history observations, and miscellaneous lore gathered by Alexander Carmichael towards the end of the 19th century and published in 1900:

> *Naoi, naodh*, nine. The number nine often occurs in these and other Gaelic compositions,--three, seven, nine, and occasionally five, being the mystic numbers. The following are some examples of the use of nine:--

An ainm Airil 's nan aingheal naodh.'	In name of Ariel and the angels nine.
'Naodh conair, is naodh conachair, Is naodha ban seanga sith.'	Nine paths and nine shouts, And nine slender fairy women.
'Bi-sa taingeil leis an aon te Ge do robh an naodh air an t-snamh.'	Be thou thankful with the one (duck) Though there should be nine on the swim.
'Chaidh Moire thar na naodh maranan A bhuain an torranain.'	Mary went over the nine waves To pluck the figwort.
'Naoi tobraiche Mhic an Lir.'	The nine wells of the Son of Lear.

> In North Uist there is a sandy plain called 'Sail Dharaich,' Oak-log. A beam of oak lay there, from which the people produced the 'tein-eigin,' neid-fire. This was done by 'naoi naoinear ciad ginealach mac', nine nines of first-begotten sons, these being in the estimation of the people the most sacred and enduring. (II p.310)

The reference to nine slender fairy women is intriguing and the reference to the nine wells of the son of Lear is apparently a reference to Mannannan mac Lir.

It is the same in Welsh folklore where nine crops up frequently, this particular charm being used for healing is from Owen's *Welsh Folklore*:

> Male eagle, female eagle,
> I send you
> Over nine seas, and over nine mountains,

> And over nine acres of unprofitable land,
> Where no dog shall bark, and no cow shall low,
> And where no eagle shall higher rise.
>
> The charmer spat first on the rash and rubbed it with his finger over the affected parts, and then breathed nine times on it. (p.332)

In early Irish material we find the same thing as can be seen in this excerpt from O' Grady's translation of the *Collquoy of the Ancients*:

> After this again until expiration of six weeks they were in the *sídh,* and Caeilte said 'it is time for us to depart, for we are now for a good while here within.' 'God's benison on thee, and that of the people inside here,' said the *sídh*-folk: 'and though it were for everlasting thou shouldst desire to abide with us, thou shouldst have it.' Ilbhrec said: 'since on going thou art bent, here for thee are nine gorgeous vestures comprising rich mantles; nine shields too, nine spears, and *nine* long swords with hilt and guard of gold; *nine* hounds besides for the pleasant chase.' (p.51)

While as in many other instances this can be seen as conventional practice, both oral and literate, it reinforces the idea of the number itself having considerable significance.

Reference has previously been made to Soltysiak's analysis of the number nine in Norse folklore and in 1897 Von Kahl published a work entitled *Die Mystische Neunzahl bei Den Deutschen* looking at the number nine in Germanic folklore. What is clear is that nine has been a significant number in traditional rituals, and their associated beliefs, in many different cultures through the ages, in many instances being linked closely to moon lore.

In various parts of the British Isles, there are stone circles known as Nine Maidens, four in Cornwall alone at Boskednan,

St Buryan, Stithians and Columb Major, though this latter is a row rather than a circle. There are others in Aberdeenshire and Derbyshire with Ninestone circles in Derbyshire and Roxburghshire. This association with standing stones can be seen as underlining the antiquity of Nine Maidens motif in Britain. Intriguingly some of these circles share the relatively common origin story of Sabbath revellers being turned into the stones, which hints at 'Pagan' activity occurring after the Christian religion had become dominant.

In considering the ritual use of nine, we should return to the semi-mythical Welsh poet, Taliesin. There is ongoing debate as to when he wrote, some people suggesting the 6th century while others consider the Welsh poetry attributed to him as having been 9th or even 12th century re-workings of traditional material. There is also the suggestion that there have been several Taliesins, the name being interpreted as some sort of bardic title. MacCulloch in his *Religion of the Ancient Celts,* writes this of him:

> Taliesin was probably an old god of poetic inspiration confused with the sixth century poet of the same name, perhaps because he identified himself, or was identified by other bards, with the god. He speaks of his splendid chair, inspiration of fluent and urgent song in Caer Sidi or Elysium. And, speaking the god's name or identifying himself with him, describes his presence with Llew, Bran, Gwydion, and others, as well as his creation and his enchantment before he became immortal. He was present with Arthur when a cauldron was stolen from Annwfn, and basing his verses on the mythic transformations and rebirths of the gods, recounts in highly inflated language his own numerous forms and rebirths. His claims resemble those of the Shaman who has the entree of the spirit-world and can transform himself at will. (p.117)

The capacity of societies dependent on oral transmission to intermingle god figures with humans has already been commented upon. Caer Sidi is itself clearly an idealised location, which does not however mean that it could not have specific locations identified with it in the physical as well as the metaphysical sense. The poems attributed to Taliesin present ideas and beliefs from a time before Christianity arrived in Britain. If the arguments in this book have merit then we must consider the possibility that some such ideas might have survived for millennia, and that they might even have come into what we now call the British Isles over 10,000 years ago with the first settlers. The magical significance of nine is underlined in the poem the *Cad Godeu*, the Battle of the Trees, taken here from JG Evans' translations of Taliesin:

> Twas not of father and mother
> whence I was born,
> Thus after a new fashion I was created
> from the nine constituents:
> From the essence of fruits
> did God begin;
> from Primrose flowers
> from the pollen of shrubs
> the pollen of Oak and Nettle,
> of Meadow-sweet and Broom;
> from the Mould of the earth;
> from the water of the Ninth wave;
> from the fire of Lightning
> of these things was I made. (p.35f)

Whether this specific combination of plants has some particular effect in combination or whether they are simply used to make up the magic number nine is not something I can comment on, but the possibility exists that we are dealing with some kind of hallucinogenic used in initiatory rites. The reference to the water of the ninth wave clearly refers to beliefs we have looked at, and the fire of lightning could be linked with the supposed Druidic belief that mistletoe was caused by lightning. In the account of the Taliesin story we saw earlier, he was originally called Gwion

Bach and was touched by three magic drops from the cauldron of Cerridwen. After a shape-shifting chase that follows, Cerridwen, in the form of a hen, ate him in the form of a grain of corn. After this she carried him for nine months before he was born as Taliesin. Despite the reference to God in this poem what we have here appears to be a remnant of something pre-Christian and very old. Despite our reliance on written materials derived from earlier oral tradition, it is impossible to discern how old the pre-Christian ideas in the *Cad Godeu* are, or to determine what were the specific practices or rituals associated with them. The linguistic analysis that is used to try and date such works can go no further back than essentially theoretical dates, which even then are late – in the sense that material recorded in the 6th century CE Wales or Ireland might have already been passed down orally for thousands of years.

As different writers like Graves and Lethbridge have commented, nine is strongly associated with the moon and this is also true of goddesses from many parts of the world. This association, deriving from the actual physical effect of the moon on all fluids, and thus on female menstruation, has created obvious links with ideas and rituals of fertility. The Nine Maidens motif would seem to incorporate some of these types of association. Further, the use of divination has been thought to derive from attempts to communicate with the spirits of the ancestors to try and ensure the future fertility of crops, and probably to plead for the success of the hunt before that. The rites of magic, like those of religion, stem from this type of early belief. Throughout human existence there have always been rites and rituals to try and ensure future fertility, of crops, of animals and of humans. Perhaps in the Nine Maidens and the single male there is an echo of some such ancient practice.

In Polson's *Scottish Witchcraft Lore* there are several mentions of the use of the number nine. He tells us of Thomas Greave who, in 1623, cured a child by wrapping it nine times in an unguent-covered cloth, while repeating prayers (p.103). From Aberdeen he tells us:

THE NUMBER NINE IN FOLKLORE, LITERATURE AND RITUAL 179

> Another method of cure was to put the patient nine times through a hasp of unwatered yarn, and then a cat as many times backwards through the same hasp, and thus the sickness was transferred to the cat. (p.122)

Davidson's analysis of folklore practices in *Rowan Tree and Red Threid* includes the spell used by the North Berwick witches who tried to drown James VI and I early in the 17th century:

> Cummer ye afore, cummer gae ye
> Gin ye wanna gae afore
> Ring o ring widdershins
> Loupin, lichtly, widdershins
> Kilted coats and fleein hair
> Three times three. (p.18)

Again this is an example of going widdershins nine times to effect black magic. It is also reminiscent of the activities of the Three Witches in Shakespeare's *Macbeth*. Davidson mentions a coven, in which the men, 'turned nine times widdershins about and the women six times' (p.62), and quotes this from the trial of Marion Rickhart in 1633. In treating sick cattle she gave the following instructions:

> Go thy way to the sea and tell nyne boares of the sea come in. that is to say nyne waves of the sea, and let the hindmost of the go back again and the nixt thereafter take thrie loofullis [handfuls] of the water and put within stoupe [jug] and quhan thou comes home put it within thy kine [cattle] and thow will get thy profeit gane [again]. (p.28)

This connects with beliefs about the ninth wave being of particular significance. Another manifestation of this magic use of nine comes from Shetland. *The County Folklore Series for Shetland* tells of the cure for a child rescued from trows or trolls (1903, p.146). The mother had to collect the 'nine mithers' mait' for her child. 'Mait' in Scots means food. She would solicit nine mothers whose first born were sons for three articles of food each, to be used during the convalescence of the child. The cure was also used in the case of the wasting diseases known locally as trowie, probably connected with the belief in trolls.

This is reminiscent of The Nine Herbs Charm used amongst the early Anglo-Saxon inhabitants of Britain, given in the Everyman edition of *Anglo-Saxon Poetry* edited by Bradley. Though superficially Christian, it does refer to Woden as the originator of the charm:

> This is the herb which is called Wergelu;
> The seal sent this over the back of the ocean
> To heal the hurt of other poison
> These nine sprouts against nine poison
>
> A snake came crawling, it bit a man.
> Then Woden took nine glory-twigs,
> Smote the serpent so that it flew into nine parts
> There apple brought this to pass against poison,
> That she never more would enter her house.
>
> Thyme and Fennel, a pair great in power,
> The Wise Lord holy in heaven
> Wrought these herbs while He hung on the cross;
> He placed and put them in seven worlds
> To aid all, poor and rich.
> It stands against pain, resists the venom,
> It has power against three and against thirty,
> Against a fiend's hand and against sudden trick,
> Against witchcraft of vile creatures.
>
> Now these nine herbs avail against nine evil spirits
> Against nine poisons and against nine infectious diseases,
> Against the red poison, against the running poison,
> Against the white poison, against the blue poison,
> Against the yellow poison, against the green poison,

Against the black poison, against the blue poison,
Against the brown poison, against the crimson poison,
Against snake blister, against water- blister,
Against thorn-blister, against thistle-blister,
Against ice-blister, against poison blister;
If any poison comes flying from the east
Or any comes from the north
Or any from the west upon the people.

Christ stood over disease of every kind.
I alone know running water, and the nine serpents heed it;
May all pastures now spring up with herbs,
The seas, all salt water, be destroyed,
When I blow this poison from thee. (p.93)

This is some kind of charm! There are some very interesting aspects to this mish-mash of the pre-Christian and the Christian. We have of course come across serpents associated with Bride and the apple is the fruit after which Avalon is supposedly named. The reference to Christ on the cross could be interpreted in different ways, given the tradition among the Germanic-speaking of Odin hanging for nine nights on the World Tree, Yggdrasil, in order to attain inspiration. Are we seeing here yet another example of the Christian world overlaying the beliefs of an earlier time? This charm also is reminiscent of Taliesin's claim that he was born of the 'nine-form faculties'.

At Beltane, even in the 19th century, it was the custom to raise the neid-fire in many countries. This is the practice as known from Scotland. All fires in the parish were put out and people congregated on a traditional hilltop spot for the ceremony. The point of the ritual was to create fire by friction, without the use of metal or chemicals, a tradition probably harking back beyond datable time. After the fire was created the Beltane bonfires were lit, cattle were driven through the smoke, special food and drink were consumed and there are hints that in earlier times there was a great deal of sexual activity. Each family would light a torch from the sacred fire at dawn and after walking around their own fields and houses with the holy fire, would go into their home and ceremonially light the hearth fire – and the fire would be kept going continuously till the next Beltane. The process of driving the cattle through the smoke (which perhaps had an antiseptic component as the fire tended to include such pungent woods as juniper) and carrying fire round holdings and homes was to sain, or sanctify, home and hearth against all evil influence and to guarantee fertility. The guarantee of fertility is the older concept as we see the idea of defence against evil becoming more dominant in the 17th and 18th centuries.

Specifically, protection was sought against witches – an idea that seems to have taken hold after the Reformation. Frazer gives us a good account of fire festivals in *The Golden Bough*: 'In some places three times three persons, in others three times nine, were required for turning round by turns the axle tree or wimble' (p.803). This describes large equipment to create fire by the friction of wood on wood – a public, ritual development of the universal fire-drill technology for creating fire.

Another interesting ritual at 1st May is reported by Pennant:

> The rites begin with spilling some of the caudle [a custard of eggs and milk, cooked in the open air] on the ground by way of libation: on that, everyone takes a cake of oatmeal, upon which are raised nine square knobs, each dedicated to some particular being, the supposed preserver of their flocks and herds, or to some particular animal, the real destroyer of them. Each person then turns his face to the fire, breaks off a knob, and flinging it over his shoulders, says, 'This I give to thee, preserve thou my horses, This to thee, preserve thou my sheep, and so on. After that they use the same ceremony to the noxious animals. This I give to thee, O fox! Spare thou my lambs! This I give to thee, O hooded crow.' (1 p.90)

This would appear to be an 18th century remnant of a very ancient ceremony indeed, possibly preserved because it was thought to have been efficacious. The pre-Reformation Catholic Church turned a blind eye to such practices but in many areas the Presbyterian Church was also unable to eradicate the remnants and practices of ancient belief. Clearly the number nine had a deep significance in many areas. The following excerpt is from Ramsay's *Scotland and Scotsmen in the 18th Century*. Talking of Highland practice he tells us that:

> After kindling the bonfire with the *tein-eigin* (neid-fire) the company prepared their rituals. As soon as they had finished their meal they amused themselves a while in singing and dancing round the fire. Towards the close of the entertainment, the person who officiated as master of the feast produced a large cake baked with eggs and scalloped round the edge, and called am bonnach beal-tine – the Beltane cake. It was divided into a number of pieces and distributed to the company. There was one particular piece which whoever got was called cailleach beal-tine – the Beltane carline, a term of great reproach. Upon his being known, part of the company laid hold of him and made a show of putting him into the fire; but the majority interposing, he was rescued. And in some places they laid him on the ground, making as if they would quarter him. Afterwards he was pelted with egg-shell, and retained the odious appellation during the whole year. And while the feast was fresh in people's memory, they affected to speak of the cailleach beal-tine as dead. (2 pp.242-3)

It seems this passage describes a remnant of what was once a sacrificial act. The notion of the scapegoat is quite clear, probably the result of Christian influence. Similarly the cry of 'burn the witches' at such Beltane ceremonies was a distortion of earlier belief where the 'wise woman' was the repository of knowledge and healing within the community. Sacrifice in many societies was seen as a method of sending a messenger to the gods on behalf of the community. The name of the chosen one in this excerpt, the *cailleach beal-tine*, takes us back to the idea of the Cailleach as the Winter Hag aspect of the Mother Goddess It was at Beltane that she went to the sacred well just before dawn, and drinking from it was transformed into the beautiful golden Bride, goddess of Summer and Fertility. This might be describing a rite that had begun in the far past and was truly pre-Christian. The types of women singled out for persecution in the witch trials were generally old and therefore full of a lifetime's learning and experience, particularly in herbalism and healing. It is also likely that some of their spells preserved some sort of continuity with ideas from much earlier.

In Banks *Calendar Customs* we are told of this Scottish belief associated with Halloween:

> [I]f, on Halloween, any person should go round one of these (fairy) hillocks nine times, contrary to the course of the sun, a door would open, by which he would be admitted to the fairy realms. (p.165)

The belief in fairies inhabiting hillocks, which were in fact often ancient burial mounds, is very reminiscent of the supposed rituals that took place at Stone Age chambered cairns. It has been suggested that 'priests' tried to communicate with the spirits of the ancestors through ritual, to bring fertility in the future. This is also undoubtedly linked to the common Scottish motif of musicians being lured into fairy hills where they spend a night playing for the fairies to dance, which then turns out to have been many years, an idea of course that is not restricted to Scotland.

In Wales the people also lit the Beltane fires and Frazer tells us:

> The fire was done in this way. Nine men would turn their pockets inside out, and see that every piece of money and all metals were off their persons. Then

> the men went into the nearest woods, and collected
> sticks of nine different kinds of trees. (p.155)

These 'nine woods' were then used to create a large fire which was started by the friction of two pieces of oak rubbed together. In the 19th century a well at Tullybelton in Strathtay was visited on Beltane morning and after drinking from the well the visitor would walk round it nine times in a clockwise direction, and then round the standing stones beside it. At Oystermouth Castle in West Glamorgan it was the custom to wish on the Wishing Post, a stone in the dungeon. It was part of the ritual to walk round it nine times. The Garrack Zans at Sennen in Cornwall was the site of a good-luck ritual where old people used to go nine times daily round a large flat stone. The Stone of Odin at Stenness in Orkney was highly venerated until its destruction in 1814. Anyone who wished to gain magical powers visited it at the full moon in nine consecutive months and went round the stone on bare knees nine times, then made his wish while looking through the hole in the stone.

There is also evidence of the ritual use of nine far beyond the British Isles. Talking of the St John's fires in Scandinavia, Frazer tells of the practice in Norrland:

> The fuel consists of nine different sorts of wood and
> the spectators cast into the flames a kind of toadstool (Bäran) in order to counteract the power of
> the Trolls and other evil spirits, who are believed to
> be about that night. (p.172)

This is Midsummer, a date for fire festivals in many parts of Europe including Britain. The trolls and evil spirits were traditionally believed to have come forth from inside mountains which opened up on this night. This is very much like the old ideas associated with Samhain or Halloween in Scotland and elsewhere and is perhaps another faint echo of ancient practices at chambered tombs when the spirits of the ancestors were contacted.

Frazer recounts numerous similar activities. At Midsummer in Moravia, now part of the Czech Republic,

> on the same mystic evening Moravian girls gather flowers of nine sorts and lay them under their pillow when they go to sleep; then they dream every one of him who is to be their partner for life. (p.175)

In Brittany Midsummer bonfires were also lit, and Frazer tells us it was believed that 'every girl who danced round nine of the bonfires would marry within the year'. This particular belief is also noted in Berry, central France, while in the Pyrenees leaping over nine of the Midsummer Bonfires would assure prosperity for the coming year. A slight variation is recorded in Flanders where women were said to leap over the fires to ensure easy childbirth.

As each village or community would have its own St John's Fire, the act of dancing round or jumping over nine different fires would involve some travelling outwith the individual's immediate community. This would in turn lead to greater romantic possibilities, thus actually helping in the search for a suitable husband.

In Wales St John's fires were common and according to Frazer:

> Three or nine different kinds of wood and charred faggots carefully preserved from the last midsummer were deemed necessary to build the bonfire, which was generally done on rising ground. Various herbs were thrown into the blaze; and girls with bunches of three or nine different kinds of flowers would take the hands of boys, who wore flowers in their buttonholes and hats, and together the young couples would leap over the fires. (p.210)

The preservation of charred wood from one fire till the next is also a feature of the Scottish Midwinter fire festivals, and

I have been blessed on several occasions by having been given shards of the Clavie, the great fire bucket traditionally burnt at Hogmanay (New Year's Eve) at Burghhead in Morayshire. Some continuities remain unbroken.

The use of the number nine in ritual also occurred at Halloween, the Christianised version of the earlier Feast of the Dead. At this time of the year it was believed the boundaries between the worlds of the living and the dead were at their weakest and it was possible to move from one realm to the other. Halloween ceremonies were probably derived from rituals designed to get in touch with the ancestors who had returned to the earth and ask them to use their magic on the seed that had been buried in the ground, to ensure the growth of crops in the coming season. In later times however much of the ritual associated with Halloween seems primarily concerned with affairs of the heart. Constant references to the activities of young people at the significant feast days of the traditional year emphasises what was general practice – these were times of sexual initiation and of heightened sexual activity. In societies not affected by the Christian concept of sin, the act of making love at these specific times was seen as a form of sympathetic magic, even worship.

Again referring to the neid-fire ceremony, but this time in Germany's Wassgaw mountains at Halloween, Frazer tells us (p.271), 'Others use a thick rope, collect nine kinds of wood, and keep them in violent motion until fire leaps forth.' On the lower Rhine he informs us, 'The bonfires so kindled were composed of wood of nine different sorts . . .' (p.278), which is echoed in 18th century Swedish practice,

> the neid-fire was kindled, as in Germany, by the violent rubbing of two pieces of wood against each other; sometimes nine different kinds of wood were used for the purpose. (p.280)

Frazer documents Halloween divination practices in County Leitrim in Ireland at Halloween which were designed to help young girls to find their husband to be. It is likely that the divination in ancient times was more to do with trying to foresee the success of planting and what the future held for the tribe or family in general. Frazer goes on to mention another method of such divination:

> Another way was to take a rake, go to a rick and walk round it nine times, saying, 'I take this rick in the devil's name.' At the ninth time the wraith of your destined partner would come and take the rake out of your hand. (ibid)

The appeal in the Devil's name suggests that here, as in so in many rural areas of Europe, the Devil was not seen as the embodiment of absolute evil.

Martin Martin writing in A *Description of the Western Islands of Scotland* gives a graphic account of the neid-fire being raised as an antidote against the plague, or murrain, in cattle:

> All the fires in the parish were extinguished, and then eighty-one married men, being thought the necessary number for effecting this design, took two great planks of wood, and nine of them were employed by turns, who by their repeated efforts rubbed one of the planks against the other until the heat thereof produced fire; and from this forced fire each family is supplied with new fire, which is no sooner kindled than a pot full of water is quickly set on it, and afterwards sprinkled upon the people infected with the plague, or upon the cattle that have the murrain. (p.113)

Martin observed this pre-Christian practice in the late 17th century on both Lewis and Skye. These fertility and saining rites were used to affect a cure for diseases. This is a clear example of how pre-Christian traditions carried on for hundreds of years after people were supposedly Christianised, perhaps because such rituals had the reputation of having worked before, and so should work again.

LC Wimberley in *Folklore in the English and Scottish Ballads* describes magical instructions from a witch in the ballad, *Broomfield Hill*, which

> tells how a maiden, under instructions from a witch woman retains her honour by using sleep charms. She puts her lover to sleep by means of a combination of herbal and circle magic.
>
> But when ye gang to Broomfield Hill
> Walk nine times round and round
> Down below a bonny bank
> Ye'll find your lover sleeping sound. (p.300)

The magical use of nine also crops up in the ballad *Willie's Lady*:

> Willie had loosed the nine witch knots
> That was ain o that ladie's locks. (p.356)

So Willie lifts the evil spell from his household. Banks in *Calendar Customs* tells of a song used in North East Scotland while scattering the ashes of the Halloween fires. This was sung by farm servants, hired on a half-yearly basis, who wished to find new positions:

> This is Hallaeven
> The morn is Halladay;
> Nine free nichts till Martinmas
> An soon they all wear away. (p.110)

In a pass through the Ochil Hills behind Newburgh on the south bank of the river Tay is the site of Macduff's Cross. Only the base now remains this ancient monument which has strong associations with the number nine. Nearby there are the Nine Wells, and here we are only a few miles from Abernethy with its Nine Maidens associations. As late as the 16th century, MacDuff's Cross was a sanctuary for those who had committed murder. Andrew Laing in *The History of Lindores Abbey and the Burgh of Newburgh* tells us that the right of sanctuary extended only to those who were within nine degrees of kinship of the Earl of Fife, which would probably have covered most of his relatives. He then continues:

> The fine of nine kye [cattle] and a colpindach [a young cow or ox] payable by the manslayer is the same as that which was payable to the king when his rights were infringed. This similarity shows that the privilege was guarded by the highest sanction which law afforded. The fine of nine kye, and the traditionary necessity of washing nine times in the Nine Wells [which rise on the lands of the town of Newburgh, in a field next to Cross Macduff], tends to show that there was a mystical property connected with the number nine, and that the tradition had its origin in some principle which is lost in the mists of antiquity. (p.329)

The fine of nine cows and a young ox, as part of the sanctuary process at MacDuff's Cross, is reminiscent of the recurring feature of nine females and a single male and this excerpt shows just how central the number nine seems to have been to magic ritual in Scotland.

Dalyell quotes a further few instances of the magical/ritual use of nine in Scottish folklore in *Darker Superstitions of Scotland*:

> Nine enchanted stones were cast or laid in a field for the destruction of the crop. A skein of yarn through which a patient had been transmitted nine times was cut into nine parts and buried in three Lairds' lands for a cure. On the 11 August 1623, a mother hired a woman to go silent to the well of Ruthven, to wash her bairn for the restoration of its health; the woman,

> the mother averred before the Kirk Session of Perth, put her bairn through ane cake made of nine curnes of meal gotten from women married maidens, and that it is a common practice used for curing bairns. A draught repeated nine times from the horn of a living ox was prescribed for hooping cough, together with putting the patient nine several times in the happer of a grinding mill. Numerous other instances might be adduced of superstitious reverence for the number nine. One of the very latest that has come under our notice, shows that the superstition is widespread, and stills bear sway over the minds of men. In 1869 the Emir of Bokhara, to propitiate the favour of the Emperor of Russia who suing for peace, sent a costly present by an embassy to the monarch, consisting of nine valuable gifts, the number nine, it was stated, being strictly adhered to, in accordance with the custom of the Turko-Tartaric races. (p.395)

He also notes an instance of, 'a distempered cow taken backwards into the sea until washed by nine surges' which is reminiscent of the belief that the ninth wave was always the strongest. He goes on:

> It has been remarked already that, at Beltane, an oaten cake was prepared in the Highlands with nine square knobs, each dedicated to the protector or destroyer of the crops. In the seventeenth century, three cakes were prepared of nine portions of meal, contributed by nine maidens and nine married women ... (p.394)

There are many instances of the magical use of nine in Scotland and here is one final one. In *Witch, Warlock and Magician*, WH Davenport Adams quotes the following:

> James Og is indicted to have passed on Rudday, five years since, through Alexander Cobain's corn,

and have taken nine stones from his avine rig [corn
rick], and cast them on the said Alexander's rig and
to have taken nine lokis [handfuls] of meal from the
said Alexander's rig and cast it on his own. He is
indicted to have bewitched a cow belonging to the
said Alexander, which he bought from Kristane Bur-
net, of Cloak; this cow, though his wife had received
milk from her the first night, and the morning there-
after, gave no milk from that time forth, but died
within a half year. He is indicted to have passed,
five years since, on Lammas Day, through the said
Alexander's corn, and having gained nyne span to
have struck the corn with nine strokes of a white
wand so that nothing grew that year but fichakis
[weeds] (p.363)

The link Butler made between the Ninewells and the Nine Maidens suggests there could be a link between the efficacy of the number nine and the Nine Maidens themselves. Where there are Nine Maidens groups we might therefore expect to see the use of nine in magic and ritual. We have already seen there are various Nine Maiden groups in Norse mythology and that nine is a significant magical number. This is how Crossley-Holland describes the significance of nine in *The Norse Myths*:

[T]he number nine recurs again and again in Norse
mythology. Odin learns nine magic songs from a
giant that enables him to win the mead of poetry
for the gods; Heimdall has nine mothers; Hermod,
Odin's son, journeys for nine nights in his attempt
to win back Balder from Hel; the great religious ceremony at the temple of Uppsala lasted for nine days
every in every ninth year, and required the sacrifice
of nine humans and nine animals of every kind.
Why nine was the most significant number in Norse
mythology, has not been satisfactorily explained,
but belief in the magical properties of the number is
not restricted to Scandinavia. In *The Golden Bough*,

> Frazer records ceremonies involving the number nine in . . . Wales, Lithuania, Siam and the island of Nias in the Mentawai chain. Nine is, of course, the end of a series of single numbers, and this may be the reason why it symbolises death and rebirth in a number of mythologies; hence it also stands for the whole. (p. xxiv)

The nine separate levels of existence in Norse mythology are all located on the World Tree Yggdrasil. At Ragnarok, the final battle of the gods, Thor staggers back nine steps before he dies from the venom of the serpent Jormangard and as noted earlier, when the seeress Groa sends her son Svipdag to win the hand of Menglod, she sings nine charms over him. In Norse as in Scottish mythology the use of the number nine is widespread and central to magical practice. Another Norse tale, *The Master Smith* tells of the making of locks and bolts of the nine gates of Hel, a cold goddess ruling over nine worlds.

However it is not just in Britain and Scandinavia that the number is significant. Just as there are nine worlds in Norse mythology, so in Chinese mythology there are nine levels of heaven and the nine cauldrons of the semi-mythological emperor Yu represented control over the nine provinces of the country. Once again here we have link between the number nine and a cauldron or cauldrons. Other peoples with a belief in Nine Worlds include some of the northern Amerindian tribes and the Kogi of Venezuela. The Kogi are an indigenous tribe who, after beating off the invading Spaniards back in the 16th century, retreated into isolation in the high mountains, only recently coming down to speak with the people they call the Younger Brothers – which seems to represent all of humanity except themselves. Their priests who control the tribe are called Mamas after a goddess who had nine daughters and they believe there are nine different stages of the world. Here we have a link between a Mother Goddess figure and nine daughters – very like Cerridwen and her cauldron maidens or Menglod and her companions. An example from North America is given by Vitaliano in his *Legends of the Earth*, where he tells us:

> The Apaches believe that the hole leading down into Mother earth is located in this Range [Superstition Mountains, Arizona], its entrance guarded by a nine-headed snake which allows no mortals to pass. (p.170)

Here we have the number nine and the serpent figure combined in a way that strongly suggests the chthonic powers of various goddess figures. Nine, as a significant number can be found in many other parts of the world. Lyall Watson noted several examples in the 1970s on the Indonesian island he called Nus Tarian in his book *Gifts of Unknown Things*. There the people believe that there were nine families of mankind, corresponding to the nine clans in their village. They hold a traditional dance in the place called the Nine Dance Grounds where the men dance in a nine-fold spiral figure round women grouped in the centre. Each clan has its own 'viewing stone', a talisman handed down through the generations round which important clan business is carried out. At all other times these nine stones are kept hidden. There are similar traditions in New Guinea, particularly on the island of West Ceram. Here the belief is that the nine families of mankind came originally from Mount Nunusak, again bringing in the motif of mountains and reminding us of the founding myth of the Kikuyu in East Africa.

CHAPTER 10
The Nine Maidens

WE HAVE SEEN that the Nine Maidens crop up in many places and in many guises, though always as women of ritual and/or power. In many instances they appear to be pre-Christian priestess groups who, with their powers of divination and shape shifting, were perhaps involved in similar activities to those of shamanism - healing, divination and the like. Additionally some are said to have had control over the weather – an ability also attributed to later witch figures. This might mean no more than that they had sophisticated meteorological knowledge, though in this respect we should remember the close relationship with Mother Goddess figures, and that such beings are often portrayed as weather creators. This is also a talent, or skill attributed till relatively recently, in many cultures, to those women called witches. We have seen how, particularly in Scotland, goddess figures are often associated with mountains known for changeable and dramatic weather. The link to shamanism however, is stronger than just their skill in divination and healing.

Mircea Eliade in his classic work *Shamanism*, refers to the Buryat people of Siberia and their beliefs:

> [T]he shaman's career begins with a message from a shaman ancestor, who then takes his soul to the sky to teach him. On the way they stop to visit the gods of the Centre of the World, especially Tekha Shara Matzkala, the god of the danced, fecundity, and wealth, who lives with the nine daughters of Solboni, god of dawn. These divinities are peculiar

> to shamans, and only shamans make offerings to them. The young candidate's soul enters into amorous relations with Tekha's nine wives. When his shamanic instruction is finished, his soul meets his future celestial wife in the sky; with her too his soul has sexual relations. (p.75)

There are several familiar motifs here – the reference to Tekha as being a god of the dance is reminiscent of Apollo and his Muses and of the dancing women at Cogul. His role as an artist and representation of fertility echoes beliefs concerning Bride, Cerridwen and possibly Menglod, who has also been interpreted as a goddess of fertility. There are obvious links to the nine sisters of Avalon, itself a symbol of fertility. Here again we have the nine as sisters – reminiscent of the Nine Maidens of Abernethy, daughters of a saint; the Maidens of the Mill, daughters of the Sea Goddess Ran and the nine sisters who founded the tribes of the Kikuyu. The reference to sexual involvement with nine women again is a familiar one from Islands of Women tales and particularly the story of Ruad, son of Rigdonn. This recurring motif of nine females and one male is perhaps linked with lunar symbolism in the same way as the widespread motif of twelve plus one has been seen as deriving from solar myth, one example being Jesus Christ with his twelve apostles. Other similar groupings are Arthur and his twelve knights, Balder and his twelve judges in Norse tradition, Odysseus and his twelve companions, Romulus and his twelve shepherds, Roland and the twelve peers of France, Jacob and his twelve sons. The single year itself is divided into twelve months and it may be that some ancient belief concerning the visible moon being divided into nine discreet periods underpins some of the ideas linked with groups of nine women. It does appear that the motif of the nine females and one male is a faint echo of some kind of fertility rite. Talking of the Teleut, another Siberian people, Eliade tells us:

> The shaman is assisted in his labours not only by his celestial wife but also by feminine spirits. In

> the fourteenth heaven dwell the nine daughters of Ülgän. It is they who confer his magical powers on the shaman (swallowing live coals, etc.). When a man dies they come down to earth, take his soul, and carry it to the heavens. (p.77)

The carrying of the soul to heaven is very like the concept of the Valkyries convoying dead warriors from the battlefield to the Paradise of Valhalla, and of the Morrigan of Irish tradition who haunts the battlefield in the shape of a crow or raven. Here it is specific that the shaman receives his powers from the nine daughters of Ülgän, a motif reminiscent not only of the arming and training of Peredur by the witches of Caer Lyow, but of traditions such as the training of Cu Chulainn by the warrior woman Scathach in Irish tradition, and the teaching and arming of Norse heroes like Sigurd and Regner by Valkyries.

Eliade extensively discusses stories of the Sky God who occurs under many names among the northern Eurasian and Asian peoples. He lives in the highest sky and has several sons or daughters who are subordinate to him and who occupy lower heavens. Their names and numbers vary from tribe to tribe; seven or nine sons or daughters are commonly mentioned, and the shaman maintains special relations with some of them. The fact that some groups of women occur as sevens as well as nines long confused me. Recently I have been told that, within Scottish tradition handed down from original pre-Christian sources in the Gaelic-speaking world, there was a belief that seven represented the colours of the spectrum and nine the spectrum plus black and white. Given the importance of colour in many aspects of traditional lore this may be relevant but how the symbolism of colours might fit our overall picture is beyond the scope of this work. It is worth noting that there are instances of groups of seven sisters in many traditions. If these were originally nine we may simply be seeing, under the influence of Christianity, an attempt to suppress the importance of nine in 'pagan', or pre-Christian ritual and belief.

Eliade shows that shamanism is not all of ancient origin and that there have been many developments over the past couple of centuries, showing that, while oral traditions can sustain ideas and beliefs over extraordinary time-scales, there is always the capacity to change and develop in response to contemporary needs.

One creature that links what we know of shamanism with any of the goddess figures we have briefly looked at is the deer. The existence of a deer goddess cult with female devotees in Scotland was suggested by JG Mackay in *Folklore* (1934). He based this on the extensive stories of hag figures being associated with deer, which were in several instances known as the cattle of the Cailleach. There are perhaps then grounds for suggesting that the deer heads on Pictish symbol stones may represent masks (McHardy 2012, p.77f). We know the Pictish artists were adept at representing animals in a true-to-life fashion, and the deer heads do not look like severed heads so much as masks with clearly defined bottom edges. If so, it seems relevant to think of such masks being used in sacred ritual, we can perhaps postulate the existence of both the Nine Maidens groups and deer-priestesses among the P-Celtic speaking peoples of Scotland. In the instance of the Seven Big Women of Jura, the Deer-isle, that feature in the Gaelic story of Mac Iain Direach (Campbell 1994, 2 p.90ff) we are perhaps seeing something similar within Q-Celtic tradition. At Abbot's Bromley in Staffordshire, England, there is an annual Horn Dance which includes a Bowman who pretends to hunt the dancers who are imitating deer and it has been suggested this ancient ritual might have originated in the Stone Age. Within Gaelic oral tradition in a tale called the *Widow's Son*, (Campbell 1994, 1 p.62-3) there is a description of what appears to be a woman taking off a deer costume; it seems likely that she is a deer priestess. There are Scottish examples of stories wherein hunters require the blessing of a powerful female, clearly a witch or hag figure, before going out to hunt deer. In the fascinating work *The Deer Goddess of Ancient Siberia*, Jacobson points out a close relationship between females and deer which may link to the Nine Maidens priestess groups and she notes the following:

> The shifting reference from deer to women to deer, found in many archaic Siberian mythic traditions, is vividly reflected in the Ngaanasan belief in a swamp where their animal mothers live as naked women with the hair and antlers of deer. (p.242)

The reference to the swamp may also be of some relevance here, given the close links we have seen between the worship of the Goddess and water, and particularly the idea of the Islands of Women. Swamps are by their nature out-of-the way places and inhabiting a swamp would be as effective a way of living apart from society as inhabiting an island. The doyenne of Pictish studies, Dr Isabel Henderson, has referred to Pictish art, with its animal symbols, as being part of a broader concept – that of Eurasian hunter art, which suggests strong links with the peoples and perhaps even the beliefs of areas across northern Eurasia as far as Siberia. The contemporary fascination with shamanism might lead us in time to identifying aspects of pre-Christian belief in different parts of pre-Christian Europe as being fundamentally shamanistic. The possible deer masks on the Pictish symbol stones might be part of that particular jigsaw of ideas. The importance of deer can also be seen in the material concerning Finn Mac Cuill in Irish and Scottish Gaelic tradition: his wife is turned into a deer by a Druid and his son is called Oisin, which means 'fawn'; according to Jean Markale, Finn's own original name, Demne, can be interpreted as *dam nijo*, 'little deer'. Dowsers have shown that deer-rutting stands, where the animals mate, show similar patterns to stone circles when dowsed. All of this makes it possible that Mackay was right in presuming the existence of deer-priestesses though I would suggest the deer goddess cult is just one aspect of the worship of an overall Mother Goddess figure.

The association of the Nine Maidens with goddess figures, such as Bride, Cerridwen, Menglod, suggests that the forms of pre-Christian ritual practised by these groups, and the underlying belief system, was Mother Goddess-based. The work of Marija Gimbutas shows that Goddess worship permeated the societies of the Balkans in the 4th/5th millennia BC and there is no reason to suppose things were substantially different elsewhere in Europe. Gimbutas also noted many examples of deer motifs being used as symbols of the Goddess. Recently I have been researching hills and mountains in Scotland that are named after the fact that they resemble the female breast. Several of these locations are associated with the Cailleach with place-names referring to women, adders, swine and the like, and with wells and a variety of prehistoric monuments either on the mountains/hills or very close by, some of which are linked to the sites by significant alignments (Scott & McHardy 2020). This, combined with specific tales of hag-type figures suggests that such mountains and hills were locations for ritual activities worshipping a goddess figure and the names and tales survive in both Gaelic and Scots language forms, indicating widespread ritual activity of this type. I am currently compiling work on this and hope it will appear in a future book. Apart from Mackenzie's reference to the Cailleach of Ben Nevis and her eight sisters (p.30) I have not, as yet, come across Nine Maidens material at many of these locations but I am convinced of the reality of such locations being associated with the Mother Goddess. And if the Nine Maidens in some way worshipped, or venerated, the Goddess, as I suggest is likely, such a spread of locales in Scotland would be supportive of their survival into recent times. The sites specifically associated with St Monenna, for instance, are almost all prominent hills in flat landscapes and some can be construed as being breast-shaped.

Repeatedly we find Nine Maidens groups being involved in divination, shape-shifting and weather control, activities also traditionally associated with witch figures. In this respect the spell given by Isobel Gowdie, referred to above, with its reference to 'the Nine Maidens in the Bourtrie bank' is perhaps of particular significance. This spell suggests at least a memory of the Nine Maidens group being active in a particular place, enhancing the potential link to the witches.

We have seen how original goddess figures have been turned into hag figures and I have suggested that such figures appear, in Scotland at least, to be linked to the winter aspect of an ancient dual goddess. One of the terms used for the Queen of the Witches is the Carlin which is the Scots equivalent of the Cailleach or hag in Gaelic tradition. The term *gwrach* in Welsh meant precisely the same thing. Comparing this again to Donald Mackenzie's portrayal of the Cailleach, riding out from Ben Nevis with eight sister hags, to spread winter over the land, we see a strong association between such hag figures and the later witches who were traditionally represented as old women themselves. As the beliefs and practices of what we think of as witchcraft were undoubtedly passed exclusively through the oral tradition another possibility faces us. It seems at least possible that some of those covens of witches that survived into the 16th and even 17th centuries may in fact have been directly descended from earlier Nine Maidens groups. The regular occurrence of a coven of female witches with one male might be seen as strengthening such a link. I hope I have shown that the association of Nine Maidens groups with goddess figures suggests an origin in a belief system focussing on the Mother Goddess. The figure of the Queen of the Witches might also be understood as a remnant of this earlier form of religion. Although covens are generally described as being of 13 members, this is not universal, and it may be that some of these groupings were ten in number, with nine women and a single male. The problem in trying to obtain a clear picture of witchcraft activity is that the relatively extensive written reports of witch trials in most post-Reformation European countries are almost exclusively focused on confessions to crimes which seem to have existed almost solely in the imaginations of the interrogators of these unfortunate women. With singularly few exceptions such interrogators were male and driven by a need to have the women confess to formulaic crimes. In the sense that the witch practices were probably descended from remnants of the Old Religion, such righteous brutality would be perfectly justifiable – to the interrogators.

An ancient pedigree is not the only noteworthy aspect of the Nine Maidens. The ongoing centrality of the motif in various pre-Christian belief systems is illustrated by the wide variety of different mythological and legendary figures with whom they are associated.

Some of the rituals involved with the existence of the Nine Maidens survived till very late, as at Sanquhar, Pittempton and perhaps in the magic practices involving the number nine. Such rituals and practices were not necessarily genteel or even gentle, the Goddess being both malevolent and beneficent. She is Goddess of both life and death. The recurring possibility of the idea of sacrifice is impossible to ignore but we should remember that some evidence exists to show that in many societies sacrificial victims went willingly to the ritual. We have a different mind-set.

The existence of the motif of the Nine Maidens across so much of the world – in this respect the Kikuyu founding myth is particularly relevant given the theories of human life originating in the East African Rift Valley – suggests the possibility of a very old belief. The similarities between widely separated groups seem to retain some sense of the continuity of that belief. The divergence of detail within the various groups might be because we are looking at a motif of human thought, and a social institution, of vast antiquity, developing independently over many millennia.

We find the Nine Maidens as mythological beings like the attendants of Cerridwen's cauldron in Welsh tradition or the Maidens of the Mill at the heart of Norse mythology, as daughters of Zeus in Greece, yet also as apparently functioning priestess groups in locations such as Mount Olympus, the Isle de Sein and Pittempton. What I suggest this shows is that the motif of the Nine Maidens is so old as to have passed into mythological traditions in many instances, like the nine daughters of Ülgän or the founding sisters of Kikuyu society, while at the same time they continued to exist in different locales as practising ritual groups. The material from Iceland suggests they were still in existence close to the arrival of Christianity there, a thousand years ago.

Whether they still existed among the tribal peoples of northwest Europe as late as this is moot, but it seems certain some such groups still existed in Roman times. The existence of the stone circles in Great Britain called the Nine Maidens, sometimes with the standard Christian explanation that they were humans turned to stone for dancing on the Sabbath, might be proof, not just of their antiquity but of their continued relevance during Christian times. In this light it is worth remembering that some witch groups were known to frequent such ancient sacred sites.

In some places these two different aspects of the Nine Maidens motif seem to have survived alongside each other. The Nine Maidens at Pittempton, with the associated dragon story and the holy well, seem to belong to the mythical tradition, while just over the hill from Martin's Stone where the dragon is said to have been slain, we have another group of Nine Maidens, surviving in story as a group of saints, who are said to have gone to Abernethy at a definite, if unspecified, date.

The locations in significant political centres in Scotland like the sites of the varied Muses groups in Classical Greece, suggests that though some such groups found it necessary to live apart from society, others were at the very heart of their own communities. What we see in these different locations, like the differentiation between actual and mythological Nine Maidens groups, is perhaps a result of their antiquity. If they were in existence over the millennia suggested, their survival shows their ongoing social importance, arising from their mythological significance, and it is possible that the actual formation of the groups in sets of nine females, became the norm for a variety of sacral and ritual functions within differing societies. This in itself might help to account for the variety of post-Christian representations of them as healers, witches and seers. Even in Christian times there were substantial presences of priests and monks in all major urban locations while others of their brethren deliberately sought out isolated spots in which to live.

Many of the locations in which we find the Nine Maidens, Iberia, Brittany, Cornwall, Wales, Ireland, Scotland, Norway and

Iceland are within relatively easy sea contact of each other at certain times of the year. We should remember also that people raised megalithic structures as far south as Africa, proving long-range contacts were taking place even in the Stone Age. The Greek material also can be fitted into this pattern as we know that their earliest geographers had knowledge of the British Isles, Iberia and Gaul – knowledge that could be very ancient indeed. The spread of megalithic structures stresses the importance of sea communication and we should not forget that communication is a two-way process. Our understanding of contact between different societies and peoples in the far past has been coloured by the portrayal of expanding Western influence over the past few centuries. This has been shown as 'advanced' Westerners coming into contact with primitive, usually taken to mean inferior, peoples. Human contact over millennia has not been restricted to colonial expansion on the part of rapacious, technologically superior peoples. The spread of both the Nine Maidens motif, and the magical/ritual use of the number nine might suggest a greater degree of commonalty between differing societies in the past than has been realised.

The ability of oral transmission to pass on factual data is only just beginning to be appreciated and material from the various storytelling traditions of all the countries considered, combined with archaeological investigation, is a procedure that could be of great assistance in helping to give us a clearer picture of our common human past.

I have suggested the relationship of the nine women to the single man might be a lunar equivalent to the notion of twelve plus one, which has been interpreted as a basic solar myth – twelve months in one year – that some commentators have seen as underlying the story of Jesus in Judaeo-Christian belief. If this is so we can construe this motif of Nine Maidens and a single male as potentially being an older, matriarchal concept that was superseded by later patriarchal ideas developed subsequent to the replacement of what we might call the Old Religion by newer, male dominated belief systems. In this light it is remarkable that male figures such as Apollo, Heimdall and Arthur, all of whom have been interpreted as sun god figures, are all so closely associated with Nine Maidens.

Throughout much of the world in pre-Christian times there were groups of Nine Maidens who had similar functions and were closely associated with that most ancient of beliefs, the Goddess as mother of us all. They appear to have been priestesses who had healing knowledge, practised the arts of divination and had specific meteorological and medical knowledge which appears to have been used for the benefit of the communities in which they existed. As such they would have had an important role within society and it seems likely that, like shamans, they were believed to have the power to communicate directly with the spirits of the ancestors, the gods, or the Goddess. Their centrality within mythological structures shown by their close connections to such diverse figures as Apollo, Arthur, Heimdall, and Zeus and to Mother Goddess figures such as Bride, the Cailleach, Cerridwen, Menglod and Morgan is reflective of such an important societal function. Other instances of nine females, such as within Kikuyu belief in Africa and Kogi belief in South America, show that the basic motif is not restricted to Europe. Likewise the magic use of nine seems to be almost universal, as are some of the symbols we have considered, like the serpent or dragon.

The suggested survival of the Nine Maidens motif from the Magdelanian cave painting at Cogul through to the faded remnants of practice such as the 19th century visits to the Nine Maidens Well at Pittempton or the 20th century rite at St Bride's Well, Sanquhar, reflects a potential continuity of belief and perhaps even practice, for 15 millennia. If this is the case then perhaps the references to the widely differing Nine Maidens groups gathered here is not so surprising, and there may be much more yet to be brought to light. I am not suggesting that the different traditions from so many diverse locations are all remnants of a single cult, though there are obvious grounds for seeing close links within the Celtic and Germanic traditions of Europe. What the chronological and geographical spread of the motif of the

Nine Maidens suggests is something more intriguing. Although, as suggested, the original motif of the Nine Maidens may well have come out of Africa with the first human Diaspora, we might consider another putative origin. What the recurring use of nine in magic and the particular significance of groups of nine women linked to fertility and magic might suggest is that our distant ancestors in many parts of the planet came up with very similar ideas. If this is so then the basis for these must lie in some appreciation of what we know we all share – experience of the planet, the seasons, the sun, the moon and the stars. In the Nine Maidens are we in fact seeing a series of essentially localised reactions to common phenomena? As the basis for such a common reaction the component parts could be female fertility and perhaps some time based analysis based on observation of the moon. Just as the number twelve is associated with solar myth so the number nine has strong lunar connotations and in the nine females and a single male we perhaps are seeing the lunar equivalent of the solar myths mentioned. If this is so then, just as belief in the Mother Goddess would appear to have pre-dated the rise of the patriarchal religions of the modern world, did the idea of the female lunar nine plus one precede the notion of the solar, twelve plus one – a concept that includes no recognition of the female principle? TC Lethbridge's suggestion of the creation of nine goddesses from one might be close to the underlying reality of how the Nine Maidens arose.

In his book *Witches,* he writes:

> In Britain the Great Mother had three aspects and three apparent personalities . . . if there were three Great Mothers all of one aspect, they must have obviously have each possessed two other aspects or personalities. You then get nine Goddesses out of one. This is probably the origin of the frequent occurrence of Nine Maidens, particularly in connection with the names of sacred springs. In Scotland in particular these maidens are often associated with Brigid. There were probably no other maidens

> originally, save Brigid alone. It is an interesting to note that the Teutonic Goddess of war became nine Valkyries . . . the Nine Maidens and their association not only with Brigid but with a dragon are certainly part of our Great Mother picture. The dragon may well be the same old beast who was cast out by Michael and worsted by Indra. (p.83)

Here we have the well and the dragon, just as at Pittempton. As we have seen the motif of the casting out of the dragon has been interpreted as a metaphor for the Christian triumph over pre-Christian belief, though we have also seen that remnants of such pre-Christian belief survived in many parts of Christian Europe at least till very recently – not least the various traditions concerning the Nine Maidens. His argument as to the development of the Nine from the One is possible. Earlier in the same work (p.82) he mentions the link between the concept of the three Mothers, found in many European traditions, and the three phases of the moon – new, full and waxing – and lunar observation through such a process could account for parallel developments of the same idea in widely divergent societies and periods.

A similar concept of the triple goddess developing into nine is discussed by Robert Graves in *The Greek Myths*:

> The moon's three phases of new full, and old recalled the matriarch's three phases of maiden, nymph and crone. Then, since the sun's annual course similarly recalled the rise and decline of her physical powers – spring, a maiden, summer a nymph, winter a crone – the Goddess became identified with seasonal changes in animal and plant life: and thus with Mother earth who, at the beginning of the vegetative year, produces only leaves and buds, then flowers and fruits, and at last ceases to bear. She could later be conceived as yet another triad; the maiden of the upper air, the nymph of the earth or sea and the crone of the underworld – typified respectively by Selene, Aphrodite and Hecate.

> These mystical analogues fostered the sacredness of
> the number three, and the moon-Goddess became
> enlarged to nine when each of the three persons –
> maiden, nymph and crone – appeared in triad to
> demonstrate her divinity. (1 p.14)

Behind this idea, certainly in northern Europe, I would suggest we have the dual goddess, in her colours of black and yellow, symbolising winter and summer, and at the most fundamental level, life and death. And with her went Nine Maidens.

There is an old cliché that says – how can you know where you're going if you don't know where you have been? At a time of major and ever-increasing global change it is important that we learn as much as we can from the past, and from those who have gone before. Perhaps, in this light, the Nine Maidens can still have a role to play in helping us understand the interrelatedness, not only of all planetary life, but of the different societies created by human beings in our time on planet Earth.

The founding myth of the Kikuyu people of Kenya survives close to where it is thought humanity first came into being but to see this as the source would require us to think of ideas surviving for many hundreds of thousands of years. The cave painting at Cogul may be over 15,000 years old and we know that the giant marsupials of Australia that exist in indigenous Dreamtime stories have been extinct for over 30,000 years. We know that in oral traditions throughout the world that modern concepts of dateable time play little if any part. Stories exist in a different time frame to history's attempted mappings of our shared past. The oft-repeated criticism of oral tradition as being just like Chinese whispers and thus unreliable is directly contradicted by the stories of the giant marsupials. That said, many story motifs that exist in all continents may well have arisen from the reality that humans are fundamentally the same in all parts of the planet, be it a San bushman or a Soviet cosmonaut. However, as with the Diprodotons, the motif of the Nine Maidens is so specific that, to me at least, the idea of a truly ancient common origin seems most likely.

CHAPTER 11

Mythical and Legendary Figures Associated with Nine Maidens

WE WILL LOOK first at male figures associated with Nine Maidens groups, most of which exemplify the motif of the Nine Maidens and the single male.

Apollo

The Greek sun god with his nine Muses. As with the Welsh goddess Cerridwen the link to poetry and inspiration is central to this group. Some scholars have suggested that Apollo originated in northern Europe and there are intriguing grounds for linking him with the great Calanais stone circle on the Isle of Lewis. Tradition tells us The Shining One walks the central avenue of the complex every Midsummer's Day and though this has been suggested as a reference to Lugh, a supposed sun god among some of the Gaelic-speaking peoples, there is a striking reference from the Roman geographer Diodorus Siculus, writing in the 1st century AD but quoting from an original 4th century BC source. He writes of an island in the ocean beyond the land of the Celts, inhabited by the Hyperboreans. This is the quote as given in Ivimy's *The Sphinx and the Megaliths*:

> [T]he following legend is told. Leto [Apollo's mother] was born on this island, and for that reason Apollo is honoured by them above all other gods. And there is also on the island both a magnificent

> precinct of Apollo and a notable temple which is adorned with many votive offerings and is spherical in shape. (p.94)

Diodorus Siculus goes on:

> They say also that the moon, as viewed from this island, appears to be but a little distance from the earth and to have upon it prominences like those of the earth, which are visible to the eye. The account is also given that the god visits the island every nineteen years. (p.95)

Many scholars have identified Britain as the island of the Hyperboreans and Stonehenge with the round temple but, rather than Stonehenge, I would suggest the Celtic-cross-shaped megalithic alignment of Calanais on the Isle of Lewis is a more likely location. Investigation over the past couple of decades shows that the Calanais complex can be used to monitor the changing position of the moon rise which reaches its westernmost point every 18.6 years (Ponting 1977). The hills in which the moon is seen to rise at this time forms the outline of a recumbent human shape in the landscape known locally as *caillich na montich*, translated as the old woman, or hag, of the moors. As we have seen, the Cailleach, here *caillich*, is more than a hag. Whatever the possibilities of linking Apollo with Calanais or elsewhere in the British Isles, it seems at least possible that his association with the Nine Maidens make him a figure from much earlier than classical Greece with perhaps his mother being a faded representation of the Mother Goddess herself. As a sun god, Apollo was of course associated with fertility but he was also strongly linked with mountaintops, healing and prophecy, with many oracles dedicated to him in both Asia Minor and Greece. These are all recurrent motifs in Nine Maidens material. Additionally, Apollo's birth took nine days and nine nights. All of this makes Apollo and the Muses a classic case of the single male and the Nine Maidens. Several commentators on Greek mythology have suggested that he originated outside

Greece and as Apollo and the Muses were often portrayed as dancing, it is tempting to see a direct link with the dancing scene at Cogul where nine women danced around a male fertility figure.

Arthur

Arguments still rage as to whether or not there was a historical King Arthur. If he did exist in the 6th century he would have been the leader of a tribal war band rather than a king. There are quite varied views as to where the putative 12 battles attributed to him in the Middle Ages were actually fought, and Scotland provides likely locations. As I have said before, the mythological and legendary stories told in pre-literate societies would normally have been presented within an environment familiar to their audience. It would be particularly important for children to hear such material set in a landscape they knew. This means that the stories of Arthur in Argyll, Lothian and Strathmore in Scotland are every bit as 'true' as those in Wales or Cornwall. At the heart of the Arthurian romance as developed in northwest Europe in the early medieval period, are links to female figures such as the lady of the lake, Guinevere, and Morgan and her sisters. The latter are a classic Nine Maidens group with fertility associations – Avalon is an idealised fertile Paradise – and healing powers. The sisters are presented as beneficent healing figures while the nine witches of Caer Lyow, are presented as inherently vicious and evil female warriors. What this perhaps illustrates is that Morgan and her sisters might preserve a direct memory of one, or more, Nine Maidens groups surviving from pre-Christian times, while the Caer Lyow witches are a Christianised version of the same groups, in which they are portrayed as evil in order to denigrate their pre-Christian aspect and undermine whatever hold they still had over the popular imagination. This could be exactly the same process underlying the story of the killing of St Samson of Dol's assistant by the wild woman of the wood. Within pre-literate societies the presentation of mythological and legendary material incorporated moral, social, political and practical information, making such stories a necessary psychological building block of society. Even when Christianity arrived, people would hear the priests once or twice a week while what we know of the storytelling tradition in such societies suggests it was an everyday, normal occurrence. The spoken word continued for a long time in many societies as the primary means of transmitting necessary information.

The arrival of literacy did not destroy the oral tradition and in the early Medieval Period, various writers developed the Arthurian material from such tales into medieval literary romances designed primarily for an aristocratic audience. The Nine Maidens motif continued to be of considerable significance within Arthurian tradition. Darrah in *Pre-Christianism in the Arthurian Romances* makes the point:

> The discussion on Avalon suggests that the place was not necessarily unique but rather one where a group of priestesses offered oracular pronouncements. Just as Delphi was not the only oracle in the classical world, we may expect to find more than one oracular site in Wales. Previous commentators on the Matter of Britain have noted a resemblance between Avalon and the various versions of the Castle of Maidens. (p.229)

It has already been noted that the Nine Maidens groups associated with St Monenna were linked with significant locations in Dark Age Scotland including Edinburgh Castle, consistently referred to as the Castle of the Maidens in 12th and 13th century annals. There is also an Arthur's Seat in the middle of the modern city of Edinburgh which several commentators have tried to maintain that its name is post medieval and inspired by early literary sources. The Dark Age name of *Mynyd Agned*, the association of St Monenna and her maidens with the castle rock and the reality that the first known mention of Arthur is in *Y Gododdin*, the 6th century P-Celtic poem accepted by many as having been composed in or near Edinburgh, disprove this.

Another probable Nine Maidens site nearby is Traprain Law 20 miles to the east of Edinburgh. This was a major site of the Votadini [Gododdin] as far back as Roman times and is mentioned in several Arthurian romances as the site of the capital of King Lot or Loth after whom the surrounding area was said to have got its name. Loth figures as Arthur's brother-in-law and as the father of Gawain and in some cases of Modred, the usurper of Arthur's kingdom and the lover of Queen Guinevere. Given we are dealing with remnants of the pre-Christian belief centred on the feminine principle it is perhaps worth reiterating that there are many strong female figures in the traditions of the Celtic-speaking peoples. The idea of Irish sovereignty being personified in a female figure and the possibility of some level of matriliny in Pictish succession suggests we should at least consider the possibility that Guinevere was the prime mover in the situation, choosing a new mate in Modred. This would make sense if Arthur was a Christian opposing the old pre-Christian ways with their reliance on matriliny and was trying to impose a new order. This might also help explain why the Arthurian stories have continued to be so popular – he can be seen as the winner in the struggle between Christianity and pre-Christian belief, and thus a worthwhile hero for Christians, just as he was previously a heroic figure, or perhaps a god among the pre-Christian tribes. His association with the Nine Maidens of Avalon seems to come straight from pre-Christian belief.

Traprain Law as a Nine Maidens and Arthurian location leads us to some other startling possibilities. Lot's daughter Thenew is said in the *Life of St Kentigern* to have converted to Christianity and having become pregnant after being seduced by Prince Ewen of Strathclyde, refused to marry him. Her father, after trying to marry her off to a swineherd, first had her thrown off Traprain Law in a chariot which floated gently to the ground, then cast her adrift in an oarless boat on the Forth. She eventually landed at Culross, considerably up river and a substantial Christian site from early times, where she gave birth to St Kentigern. The child was taken under the care of St Serf, an early Scottish dragon-slaying saint. Kentigern is a major figure who is difficult to authenticate but it is in his life that we have possibly the earliest reference to Merlin. In the *Life of St Kentigern* the character is known as Lailoken (Historians, p.371) and in the light of what has gone before it is worth noting that Merlin is associated strongly with deer and falls under the power of a woman, Niniane.

Arthur is a classic case of the single male associated with the Nine Maidens and the idea of his being taken off to Avalon to be healed, and that he is still alive awaiting the call to come to the help of Britain when needed, has been reworked time and again in literature. There are those who see him essentially as a god figure and others as the prime model of the Celtic hero. Whatever his origin, and location, Arthur is closely linked to the Nine Maidens and in the references to him in Celtic-speaking traditions we perhaps are seeing a remnant of a much older figure.

Heimdall

Like Apollo, Heimdall has been interpreted as a sun god and also as the father of the Norse people in his character Rig. He could hardly have a more central role within Norse mythology. Heimdall is also a liminal god – he is at the edge of things and in tales from cultures all over the world, edges are where magic is often worked. Mentioning Heimdall's nine mothers, HRE Davidson tells us in *Gods and Myths of Northern Europe*:

> These appear to be sea-giantesses, or perhaps waves of the sea. We have already seen that the idea of maidens of mighty strength, dwelling beneath the sea, is familiar in both Scandinavian and Irish tradition, and that they are linked with the giantesses of the underworld who play an important part in Norse mythology. (p.175)

Talking of Heimdall she says, '. . . to him was added the might of earth, of the ice-cold sea, and sacred swine blood' (ibid). Davidson draws attention to the fact that swine were associated with

Freyr and the Vanir, and that they in turn were closely linked with the giantesses. She suggests there were also links between Heimdall and Menglod, who had her own Nine Maidens, and to the fertility goddess Freyja. It seems Heimdall was also involved with the powers of the underworld. We have already seen there are grounds for thinking that prayers to the spirits of the underworld were a means of invoking fertility. Heimdall was also known as the White God and white in many societies has been considered especially sacred. Davidson also refers to the concept of the White Youth among the Yakut peoples of Siberia (1990, p.174), a people who practise shamanism, and this youth was said to have been protected by the spirit of the World Tree and fed on milk. This is reminiscent of the central role of the World Tree in so much northern mythology but it is also notable that the Mamas, the priests of the Venezuelan Kogi, are raised on milk and white foods only. Yet again there are resonances between belief patterns in widely spaced locations with links to the magical use of nine. The reference to sacred swine blood also echoes the associations of the sow with British goddesses and particularly Cerridwen.

Heimdall's mothers have been extensively suggested as the daughters of the sea goddess Ran but they may also be linked to the Maidens of the Mill who are the creators of the physical world from the bodies of the Frost Giants. This is classic foundation mythology and underlines the importance of the group. They are at the foot of the roaring cauldron, Hvergelmer, and as previously noted this can be compared to the Corryvreckan whirlpool between the Hebridean islands of Scarba and Jura. Since humans have gone into space, photographs of the earth have been taken from a considerable distance. This has led to the discovery that there are great eddies, or whirlpools, in the oceans that circulate warm surface water to the layers of cold water far below, thus providing nutrition for deep sea life. As all life originally came from the sea, the idea of the cauldron of the goddess as the fount of life seems to be based on observable reality!

Heimdall is both shaman and poet, linking him with the notions of poetic inspiration common to the Muses and Cerridwen. His Nine Maidens can be linked to the Valkyries whose warrior aspect is similar to other Nine Maidens groups like those associated with St Samson of Dol, the nine black spirits in the story of Thidrandi and the witches of Caer Lyow. Odin is magically associated with the number nine as well. His hanging on the World Tree Yggdrasil for nine nights to acquire wisdom after having been pierced by a spear has been compared to the Crucifixion but the use of nine here probably predates Christianity.

One of the problems we face in the modern post-literate world is that we tend to see symbolism as simple. Symbolism in pre-literate societies is generally complex. Just as a circle can refer to a cauldron, the sun, the turning of the seasons and particular figures associated with any of these, so there can be many levels of symbolism associated with one individual. To us, some of these might appear contradictory but it is a general rule of thumb that the more one knows of the thought patterns of any people the more one can understand their symbolism. This would also apply within societies where those with more knowledge than their fellows – the initiated – could read more meanings into visual and linguistic symbols. Thus Odin might represent a series of different things to different groups within Norse society.

These male figures are all of significant importance in the contemporary mythologies of the societies in which they originated. Other figures like Martin; Ochonochar; Peredur; Ruad, son of Rigdonn; Thidrandi, the widow's son accompanying Monenna, while of apparent lesser importance, carry on the motif of a single male associated with Nine Maidens who are in some way sacred. While the specific rituals of the Nine Maidens groups are probably unknowable, their divinatory and healing activities clearly show them as acting within the religious sphere. In this respect, it is perhaps worth remembering the nine daughters of Ülgan in shamanic tradition with whom the shaman sleeps. Apart from the obvious links with Ruad son of Rigdonn and the mangled remnants of tales concerning lusty nuns, what we have here is perhaps a reference to a stage on a journey, whether of healing or prophecy. It is part of the role of the male in this situation to deal with these Nine Maidens before he can attain his goal. Of all the single male figures linked to the Nine Maidens groups, only St Samson's acolyte, Ruad's son and perhaps Arthur, are said to have been killed and in the latter's case although mortally wounded, the prospect of recovery is strongly attested.

The role of the Nine Maidens and one male might be something like a rite that had to be re-enacted, annually, every full moon or at some period that we can no longer discern. This would account for the survival of the motif over such a wide geographical and geological span and it is tempting to see in the almost universal magic use of nine something of this same idea.

The supernatural females who have Nine Maidens associated with them are likewise varied.

Bride

We have looked at the fact that Bride is common to both Scotland and Ireland, and I have suggested that she could date back to a time before Celtic languages were spoken in Britain. Problems of understanding this clearly delineated fertility goddess have arisen from the assumption that the first place we find a written source for anything must be its original source. This has led to the situation where Scottish Gaelic culture is seen as ultimately deriving from Ireland, as if language both defined ethnicity and culture in some specific 'Celtic' fashion. This overstates the importance of language. Works such as Professor Simon James' *The Atlantic Celts* point out that the very notion of Celticity is based on a reaction to Britishness. According to Professor Markale the name Briton, and thus Britain and British, actually derives from the name the Britons called the P-Celtic speaking Picts – Pretani, which is ironic.

Bride seems to be, in a truly ancient idea, the summer half of a dual Mother Goddess with the Cailleach as the winter goddess.

Such a duality could encompass life and death, cold and warmth, night and day, peace and war. This underlines the capacity of the Mother Goddess concept to incorporate all aspects of human thought and experience. The extent of Bride place-names in Scotland, Ireland, England and Wales points to her widespread influence and it seems likely the Brigantes a P-Celtic-speaking tribal group from north-eastern England were named directly after her. The wells named for her at Abernethy, Kilbride, Sanquhar and many other locations throughout the British Isles all evince the strong connection between the idea of the Mother Goddess and the inherent sanctity of water. This is practical – no water, no life. Bride is, like water itself, symbolic of fertility and thus of ongoing life. Her dominant role in the Christian beliefs of the Celtic-speaking peoples of western and Hebridean Scotland was remarkable. The notion that she was the birthmaiden of Christ, transported in the hour of need to the Middle East, is a clear exposition of her importance. It is intriguing that even in post-Christian times she was associated with the serpent. This I believe is illustrative of the reality that people hold on to old ideas even when they have apparently adopted new ones. This is what is behind the Scottish Kirk's previously noted repeated attempts to stop visitation to sites of 'pagan' activity. It can also be seen in the use of Christian ideas in spells and incantations attributed to witches. Bride might have been superseded to some extent by a saint figure but the ideas of which she was representative could apparently not be replaced.

The Cailleach

I have suggested that the Cailleach is the other, complementary half of an ancient dual Goddess. The story of the Cailleach turning to Bride at Beltane makes this explicit. The suggestion here is that what we are dealing with in this dual Goddess is a concept from so far back in human time we cannot even guess at its antiquity. The suggestion that the Cailleach is not an imported idea from Ireland was noted by DA Mackenzie in

Scottish Folk-Lore and Folk Life, where he quoted Eleanor Hull as saying, 'The Scottish stories about the Cailleach are far more alive and widely spread than in Ireland . . .' (p.169). Mackenzie talks of the Cailleach and Nine Maidens being linked to Ben Nevis and the Corryvreckan. This makes sense as Ben Nevis is Britain's highest mountain and a natural place to locate the Winter or Hag aspect of the Goddess, while the Corryvreckan was, and is, the most dramatic geophysical event in Europe. The association of the Cailleach in many parts of the country with significant local mountains, usually the highest and thus the focal point for changing weather patterns, reminds us of the supposed weather-working powers of Nine Maiden groups, many of whom are also found on hill or mountaintops. This can be interpreted as stressing their link to the Mother Goddess and is perhaps a direct expression of it – they control the weather because they are her representatives among the people. Perhaps like the shamans who intercede with ancestral spirits, they were officiants who could intercede with the source of all life, the Mother Goddess herself. It is noticeable within a Scottish context that several of the mountains with strong links to the Cailleach have names referring to the female breast. In Gaelic place-names the term is generally *Cioch* and in Scots, Pap. Several of these hills and mountains have Cailleach place-names, wells and archaeological remains of different kinds. Elsewhere I have commented on the fact that all hilltop sites have been interpreted as essentially military but this would appear to owe more to the interpreters' preconceptions than any archaeological certitude.

Breast-shaped mountains and hills could have been seen by people who understood life as having a fundamental feminine source, as being an actual marker of the Goddess. If she created all life – and therefore the planet itself – then there is no great imaginative leap in believing that the creation of such obvious female characteristics in the landscape must have been put there to have been noticed. Thus they could become even more important as mythological and thus sacred sites. The habit of mountaintop pilgrimages which many commentators have seen as deriving from pre-Christian times is still not dead. This type of idea might help explain mythological references, relevant place-names, wells and possibly other artefacts on hilltops underlining the importance of such sites to a variety of Nine Maiden groups in different locations.

Cerridwen

Cerridwen is a Welsh Mother Goddess figure strongly associated with poetic inspiration and prophecy. She sometimes is represented by the sow, as are many other Mother Goddess figures in different traditions. The location of her magic cauldron and its attendant Nine Maidens at Caer Sidi is said to have been on an island. Many islands have been suggested, most of the potential candidates being off the western coast of Britain. Before seeing them as rival candidates, we should remember not only the commonalty of mythological material but also that the easiest means of communication until only a couple of centuries ago was by water. Darrah talked of the possible locations of Avalon, Sein and Grassholm but as we have seen there are more candidates for that magic island. Given the widespread provenance of Arthurian material, it is likely that there are such locations off the east and west coasts of both England and Scotland. One candidate would be the Isle of May, meaning the Maiden, in the Forth estuary.

Darrah in his *Paganism in Arthurian Romance* realised the continuity with the far past, but in attempting to locate all of the original Arthurian material specifically in Wales he overlooks the wider provenance of Arthurian place-names and traditions. He mentions that Glastonbury, once an island, is a good fit for Avalon but concludes, as I do, that there was no one original location but that all the possibilities were probably early cult sites, and effectively, where you can locate Avalon, you can locate the Nine Maidens.

Cerridwen has been seen by some commentators as being primarily a witch type figure, but we should remember that the Hag and the Cailleach are one and the same. Jean Markale in *Women of the Celts* links Cerridwen to the *groa'ch*, a witch figure in a Breton traditional tale. She is connected with the Isle of Lok and entrapped men whom she turned into fish. This association with an island is striking as is the similarity to the term used for the Druidesses of Sein, *gra'ch*. In Welsh the term *Gwrach* has much the same meaning as Cailleach. It has also been noted that Cerridwen's cauldron boils the magic drops which give inspiration to Taliesin and thus might be one of the original ideas behind the Holy Grail of medieval romance. Taliesin becomes inspired by drinking from the potion distilled in the cauldron of the goddess Cerridwen, which is kept boiling by the breath of Nine Maidens. This might suggest that Taliesin too is akin to the single male figures mentioned above. In Cerridwen's pursuit of Taliesin mentioned earlier, both of them are said to shape-shift, an attribute of some of the Nine Maidens groups themselves. Taliesin, by effectively being born again after Cerridwen swallows him at the end of the shape-shifting chase is clearly an initiate into the mysteries. Pre-Christian mysteries probably required initiation ceremonies and such types of ritual are the norm rather than the exception among tribal peoples all over the earth. Although they are not the norm in modern Western societies, even here we find remnants of them in various types of social groupings. This is only to note the general importance of initiation which can end up as little more than acknowledgement of a rite of passage. Taliesin is doing something altogether much more significant when he is reborn by Cerridwen. This is a form of religious or magical initiation through which the individual either develops new powers or at the very least learns a great deal about himself/herself and thus about human psychology and, perhaps, how to use that knowledge. It is worth considering that what we have been seeing in all these various groups where there is a single male and nine women is partially remembered rites of initiation into the mysteries of a Goddess cult.

The links between the Isle de Sein, Grassholm and the mythical Avalon that Darrah points out can be seen as supportive of the idea that their inhabitants, or the inhabitants of communities to which they were linked, were in touch by sea. The significance of islands would perhaps be stronger amongst people living beside the sea and might even account for the importance of islands in lakes in areas that were settled later than the coasts and rivers. Whatever the reality of this, the idea of initiation on islands or hilltops – places apart from the rest of society is not a difficult one.

Monnena

Although we only know of Monnena in a Christian guise, and under other names such as Modwenna and Darerca, she does seem to correspond to Bride in some ways. Skene and others recognised patterns in the stories of different saints suggesting that in such tales we are seeing Christianised figures based on earlier ideas that occurred in different locales. Her association with wells and caves in the south-east of Scotland strengthens the idea that we have a figure derived from pre-Christian times. The fact that churches were dedicated to her on significant Dark Age sites suggest these as having particular relevance in pre-Christian ritual behaviour. This centrality within such different Dark Age tribal groupings as the Britons, Gododdin and Picts is suggestive of a powerful mythological figure. Whether this was accompanied by any political or temporal influence on the part of the Nine Maidens groups is impossible to say. It would appear likely that their role would give them some influence, and it is possibly this that gave rise to the titles of Mynyd Agned and subsequently the Castle of Maidens, for what was to become Edinburgh Castle. This takes us back again to the idea of significant mountains and hills being relevant in pre-Christian symbolism. At one time the fire-festivals of Beltane and Samhain took place in most parts of the British Isles, generally on prominent hilltops. The recent revival of such practices on Edinburgh's Calton Hill and elsewhere certainly seems to strike a strong chord in many people, not only the party-hungry young folk, and it may be that there are deep-seated psychological reasons for the choice of hill or mountaintops for sacred practices and mythological concepts.

Morgan

Jean Markale in *Women of the Celts* has this to say of Morgan as she appears in the medieval romance called the *Estoire de Merlin*:

> This is undoubtedly a portrait of the ambiguous, original mother Goddess, both good-natured and spiteful, the very image of the divinity who both gives and takes away, warm and sensual like the great Eastern Goddess, but a virgin nevertheless, because unwilling to submit to masculine authority. (p.137)

Here he realises that the original concept behind Morgan, like so many of the other examples of figures associated with the Nine Maidens, is that of the all-encompassing Mother Goddess. Within the Arthurian tradition we have both Morgan of Avalon who comes to help the dying Arthur and in various other versions Morgan la Fee who sets out to bring him down. This can be seen as a clear exposition of the dual nature of the Mother Goddess as 'she who gives and she who takes away'. It is not that remarkable that such a duality has survived in the Arthurian material from the Middle Ages when all of Europe was ostensibly Christian. Although the official religion was Christianity, there were many, and not only among the 'common folk', who held on to aspects of much older, pre-Christian beliefs. Some of this might account for practices mentioned in a few witch trials, though most were, as has been stated, opportunities for the persecutors to indulge their own twisted fantasies rather than the persecution of women actively working to the detriment of the society to which they belonged. It might also account for many practices that have been gathered under the general heading of folklore from all over Europe well into this century. Within this material I would include the magical use of nine and the continuing visits to wells even though many were Christianised centuries ago. Hope in *A Midsummer Eve's Dream* suggests an active fairy cult in 15th century Scotland and this would necessarily have involved continuity with earlier beliefs.

In the *Vita Merlini*, Morgan is one of the Nine Maidens of Avalon and clearly their leader. This can be contrasted with the figures of Bride, Cerridwen, Menglod and Monenna who all have Nine Maidens as priestesses, acolytes or followers. Perhaps this came about because Morgan entered the literary romance tradition in Christian times and became one of the maidens to make her essentially pre-Christian aspect less blatant to the courtly audience. Much of what we know of these other female figures comes from oral tradition that continued long after Morgan had attained fame within Arthurian literature.

Darrah makes the following point about Morgan and her sisters:

> At Avalon the Goddess and her priestesses are Morgan and her bird-transforming sisters. Morgan is also resident, with many maidens, in the Castle of the Marvel, one of the equivalents of the Castle of the Maidens; and in another Castle of Maidens the Goddess is the Queen of Danemarche who has many attendant maidens in her garden, surrounded by a hedge of air. (p.229)

This hedge of air is reminiscent of the hedge around Bride's sacred flame at Kildare into the Christian period. No men were allowed to cross, or look over this hedge, on pain of death. Here Darrah is seeing Morgan as the Goddess and many scholars have seen some resemblance with the Irish Morrigan. It is interesting that Darrah mentions an Arthurian instance of a raven attacking a knight at a ford; the raven, when killed, turned into a maiden whom Darrah sees as one of Morgan's companions (ibid p.226). The Morrigan is of course seen on battlefields in the shape of a raven and the idea of the battle attendant finds some further echo in the figures of the Valkyries in Norse tradition. Here we also have the recurring motif of shape-shifting among Nine Maidens groups which may be related to the idea of spirit journeying in shamanism. Darrah also notes that there are references to the Nine Maidens of Sein flying through the air and as with the raven-maiden here mentioned this is redolent of the supposed capacity of witches to fly through the air, interpreted in modern times as being descriptive of spirit journeys taken under the influence of drugs of one kind or another.

Morgan is an obvious otherworldly figure and in Breton traditions the term Morgan actually became associated with specific types of fairy. As an Otherworld female her links with the figure of Arthur perhaps suggest he is an initiate into the pre-Christian mysteries – he does after all go into the underworld to seek a magic cauldron in the poem by Taliesin we have looked at. RS Loomis tells us that:

> Giraldus Cambrensis speaks of Marganis as . . . a certain imaginary Goddess; and even late in the fourteenth century the author of Gawain and the Green Knight speaks of her as Morgne the Goddess.
> (1993 p.192)

Whomever she was originally, the Goddess herself or her chief priestess, or both, there is no doubt that the figure of Morgan has continued to inspire generation upon generation of writers and has retained a considerable amount of the ambiguity originally associated with the Mother Goddess herself.

Ran

As the Norse goddess of the sea, Ran has great importance for the Norsemen who were great seafarers, the dominant image we have of them being of the gold- and battle-hungry Vikings. We should remember however that much of the British Isles was actually settled by people from Scandinavia, a fact discernible in a host of place-names in areas now portrayed as essentially Celtic. The fact is that orally transmitted traditions can and do transcend language shifts, which have themselves too often been interpreted as a result of mass immigration or invasion and suppression. That there are ideas from Norse mythology inherent in different parts of what has been called the Celtic world and vice versa suggests we might better look to interpret the past in terms of cultural contacts between different groups instead of looking for military explanations. Ran is portrayed as a being who actively welcomes drowned sailors and HRE Davidson tells us of how she was seen in Iceland:

> A folk belief quoted in one of the Icelandic sagas is that when people were drowned they were thought to have gone to Ran, and if they appeared at their own funeral feasts, it was a sign that she had given them a good welcome. In a late saga, Fridjof's Saga, it is said to have been a lucky thing to have gold on one's person if lost at sea. The hero went so far as to distribute small pieces of gold among his men when they were caught in a storm, so that they should not go empty-handed into Ran's hall if they were drowned. The idea of the hospitality of Aegir and Ran, who were so anxious to throng their underwater world with the hosts of the dead, may be compared with that of the god of battle. (1990 p.129)

It can also clearly be compared to the goddesses of battle like the Morrigan and therefore directly to the destructive aspect of the Mother Goddess. Ran's nine daughters are represented as the waves themselves and this is perhaps the agency of her drawing sailors into her net. Sailors throughout the world have a particular attitude towards the sea. In many parts of the world, including Scotland, seamen traditionally refused to learn how to swim. They were entirely at the mercy of the sea, which would spare them if their fate decreed it. Here we are very close to the idea of the giving and taking Goddess, in that fishermen or traders might flourish through her agency, or they might drown. Such ideas are ancient indeed. We know that in much of the period since the last Ice Age, over 10,000 years ago, people have been travelling around northern Europe by sea and weather changes at sea can be dramatic at any time of the year. In Norse mythology we have Ran and her husband Aegir, while in the Q-Celtic areas, we have the male Manannan mac Lir alone, perhaps suggesting an older stratum existing among the Norsemen. Manannan has a counterpart in Welsh literature Manawydan, son of Lir who marries the goddess Rhiannon. She had birds who were said to have the ability to bring the dead back to life and send the living to sleep with their singing. This seems to echo the associations that Morgan has with the raven mentioned above and underlines the fact that many of the goddess figures seen in material derived from the oral tradition in both P- and Q-Celtic speaking areas seem to hark back to much older ideas of the Mother Goddess. This is not to suggest a specific link between Ran and Rhiannon but to show the complexity of, but also the continuity inherent in much of this material.

In the Irish saga of Ruad, son of Rigdonn the nine maidens he meets can be seen as the daughters of Ran and it is worth noting that Heimdall, of the nine mothers, was known in some sagas as Rig, which most commentators have seen as linked to Celtic ideas. The name Rigdonn has the component Donn here which is reminiscent of the goddess Danu from Irish tradition.

Menglod

We saw in the story of Svipdag, son of the witch Groa, that Menglod lived on a mountain of healing surrounded by her Nine Maidens. She was said to have been the daughter of a giant of the underworld, who might be linked to Heimdall as both are referred to in different locales as being 'nail-resplendent'. However Menglod means 'necklace-glad' and this seems to link her directly with the Norse goddess Freyja, who was the owner of a famed necklace, Brisingamen. Freyja is clearly a fertility goddess and HRE Davidson in *Roles of the Northern Goddess* writes of the goddesses Frigg and Freyja:

> Both are associated with fertility, and while Frigg is presented as the divine mother, queen of heaven, Freyja is apparently of a younger generation, the

> daughter of Njord and Skadi, and is said to hold the
> title 'Bride of the Vanir'. (p.86)

This is somewhat like the duality of the Cailleach and Bride in that we have two generations of goddesses though it is not an exact match, and Davidson also tells us that Freyja was associated with the sow – redolent of the Welsh goddess Cerridwen among others. So we have Menglod linked to healing, a mountain site and the sow, as well as fertility. All of these are recurrent themes in the motif of the Nine Maidens. Svipdag who woos her, has help from beyond the grave, again taking us into the realms of Life and Death. All of this, like the turning of the seasons, seems very much the realm of the Mother Goddess.

The Number Nine

We have already seen that nine crops up extensively in the folklore of many lands and some of this material is linked directly to magical practices.

The number nine has been seen in some esoteric traditions as representing perfection and truth. One of the strange things about the number nine is that it always reproduces itself, e.g:

$2 \times 9 = 18: 1 + 8 = 9;$

$32 \times 9 = 288: 2 + 8 + 8 = 18: 1 + 8 = 9;$

$65 \times 9 = 585: 5 + 8 + 5 = 18: 1 + 8 = 9$

and so on. This can be interpreted as the number reproducing itself so it is therefore the optimum number to represent regeneration and fertility. Mathematically, I have been told, this capacity to reproduce itself would happen with the number 5 if we counted to base 6, or the number 12 if we counted to base 13, but humans count to base 10, because of the fact that we have 10 digits on our hands.

Bibliography

Aberdeen Breviary, The (Spalding Club, Edinburgh, 1854)
Adams, WHD. *Witch, Warlock and Magician* (Chatto & Windus, London, 1889)
Anderson, AO. *Early Sources of Scottish History* (Paul Watkins, Stamford, 1990 repr)
Anson, PF. *Fisher Folk Lore* (Faith Press, London, 1965)
Banks, MM. *British Calendar Customs: Scotland* (Folklore Society, London, 1937-41)
Baring-Gould, S. *Lives of the British Saints* (Llanerch, Felinfach, 1990 repr)
Barrow, GWS. 'Religion in Scotland on the eve of Christianity' in *FS Peter Herde (Reich)* Karl Borchardt & Enno Bünz (eds) 2 vols (Stuttgart, Hiersemann, 1998)
Barrett, M. *Footprints of the Ancient Scottish Church* (Sands & Co., London, 1914)
Bawcutt, P & Riddy, F. *Longer Scottish Poems* (Aberdeen University Press, Aberdeen, 1987)
Bede, *A History of the English Church and People* tr. L Shelley-Price (Penguin, London, 1955)
Bellenden, J. *Translation of Boece's History and Chronicles of Scotland,* ed. W Seton, RW. Chambers, EC Batho (Scottish Text Society, Edinburgh, 1821)
The Black Book of Carmarthen reproduced and edited by JG Evans (Pwlhelli, Wales, 1906)
Black Book of Taymouth, The by W Bowie, ed. C Innes (Bannatyne Club, Edinburgh, 1855)
Black, GF. *County Folklore, Vol III Orkney and Shetland* (David Nutt, London, 1903)

Boece, see Turnbull, W.

Bonwick, J. *Irish Druids and Old Irish Religions* (Dorset, USA, 1986 repr)

Bord, J., & Bord, C. *The Secret Country* (Paladin, London, 1976)

Bovet, R. *Pandaemonium* (London, 1684)

Bradley, SAJ. ed, *Anglo-Saxon Poetry* (Everyman, London, 1982)

Brown, GB. *The Art of the Cave Dweller* (John Murray, London, 1932)

Brown, J. The *History of Sanquhar* (Anderson & Sons, Dumfries, 1891)

Burt, E. *Burt's letters from the north of Scotland* ed. A Simmons (Birlinn, Edinburgh, 1998)

Butler, D. *The Ancient Church and Parish of Abernethy* (Blackwood & Sons, Edinburgh, 1897)

Campbell, D. *The Book of Garth and Fortingall* (Inverness, 1888)

Campbell, JG. *Popular Tales of the Western Islands* (Birlinn, Edinburgh, 1994 repr)

Campbell, J.G. *Superstitions of the Scottish Highlands and Islands* (McLehose Glasgow, 1900)

Carmichael, A. *Carmina Gadelica* ed. CJ Moore (Birlinn, Edinburgh, 1994)

Chadwick, HM. *Early Scotland* (Cambridge Uni Press, Cambridge, 1949)

Christie, J. *The Lairds and Lands of Tayside* (Cameron & Sons, Aberfeldy, 1892)

Cockburn, JH. *The Celtic Church in Dunblane* (Society of the Friends of Dunblane Cathedral, Dunblane, 1954)

Crawford, OGS. *The Eye Goddess* (Phoenix House, London, 1957)

Crossley-Holland, K. *The Norse Myths* (Deutsch, London, 1982)

Dalyell, JG. *Darker Superstitions of Scotland* (Griffin, Glasgow, 1835)

Dames, M. *The Silbury Treasure* (Thames & Hudson, London, 1976)

Darrah, J. *Paganism in Arthurian Romance* (Boydell, Woodbridge, 1994)

Davidson, HRE. *Gods and Myths of Northern Europe* (Penguin, London, 1990)

Davidson, HRE. *Myths and Symbols in Pagan Europe* (Manchester University Press, 1988)

Davidson, HRE. *The Lost Beliefs of Northern Europe* (Routledge, London & NY, 1993)

Davidson, HRE. *Roles of the Northern Goddess* (Routledge, London & NY, 1998)

Davidson, T. *Rowan Tree and Red Thread* (Oliver & Boyd, Edinburgh, 1949)

De Santillana, G & von Dechend, H. *Hamlet's Mill* (Macmillan, London, 1970)

Dillon, M & Chadwick, N. *The Celtic Realms* (Weidenfield & Nicolson, London, 1972)

Dindshenchas URL: https://celt.ucc.ie/published/T106500B/text004.html

Diodorus URL: https://penelope.uchicago.edu/Thayer/E/Roman/Texts/Diodorus_Siculus/1A*.html

Douglas, S. *The King of the Black Art and other stories* (Aberdeen University Press, 1987)

Dumezil, G. *Gods of the Ancient Northmen* (University of California Press, Berkeley, 1973)

Eliade, M. *Shamanism* (Arkana, London, 1989)

Evans, JG. *Poems from the Book of Taliesin* (Llanbedrog, N.Wales, 1915)

Forbes, AP. *Kalendars of Scottish Saints* (Edmonston & Douglas, Edinburgh, 1872)

Frazer, J. *The Golden Bough* (MacMillan, London, 1922)

Gaeyang URL; https://www.magoism.net/2012/08/gaeyang-halmi-the-sea-goddess-of-korea-by-helen-hye-sook-hwang/

Gimbutas, M. *The Goddesss and Gods of Ancient Europe* (Thames & Hudson, London, 1982)

Glennie, JS. *Arthurian Localities in Scotland* (Llanerch, Felinfach, Wales, 1994 repr)

Gollancz, I. *Hamlet in Iceland* (Nutt, London, 1898)

Grant, J. *Old and New Edinburgh* (Cassell's, London, 1885-7)

Graves, R. *The Greek Myths* 2 vols (Harmondsworth, London, 1960)

Graves, R. *Mammon and the Black Goddess* (Cassell, London, 1965)

Graves, R. *The Greek Myths* (Book Club Associates, London, 1985)

Graves, R. *The White Goddess* (Faber & Faber, London, 1961)

Gray, J ed. *Mythology of All Races* 13 vols (Marshall Jones, Boston, 1916-1964)

Gregor, W. *Notes on the Folklore of the North East of Scotland* (London, 1881)

Grenfell, BP & Hunt, AS. *The Oxyrhynchus Papyri* (Kegan Paul, London, 1898)

Grimm, J. *Teutonic Mythology* 4 vols (Swan, Sonnenschein & Allen, London, 1880-88)

Guerber, HA. *The Norsemen* (Senate, London, 1994 repr)

Guthrie, JC. *The Vale of Strathmore, its scenes and legends* (Edinburgh, 1875)

Gwynn, E ed. *The Metrical Dinshenchas* (Royal Irish Academy, Dublin, 1903-35)

Hansen, W. *Saxo Grammaticus and the Life of Hamlet* (Uni. Nebraska Press, Lincoln and London, 1983)

Harmon, M. *Dialogue of the Ancients of Ireland* (Carysfort Press, Bray, 2009)

Helgi URL; https://web.archive.org/web/20090522103123/http://www.angelfire.com/on/Wodensharrow/helgakvidha2.html

Heywood, T. *Gunaikieon* (printed by Adam Islip, London, 1624)

Historians of Scotland v5, *Lives of St Ninian and Kentigern* (Edmonston & Douglas Edinburgh, 1874)

Hollander, L. *The Poetic Eddas* (University of Texas Press, Austin, 1924)

Hope, AD. *A Midsummer Eve's Dream* (Oliver & Boyd, Edinburgh, 1971)

Hull, E. *Folklore of the British Isles* (Methuen, London, 1928)

Hutton, R. *Pagan Religions of the Ancient British Isles* (Blackwell, Oxford, 1991)

Isaacs, J. *Australian Dreaming; 40,000 years of Aboriginal history* (Lansdowne Press, Willoughby, NSW, 1980)

Ivimy, J. *The Sphinx and the Megaliths* (Abacus, London, 1976)

Jacobson, E. *The Deer Goddess of Ancient Siberia* (E.J. Brill, NY, 1993)

James, S. *The Atlantic Celts* (British Museum Press, London, 1999)

Jervise, A. *Epitaphs and Inscriptions* (Edmonston & Douglas, Edinburgh, 1875)

Jervise, A. *The History and Traditions of the Land of the Lindsays* (David Douglas, Edinburgh, 1882)

Joceline, 'Life of St Kentigern' in The Historians of Scotland 10 vols (Edinburgh, 1871-80)

Jones, G & Jones, T. *The Mabinogion* (Everyman, London, 1994)

Jones, G. *Erik the Red and other Icelandic Tales* (Oxford University Press, London, 1961)

Kelly, L. *The Memory Code* (Pegasus, Cambridge, 2017)

Kenyatta, J. *Facing Mount Kenya* (Heinemann, London, 1979)

Knight, GAF. *Archaeological Light on The Early Christianising of Scotland* (J. Clarke & Co, London, 1933)

Koch, JT. *The Gododdin of Aneurin* (University of Wales Press, Cardiff, 1997)

Laing, A. *Lindores Abbey and the Burgh of Newburgh* (Edinburgh, 1876)

Leslie, F. *The Early Races of Scotland* (Edmonston & Douglas, Edinburgh, 1866)

Leslie, Jhone. *Historie of Scotland* 8 vols (Blackwood, Edinburgh, 1888-95)

Lethbridge, TC. *Witches: investigating an ancient religion* (Routledge & Kegan Paul, London, 1962)

Loomis, RS. *Arthurian Literature in the Middle Ages* (Clarendon Press, Oxford, 1959)

Loomis, RS. *Arthurian Tradition and Chretien de Troyes* (Columbia University Press, NY, 1949)

Loomis, RS. *Celtic Myth and Arthurian Romance* (Constable, London, 1995 repr)

McArthur, H. *Arthur's Battle Against the Whirlpool* (Glasgow, 2010)

MacCulloch, JA. *The Celtic and Scandinavian religions* (Constable, London, 1994 repr)

MacCulloch, JA. *The Religion of the Ancient Celts* (Constable, London, 1992 repr)

McHardy, SA. *The Folklore of the Picts* in *stones, symbols and stories; Aspects of Pictish Studies* (Pictish Arts Society, Edinburgh, 1994)

McHardy, SA. *The wee dark fowk o Scotland*, in *the worm, the germ and the thorn, Essays presented to Isabel Henderson* (Pinkfoot Press, Forfar, 1997)

McHardy, SA. *The Quest for Arthur* (Luath Press, Edinburgh, 2001)

McHardy, SA. *The Pagan Symbols of the Picts* (Luath Press, Edinburgh, 2012)

McHardy, SA. Gruagach; https://www.academia.edu/4402183/The_Gruagach_a_remnant_of_somethng_bigger

Mackay, JG. *The Deer-goddess and the Deer-Goddess Cult in Scotland in Folklore* vol 51 (1934)

Mackenzie, DA. *Crete, Myths and Legends* (Senate, London, 1995 repr)

Mackenzie, DA. *Egyptian Myth and Legend* (Gresham, London, 1913)

Mackenzie, DA. *Pre-Hellenic Myths and Legends* (Senate, London, 1995 repr)

Mackenzie, DA. *Scottish Folklore and Folklife* (Blackie, London & Glasgow, 1935)

Mackenzie, DA. *Teutonic Myth and Legend* (Senate, London, 1995 repr)

Mackinlay, JM. *Ancient Church Dedications in Scotland* 2 vols (David Douglas, Edinburgh, 1910-14)

Mackinlay, J. *Folklore of Scottish Lochs and Springs* (W. Hodge & Co., Glasgow, 1893)

Mackinlay, JF. 'Traces of the Cultus of the Nine Maidens' in *Proceedings of the Society of Antiquaries of Scotland* vol 38 (1904)

Maclean, J. *Translations of names of places on the Breadalbane Estates* (Edinburgh, 1887)

MacLeod, N. *Reminiscences of a Highland Parish* (London, 1871)

McNeill, M. *The Silver Bough* 4 vols (Wm. McLellan, Glasgow, 1953-61)

Malory, T. *Morte d'Arthur* (Penguin, London, 1969)

Markale, J. *The Celts* (Inner Traditions International, Vermont, 1993)

Markale, J. *The Women of the Celts* (Inner Traditions International, Vermont, 1986)

Martin, M. *A Description of the Western Isles of Scotland 1697* (J.Thin, Edinburgh, 1970 repr)

Miscellany, *A Miscellany presented to John MacDonald Mackay* (Constable, London, 1914)

Morris, K. *Sorceress or Witch* (University Press of America, Lanham & London, 1991)

Navaratri URL; https://en.wikipedia.org/wiki/Navaratri

New Larousse Encyclopaedia of Mythology (London, 1968)

Newall, V. *The Witch Figure* (Routledge & Kegan Paul, London, 1973)

Newman, P. *The Hill of the Dragon* (Kingsmead, Bath, 1979)

Njord URL; http://www.voluspa.org/solarljod76-80.htm

O'Grady, S. *Colloquy with the Ancients* in *Silva Gadelica* Vol II (Williams & Norgate, London, 1892, pp.101-265)

Owen, EO. *Welsh Folklore* (Woodall, Minshall & Co, Oswestry, 1887)

Parry, JJ. The Vita Merlini in *University of Illinois Studies in Language and Literature* (Uni. Illinois Press, 1925)

Paton, LA. *Studies on the Fairy Mythology of Arthurian Romance* (Burt Franklin, NY, 1960 repr)

Pennant, T. *A Tour in Scotland* (Printed for Benj. White, London, 1774)

Polson, A. *Scottish Witchcraft Lore* (W. Alexander & Son, Inverness, 1932)

Ponting, G & M. *The Standing Stones of Callanish* (Stornoway, 1977)

Pratt, J. *Buchan* (Lewis Smith, Aberdeen, 1870)

Ramsay, J. *Scotland and Scotsmen in the 18th Century* (Wm. Blackwood & Sons, Edinburgh, 1888)

Rees, A & Rees, B. *Celtic Heritage* (Thames & Hudson, London, 1990 repr)

Rolleston, TW. *Celtic Myths and Legends* (Bracken Books, London, 1995 repr)

Ross, A. *Pagan Celtic Britain* (Constable, London, 1992 repr)

Rufus, A & Lawson, K. *Goddess Sites in Europe* (HarperSanFrancisco, NY, 1990)

Rydberg, V. *Teutonic Mythology* trans. Anderson, RB (Swan Sonnenschein & Co., London, 1889)

Scott, D & McHardy, SA. *Stones of the Ancestors* (Luath Press, Edinburgh, 2020)

Sebillot, P. *Le Folk-lore de France* (Maisonneuve et Larose, Paris, 1968)

Sinclair, D. *Satan's Invisible World Discovered* (Glasgow, 1840)

Skene, WF. *Celtic Scotland* 4 vols (David Douglas, Edinburgh, 1886-90)

Skene, WF. *Arthur and the Britons in Wales and Scotland* (Llanerch, Felinfach, Wales, 1988)

Small, A. *Some Interesting Roman Antiquities recently discovered in Fife* (Anderson, Edinburgh, 1823)

Smyth, ALF. *Warlords and Holy Men* (Edward Arnold, London, 1984)

Soltysiak, A. 'The Number Nine in the Tradition of the Norsemen' in *Między Drzewem Życia a Drzewem Poznania. Księga ku czci profesora Andrzeja Wiercińskiego*, MS Ziółkowski & A Sołtysiak (eds), (Warszawa–Kielce, 2003, pp. 231–242)

Spalding Club, *Collections on the shires of Aberdeen and Banff* (Aberdeen, 1863)

Spence, J. *Shetland Folk Lore* (Johnson & Greig, Lerwick, 1899)

Spence, L. *The History of Druidism* (Newcastle Publishing, California, 1995 repr)

Spence, L. *Legends and Romance of Brittany* (Constable, London, 1977 repr)

Spence, L. *The Magic Arts in Celtic Britain* (Constable, London, 1995 repr)

Spence, L. *Minor Traditions of British Mythology* (Rider & Co., London, 1948)

Spence, L. *The Mysteries of Britain* (Newcastle Publishing, California, 1993 repr)

Swire, O. *The Inner Hebrides and Their Legends* (Collins, London, 1964)

Swire, O. *The Outer Hebrides and Their Legends* (Oliver & Boyd, Edinburgh, 1966)

Tacitus, (Ed. Mattingly, H), *Tacitus on Britain and Germany* (Penguin, London, 1990)

Taliesin, *The Book of Taliesin*, ed. JG Evans (Llanbedrog, 1910)

Thompson, DP. *On the Slopes of the Sidlaws* (Munro Press, Perth, 1953)

Third Statistical Account of Scotland; *Perth and Kinross* (Edinburgh,1979)

Tranter, N. *Argyll and Bute* (Hodder & Stoughton, London, 1977)

Turnbull, W ed. *Stewart's Metrical translation of Boece* (London, 1858)

Vitaliano, DB. *Legends of the Earth, their geologic origin* (Indiana University Press, Bloomington, 1973)

Walters, D. *Chinese Mythology* (Aquarian, London, 1992)

Warden, AJ. *Angus or Forfarshire* 5 vols (C. Alexander & Co., Dundee, 1880-85)

Watson, L. *Gifts of Unknown Things* (Coronet, Sevenoaks, 1977)

Watson, WJ. *The Celtic Placenames of Scotland* (Birlinn, Edinburgh, 1993 repr)

Wheater, H. *A Guide in hand to Kenmoreand Loch Tay* (Keltneyburn, Perthshire, 1980)

Wilson, D. *Memorials of Edinburgh in the Olden Time* (A&C Black, Edinburgh, 1891)

Wimberley, LC. *Folklore of the English and Scottish Ballads* (Chicago, 1928)

Luath Press Limited

committed to publishing well written books worth reading

LUATH PRESS takes its name from Robert Burns, whose little collie Luath (*Gael.*, swift or nimble) tripped up Jean Armour at a wedding and gave him the chance to speak to the woman who was to be his wife and the abiding love of his life. Burns called one of the 'Twa Dogs' Luath after Cuchullin's hunting dog in Ossian's *Fingal*. Luath Press was established in 1981 in the heart of Burns country, and is now based a few steps up the road from Burns' first lodgings on Edinburgh's Royal Mile. Luath offers you distinctive writing with a hint of unexpected pleasures.
Most bookshops in the UK, the US, Canada, Australia, New Zealand and parts of Europe, either carry our books in stock or can order them for you. To order direct from us, please send a £sterling cheque, postal order, international money order or your credit card details (number, address of cardholder and expiry date) to us at the address below. Please add post and packing as follows: UK – £1.00 per delivery address; overseas surface mail – £2.50 per delivery address; overseas airmail – £3.50 for the first book to each delivery address, plus £1.00 for each additional book by airmail to the same address. If your order is a gift, we will happily enclose your card or message at no extra charge.

Luath Press Limited
543/2 Castlehill
The Royal Mile
Edinburgh EH1 2ND
Scotland
Telephone: +44 (0)131 225 4326 (24 hours)
Email: sales@luath.co.uk
Website: www.luath.co.uk